A quarterly journal of socialist theory

Autumn 1992
Contents

Editorial

Chris Harman	*The return of the national question*	3
Dave Treece	*Why the Earth Summit failed*	63
Mike Gonzalez	*Can Castro survive?*	83
Lee Humber and John Rees	*The good old cause— an interview with Christopher Hill*	125
Ernest Mandel	*The impasse of schematic dogmatism*	135

Issue 56 of INTERNATIONAL SOCIALISM, quarterly journal of the Socialist Workers Party (Britain)

Published September 1992
Copyright © International Socialism
Distribution/subscriptions: International Socialism,
PO Box 82, London E3.
American distribution: B de Boer, 113 East Center St, Nutley, New Jersey 07110.
Subscriptions and back copies: PO Box 16085, Chicago Illinois 60616
Editorial and production: 071-538 1626/071-538 3307
Sales and subscriptions: 071-538 5821 x133
American sales: 312 666 7337

ISBN 0-906224-76-4

Printed by BPCC Wheatons Ltd, Exeter, England
Typeset by East End Offset, London E3

Cover: 'Fools' Cap Map of the World', circa 1590, artist unknown (copyright: Wychwood Editions). The main Latin inscription reads:
 'Democritus mocked it, (i.e. the world)
 Herachtus wept over it,
 Epichthanius Cosmopolites portrayed it.'
Epichthonius Cosmopolites, or Everyman, is a pseudonym for the artist.

Cover design: Ian Goodyer

For details of back copies see the end pages of this book

Subscription rates for one year (four issues) are:

Britain and overseas (surface):	individual	£12.00 ($25)
	institutional	£20.00
Air speeded supplement:	North America	nil
	Europe/South America	£1.00
	elsewhere	£2.00

Note to contributors
The deadline for articles intended for issue 58 of *International Socialism* is 1 November 1992
All contributions should be double-spaced with wide margins. Please submit two copies. If you write your contribution using a computer, please also supply a disk, together with details of the computer and programme used.

A quarterly journal of socialist theory

NATIONALISM SEEMS to be the most powerful political force in the modern world. From the Middle East to the Caucasus, from Ireland to Croatia, from South Africa to Slovakia no one remains untouched by nationalism. 'The return of the national question' unravels the enigma of nationhood, tracing its roots in early capitalism and using the legacy of the classical Marxist tradition to chart the development of more recent national liberation movements.

Chris Harman shows how even the most progressive of such movements have close ties with the growth of the capitalist system. Yet there is an alternative to fashionable pessimism about the world's descent into communalism. It is to be found in class politics—providing socialists build on their own traditions' strengths, not its weaknesses.

THE EARTH SUMMIT in Rio earlier this year was a spectacular failure. Dave Treece explains why the world's leaders are incapable of coming to grips with the environmental crisis and outlines the only kind of political response that stands a chance of dealing with a problem so deeply rooted in the make up of late 20th century capitalism.

US IMPERIALISM has its greedy eye on Cuba. Every socialist will hope that Cuba remains a thorn in the American ruling class's side. But does that mean uncritical support for Castro's repressive regime? Mike Gonzalez analyses a turning point in history.

CHRISTOPHER HILL, the best known historian of the English Revolution, marks the 350th anniversary of the outbreak of the civil war with an interview which outlines the current state of historical debate on the revolutions' causes and consequences.

ERNEST MANDEL closes this issue with another contribution to the discussion of the class nature of the Russian and East European states begun in issue 49. *International Socialism* will reply in a future issue.

Editor: John Rees, Assistant Editors: Alex Callinicos, Sue Clegg, Chris Harman, John Molyneux, Lindsey German, Pete Green, Costas Lapavitsas, Colin Sparks, Mike Gonzalez, Peter Morgan, Ruth Brown, Mike Haynes and Rob Hoveman.

The return of the national question

CHRIS HARMAN

Introduction

It has become almost an orthodoxy to say that the great divide in the world today is between nationalisms. The talk of 'a new world order' and 'the end of history' may not have lasted long. But what has replaced it does not seem to have been class politics, but rather the rivalry of reborn—or sometimes completely new—nationalisms.

Yet those who speak in these terms have great difficulty in defining what makes up a 'nation'. It cannot just be those people who inhabit a certain geographical entity—otherwise what sense are we to make of minorities declining to be part of the 'nation' of the majority among whom they live? It cannot just be language—or what are we to make of Serb, Croat and Bosnian speakers of a single language declaring themselves to be separate nationalities, or of the founders of India attempting to impose Hindi, their own recently sanitised version of a regional dialect, Hindustani, as the 'national language' of a whole subcontinent? It cannot be that fashionable catch-all 'culture', since everywhere differences in culture, or ways of living, are greater between the rich and poor, or the workers and peasants, within a national state than they are between neighbours from the same class on different sides of national borders.

There is no single objective criterion by which to determine whether a group of people—or their would be leaders—will decide they should constitute a nation. On this, at least, such diverse authorities as 'old left' academic Eric Hobsbawm,[1] 'new left' academic Benedict Anderson,[2] liberal academic Ernest Gellner[3] and former editor of this journal Nigel Harris[4] are in agreement. Nations are, in Anderson's words, 'imaginary' entities—although in this case imagination in power can use all the nastiest weapons of the state to impose its beliefs on those who dissent from them.

The ideologists of nationalism nearly always try to trace the ancestry of their particular nation back many hundreds of years—as when English history is said to begin with King Alfred and his burnt cakes and Ethelred the Unready, when Tudjman's government speaks of 'the thousand year old Croatian nation', when the Serbian government invokes the battle of Kosovo in 1389, or Romanian nationalists claim a continuity going back to the Roman Empire's settlement of Dacia.[5] But these claims are invariably based on fictitious histories. For nations as entities have not always existed.

The modern nation, with its ideal of a homogeneous body of citizens, enjoying equal rights, expressing loyalty to a single centre of sovereignty and speaking a single language, is as much a product of relatively recent history as capitalism itself. It is a notion as out of place in any serious account of the pre-capitalist societies which dominated the whole world until the 16th century, and more than 90 percent of it until little over a century ago, as that of the motor car or machine gun.

In fact, it is the connection between the rise of the nation state and the rise of capitalism which enables us to understand the strength of the myths that lead people to slaughter each other—as always with wars, most of the slaughter being of the poor by the poor, not the rich by the rich.

Capitalism and the nation

The class societies that existed before the rise of capitalism were organised through states. But these states were external to most of the activities of the great mass of people. They robbed them through taxation and pillage and they coerced or bribed them into joining their armies. But they left untouched their basic everyday activity of getting a living, which took place mainly through subsistence agriculture even if a small portion of their output was traded. The peasantry were, of course, heavily exploited and subject to vicious legal repression but it was by particular lords and particular clerics (often the same people), who themselves owed only a distant and fragile allegiance to any central state.

In such a society the situation which existed in the 12th century monarchy called England (in fact made up of modern England, much of western France and parts of Wales, Ireland and Scotland) was typical, with the military rulers using one language (Norman French), the literate elite of administrators using another (medieval Latin), and the mass of the population using a variety of disparate dialects (various forms of Anglo-Saxon, French, Welsh and Gaelic).

The state in such a society might be centralised and powerful or weak and fragmented. But in neither case was it a *national* state as we understand it today. Whatever else its subjects thought, they did not think of themselves as citizens speaking a common language or owing an undivided loyalty to a single geographic entity.

Under capitalism things are very different. The market impinges on every aspect of everybody's life, from the work they do through the food they eat and the clothes they wear to how they amuse themselves. And with the growth of the market there is a massive growth of administration, both within individual companies and in the state.

The ideological mythology of capitalism claims it needs only a minimal state. But, in fact, the market can only function on an extensive, enduring basis if it is backed up by an equally pervasive state—issuing money, ensuring debts are paid, limiting the scale of fraud, building roads and ports, keeping the poor from getting their revenge on the rich, engaging in wars and, above all, enforcing regular taxation on the mass of people.

But an administrative apparatus cannot operate efficiently without an easy means of communication between its functionaries, a language in which they are all fluent. It also prefers this to be the language of most of those who live under it: it makes the prying of the secret police and the tax collectors so much easier, the cohesion between those who give orders at the top and those who enforce them at the bottom so much more efficient.

The first national states

Capitalism first began to develop fully in Holland and England from the 16th century onwards—although market relations and, with them, the first nuclei of capitalist production, were already present in parts of 14th century Italy and Flanders, and 16th century Germany, France and Bohemia. In each case the rise of the market began, spontaneously, to give rise to the elements that were to come together to create the national state.

The spread of trade caused people in different regions to have increasing direct and indirect contact with each other. Traders from the towns travelled through the countryside, buying, selling and talking to people in the most remote villages, picking up the bits of dialect they needed to make themselves understood and mixing them into the colloquial idiom of the town, creating, without thinking about it, new standard forms of communication which it was an advantage for everyone connected with the new commerce to learn. Along with the traders went itinerant preachers—often out to profit their pockets as well as their souls—and recruiters looking for men for the new mercenary armies. Meanwhile, the poorest in the villages would leave for the towns in search of work, and the richest to cut out the middleman and to trade directly themselves. While in rural France, the average peasant never travelled more than about five miles from his or her home in a lifetime of toil, by the late 17th century one in seven of England's population would pass at least part of their life in London.[6]

Spontaneously, unconsciously, trading networks started to become linguistic networks. It was then that the administrators of the state, keen to tax the profits of trade, saw the point in carrying out their transactions in the language of the market, not that of the court or the church. It was then, too, that the innovative writers saw that using the new colloquial tongue was the way to win an audience—as Dante did in early 14th century Florence, Chaucer in England half a century later, and Luther and Rabelais in 16th century Germany and France.

The change took a long time to complete—even as late as the 17th century, Hobbes in England and Spinoza in Holland could still write major works in Latin—but where capitalism conquered, so did the new tongues. By contrast, where capitalism had a false start and then succumbed to a revival of the old order, so too the new languages suffered: the increasing refeudalisation of late Renaissance Italy meant much literature was in Latin rather than in Dante's Italian;[7] the smashing of Bohemian Protestantism by the armed counter-reformation at the battle of the White Mountain in 1618 was also the destruction of Czech as a written language for nearly 200 years; Latin continued to be the language of adminstration in the Habsburg empire until the 1840s.

What became the first nations began their life as networks of trade, adminstration and language which grew up in the hinterland of major cities. Everywhere in Europe the administrators of late feudal monarchies tried to increase their power over members of the old feudal ruling class by allying themselves with the traders and manufacturers of the towns. These 'burghers' were often already at the centre of geographically compact networks of trade and language. Some of the administrators could see great advantage to themselves in making the language of the burghers the language of the state, so cementing the alliance and beginning to create a linguistically homogeneous state, able as none previously had been to insist on the allegiance of all those who lived within its boundaries.

The growth of the new linguistically based state had great advantages for the rising bourgeoisie. It made it more difficult for traders from elsewhere, who spoke 'foreign' languages, to challenge their 'home' markets. And it made the administrators of the state increasingly subject to their influence and eager to pursue their interests, especially when it came to helping them compete with rival groups of traders on world markets—as with the state backed struggle for control over the East India trade between the English and Dutch chartered companies in the 17th century. Even where the form of the state remained feudal, as in 17th century France, it was increasingly attentive to the interests of the nascent capitalists.

But if the creation of the national state began spontaneously, elements of consciousness were soon involved as well. Political philosophers from the time of Machiavelli (at the very beginning of the 16th century) onwards began to urge policies on states which would speed up the spontaneous process.[8] Political economists elaborated the 'mercantilism' doctrines, which identified the interests of the state with the accumulation of trade surpluses by its merchant class. Playwrights, poets and pamphleteers began for the first time to celebrate what would later be called 'national' traditions.

The new 'national' state proved in practice to have an additional advantage for those who ruled over it, whether they came from the old aristocracy or from the rising class of capitalists. It provided an apparent tie between the exploiters and the exploited. However much they differed in their incomes and lifestyles, they had one thing in common: they spoke a language which others could not understand. This became particularly important to a section of the middle class who, knowing the language and proving their loyalty to the state, could get jobs in the state machine itself which were denied to national minorities at home and colonised populations abroad.

The drive to create new national states

The spread of capitalism through the globe was characterised by combined and uneven development. The first centres of capitalist accumulation in Britain and Holland had a double effect on the rest of the globe. They robbed and impoverished whole regions. But they also drew them into a worldwide network of market relations and so eventually encouraged the rise of new groups of capitalists—or of new middle classes who saw their future as lying with capitalism.

But these groups found themselves in a world already dominated by existing capitalists using national states to protect their interests. If new centres of capitalism were to develop beyond a certain point, they needed states of their own to fight for their interests. So it was that French mercantile interests looked to the absolutist state that had grown out of feudalism to fight for its interests in a war for global influence with Britain, that land owners and traders in the North American colonies began to resent the dictates of the British state and create state structures of their own in opposition to it, and that sections of the middle class in Dublin and Belfast began to mutter about their own 'right' to independence from Britain.

Those who looked to the creation of new national states to advance their interests could not wait hundreds of years for spontaneous economic and social developments to bring such states into being. The path forward was at least partially blocked by the existing capitalist nation states, particularly Britain, on the one hand, and by the old absolutist, pre-capitalist states on the other. Conscious revolutionary action was required if they were ever to emulate, let alone out-compete, British capitalism. And revolutionary action had to be motivated by an ideology that laid out, in however confused a way, the key points about the sort of state they wanted.

The French revolutionaries went furthest in this direction, with their proclamation of 'the French republic, one and indivisible'. They forcibly replaced the old administrative divisions, with their plethora of differing taxes and privileges, by a centralised structure run through government appointed prefects. They imposed a single standard of citizenship, demanding the allegiance of everyone, an allegiance which found expression in the universal conscription of young males to fight for 'the nation in arms'. They established a single national educational system, and used it to propagate a single language in place of the regional dialects of the southern half of France, the Breton of the west and the Germanic tongue of the northern frontiers.

Theirs became the model of what the national state should be for all those who sought to make the breakthrough to a 'modern', capitalist development of society elsewhere in the world. Soon young revolutionaries were striving to copy it in Ireland, Latin America, Greece, Italy, Germany, Poland, Hungary and Spain. By the beginning of the 20th century there were carbon copy nationalisms in the Czech speaking regions of Austro-Hungary, the Balkans, Asiatic Turkey, China, India, the Ukraine and the Russian Caucasus. The next half century saw their spread through the empires of Britain and France, which between them controlled all of Africa and most of South Asia and the Middle East.

Nation, language and religion

The new nations were conscious products, in a way that the earlier ones had not been. There were Italian and German, Greek and Czech, Indian and Indonesian national movements long before the nation states themselves were established, whereas in the earlier English, American and French cases the idea of nationality had only taken hold as, or even after, the national state was coming into being. However, life was usually much harder for the creators of the new nations than for their predecessors. Not only did they often encounter vicious persecution from those in charge of the states they wanted to replace or reform, but the raw material—the people—from which they wished to construct a nation, was far from ready.

Centuries of long drawn out capitalist development had created in north west Europe—and in its transplant in North America—fairly large geographic regions in which single languages predominated: in most of England and part of Scotland, in much of northern France, even in Germany as a result of Luther's success in establishing a church which used a single local dialect. By contrast, in southern and eastern Europe, in Asia and Africa, the late arrival of capitalism meant the task of linguistic homogenisation had hardly begun.

It was still quite usual to find the same picture as in medieval Europe: a state administration using one language, a church another, local landlords a third, the peasantry a fourth and often the inhabitants of the towns a fifth. Thus in any particular part of the Balkans, the religious language would be a dead language—Latin, Old Church Slavonic, archaic Greek or classical Arabic. The language of administration would be German, Hungarian, Turkish or Greek. The language of the peasantry would be a Slav or occasionally a Romance or Hungarian dialect, and the language of the towns quite likely a German dialect. What is more, the language of the peasantry would vary from village to village, or sometimes from household to household within the same village.

This did not lead to any great problems so long as pre-capitalist forms of production dominated. The peasants would know enough of the languages of administration and of the towns to cope in their limited number of transactions with them and indeed would often switch from one language or dialect to another without difficulty as the occasion demanded. They might not have been able to achieve examination level standards of competence—particularly written competence—in any of them, but they could cope very well without doing so.

But this plethora of languages and dialects was a headache for the modernising nationalists, with their aim of achieving linguistic homogeneity not only in the spoken language, but also in the written forms required for the advance of the market and the modern state. The only way they could achieve their goal was to pick on one or other spoken idiom and proclaim this was the 'national' language that everyone had to learn, not merely to speak, but to read and write.

The choice was not always completely arbitrary. Capitalist development, however slow, usually meant there were sections of the peasantry already in continuous contact with part of the urban population, with a dialect that was already more influential than others. So for instance in early 19th century Prague there was already a growing Czech speaking petty bourgeoisie that could act as the link with the peasantry that the nationalists wanted. But there was often a powerful, arbitrary element to it—as when Italian nationalists finally opted for the Tuscan dialect[9] (spoken by only 2.5 percent of the population of the peninsular) as the 'national language', or when the first Indian nationalists decided the regional dialect of Delhi, Hindustani, could be the national language once it was purged of all words of Persian origin, or when South Slav nationalists residing in Vienna rejected the idea of using Old Church Slavonic as the national language and instead gave the accolade to the Stokavian dialect (spoken by sections of both Croats and Serbs, but not by all of either) which they baptised 'Serbo-Croat'.[10]

But deciding what was the national language was only the beginning of the problem. The mass of people then had to be persuaded to accept it. Here again, things were much harder with most late arriving, more economically backward nations than with their predecessors. For where capitalist development was successful, providing markets for peasants and jobs for growing urban populations, it was not that difficult to get people to put up with the discomforts of not being fluent in the official language. In France most of the non-French speaking minorities embraced the revolution and the nation because it seemed to offer them a better life. In the US generation after generation of non-English speaking immigrants treasured their new nationality, even if they could not speak its language very well. By contrast, in Spain Catalans resented having to speak the language of economically more backward Castille and Andalusia, in Romania Hungarians and Saxons insisted on using their own languages, in Ireland a mass of inducements by the state could not stop the people of the far west abandoning their native Gaelic for the economically much more useful English, and in India the peoples of the south simply refused to accept the Hindi of the north.

The latecoming nationalists had similar problems when it came to the question of religion. The model for nationalists was strongly secularist. For religion was a product of the pre-capitalist societies they were trying to transform. It usually encouraged them to take on obligations that cut right across the new state boundaries they were trying to establish. And it often encouraged divisions among the people they were trying to win to a sense of a single national identity. So 19th century South Slav nationalists wanted the unity of Catholic, Orthodox and Muslim; Indian nationalists of Hindu and Muslim; Irish nationalists of Catholic and Protestant; Arab nationalists of Muslim and Christian.

But the temptation was always to compromise with religion so as to find a base among a mass of peasants who were still fairly remote from the market and the modernising schemes that went with it, and who found the 'national language' incomprehensible. So the leaders of the Irish national movements always combined talk of secularism with attempts to win at least limited support from the Catholic Church, the Indian National Congress's most popular figure, Gandhi, sought to compromise with peasant prejudice by adopting the garb of a Hindu saint, and the founder of the Arab nationalist Ba'ath party, Afleck, converted to Islam towards the end of his life.

These problems over language and compromises with religion had very important effects. The founder nationalists did not usually identify with one ethnic group against another, and did not embrace what today is euphemistically called 'ethnic cleansing'. Their aim was to unify the population of a particular region so as to enable them to 'modernise' it in a capitalist sense. They were ready if necessary to force a certain language and culture on people, and if necessary to use the full power of the state against those who resisted—as the French Revolution did in Brittany, or the combined forces of the English and Scottish bourgeoisies did in the Highlands. But their aim remained to unite the whole population, not to use one section to eradicate another.

However, they began to move away from this aim every time they picked on one minority dialect as *the* national language or identified with one particular religion. The national movement became based in one part of the population, not the rest. And it was very easy to make a virtue of necessity—to see the German speakers as excluding themselves from the Czech nation, the Protestants from the Irish nation, the Muslims from the Indian nation, the Catholics and Muslims from the Serbian nation.

The class base of nationalism

Nationalism grew up as part of the ideology of capitalist development. The idea of the nation is inseparable from a range of other ideas associated with the bourgeois revolution. If nationalism has conquered the globe, with every individual anywhere in the world today slotted into one national identity or another, it is because capitalism has conquered the globe.

This does not mean, however, that the pioneers of nationalism have necessarily been capitalists themselves. There have been such cases. For instance, the first nationalist party in Catalonia, the Lliga, was the party of the Catalan capitalists.[11] More commonly, however, the promoters of new nationalisms have come from sections of the middle class frustrated by the stagnation and backwardness of the society in which they have found themselves. They have seen the only way out as being to turn their country of origin into a 'nation' like every other nation, and using that to encourage economic advance. Since every other nation is capitalist, this involves, in reality, encouraging capitalist development, however much it is dressed up in talk of the virtues of the traditional way of life: the Celtic twilight may have inspired Irish nationalists of a century ago, but the programme of the founder of Sinn Fein, Arthur Griffiths, was to create 'a Gaelic Manchester';[12] Mahatma Gandhi may have preached the virtues of homespun cloth, but his Congress was financed by the big Indian capitalists and the building up of heavy industry was central to its economic programme; Nkrumah of Ghana may have praised African 'communalism', but on gaining control of state power he set about trying to build modern industry.[13]

The nationalists were more often middle class intellectuals—poets, playwrights, teachers, lawyers—than big capitalists. But their programme depended on the encouragement of capitalism, even if this meant turning some of their own number into state capitalists by the establishment of new nationalised industries. Before being able to do any of these things, the nationalists had to find a base of support in society at large.

The middle class itself, or, rather, certain sections of the middle class, was usually an important part of the base. The backwardness of society was reflected in the feebleness of career opportunities for the literate middle class, especially when state power was in the hands of a pre-capitalist ruling class or some already existing foreign nation state. Then an obvious way for the middle classes to improve their chances in life was to fight for their own right to work in the state machine—using their own language if this was a problem—and to go even further and fight for a revolutionary reconstitution of the state machine under their own 'national' control.

In a similar way the small shopkeeping, trading and petty manufacturing bourgeoisie could rally behind the nationalist course. They did not have the ability to extract concessions from a pre-capitalist or foreign state machine which big capital sometimes had. The creation of a new national state would provide them with influence over political decisions and with the government contracts and protected markets that went with it.

Finally, the peasantry and the incipient working class were always possible allies for the national cause. They suffered from the general backwardness of society and faced continual humiliation and repression from those who ran the old state machine. Nationalist agitation could act as a focus for a mass of discontents and stir the lower classes into action.

But there was always a problem for the nationalist in relying on the workers and peasants. Their discontent was not merely with pre-capitalist forms of exploitation or the behaviour of the old state; it was also with the new, rising forms of capitalism, often presided over by the new 'national capitalists', and with the privileges of the 'national middle class'. A movement of workers and peasants which began with hostility to the old rulers and exploiters could all too easily spill over into confrontation with the new, home born variety. This could destroy all the plans of the nationalist leaders. That is why the history of nationalist movements often involves spells of agitation among workers, but these spells have always been brought to an end with a sharp turn to placate 'national' propertied interests, even if the price of doing so is to derail the national movement itself. Hence the 'betrayals' of Germany in 1848-9, Ireland in 1921-2 or China in 1925-7.

The workers movement may be a temporary ally for the nationalists. But it cannot constitute a firm and reliable base for their schemes. For this they have to look to sections of the bourgeoisie or petty bourgeoisie.

Reactionary nationalist movements

The classic nationalist movements were part of the bourgeois revolution which swept Europe and the Americas in the 18th and 19th centuries. Later nationalist movements were often associated with the struggle of colonial peoples to throw off imperialist rule. To this extent they involved a challenge to existing oppressive state structures—even if they intended only to replace them with new oppressive state structures.

But from very early on movements arose which seemed to have certain 'national' characteristics, but which served to protect, not undermine, the old structures. One such movement was that of Highlanders who joined the reactionary risings of the Stuart pretenders to the British throne in 1714 and 1746 in the belief that this would protect them against the new, bourgeois organisation of society being imposed by the Lowlanders and the English. Another was the *chouan* movement in Brittany in the 1790s, with priests and royalists manipulating the fears of Breton peasants about threats to their traditional way of life so as to ignite a counter-revolutionary revolt. A third was the Carlist movements of northern Spain in the 1830s and 1872, with Basque and Navarese peasants expressing resentment at the loss of traditional rights by fighting under the leadership of the most reactionary forces (their first demand was the restoration of the Inquisition!).

In the same league, although with a rather different social base, was the Orange Order in Ireland—consciously established by the British state around the slogan of Protestant supremacy to help smash the Irish national movement in the late 1790s, and revived for the same purpose in 1832, 1848, 1884, 1912 and 1920-1. These movements did not proclaim themselves to be national, although some present day nationalists have claimed them as precursors. But a movement which emerged during the revolutions of 1848 did present itself as part of the more general nationalist upsurge. This was the movement of the Slavs living within the Austro-Hungarian Empire. Its leaders aimed to create new national entities for the Czechs, the Ruthenes (western Ukrainians) and the South Slavs (the common name for Serbs, Croats and Slovenians). But with the partial exception of the Bohemian Czechs, these peoples were still in their overwhelming majority economically backward peasants, speaking mutually incomprehensible dialects, with the idea of any common national ties restricted to a handful of urban intellectuals. The mass of peasants could not be drawn into battle to replace the old traditions of economic backwardness and local parochialism by some new model of national unity. But some of them could be persuaded to play the role of the Bretons and the Basques—to fight in defence of the old feudal order against the challenge to it from the German and Hungarian nationalists. So in 1848 they fell in behind the counter-revolution and helped the Habsburg monarchy to crush the revolution in Vienna. As Marx wrote at the time, 'In Vienna we have a whole swarm of nationalities which imagined the counter-revolution will bring them emancipation'.[14] No wonder, 'in those months all of Europe's democracy came to hate the small Slavic nations...'[15]

As 'nationhood' became the established, generally recognised symbol of legitimacy in an increasingly bourgeoisified world, so not only movements fighting the old order but those striving to reinforce it inscribed 'national' slogans on their banners. By the second half of the 19th century even the dynastic empires which had previously been the most bitter opponents of national movements began to redefine themselves in nationalist terms. The Prussian monarchy took over the German nationalist ideology. The Habsburg monarchy split its domains into two halves, in one of which Hungarian replaced Latin as the official language, in the other, German. The 'Tsar of all the Russias'—whose court had spoken French and relied to a considerable extent on German speaking administrators—for the first time began to encourage a Great Russian nationalism, which regarded other ethnic groups as innately inferior. 'It was not until Alexander III (1881-94) that Russification became official policy.'[16]

The absolutist monarchies, which had established themselves in the late middle ages by using the urban burghers as a counterweight to the feudal lords, were now trying to prolong their life by renegotiating terms with sections of the bourgeoisie and petty bourgeoisie. The monarchy would give privileges to traders, bankers, manufacturers, gentry and literate intelligentsia which spoke one language, if they would ally with it against its enemies—inducing those sections of the bourgeoisie and petty bourgeoisie who spoke other languages.

But it was not only the old absolutist monarchies who adopted the policy of pushing one nationalism and oppressing others. So did the already capitalist states which were dividing the whole of Africa and most of Asia between them. The second half of the 19th century saw a new celebration of 'British' nationalism, with the establishment, for the first time, of a state run educational system that indoctrinated children in the glories of 'national' history, the writing of nationalist popular novels, plays, poetry and songs by literary admirers of the empire and the conscious invention of traditions aimed at encouraging popular identification with the monarchy. For the middle classes the identification with 'nation' and empire was not to be simply ideological but contained crude material incentives: the bureaucracy that administered the empire was English speaking, and the career structures in it were open to the middle class English or Scots in a way in which they were not to the Irish Catholic or the Australian, still less the Indian or African.

The use of reactionary nationalism was combined with the deliberate exploitation of linguistic and religious differences to weaken movements against British rule in the colonies. Just as the Orange slogans of Protestant ascendancy had been used with effect in Ireland, in India the British sought to play the Muslim card against the incipient national movement by splitting Bengal along religious lines in the early 1900s, in Palestine they encouraged European Jewish immigration at the end of the First World War to undercut the power of Arab resistance to British rule. In Cyprus they recruited the police force mainly from the Turkish speaking minority, and in Ceylon (present day Sri Lanka) from a section of the Tamil speakers.

Contradictory nationalisms and communalism

There was one further twist to the spread of the national ideal across the whole world from the late 19th century onwards. Rival nationalities were soon battling for the same territory.

The model of the early nationalists assumed they would easily be able to absorb minorities into their new national states. And so it was with many of the first national states: the English did succeed in getting the Scots to identify with 'Britain' and the empire, the French did absorb the southerners who spoke the Occitanian dialect and even gained the support of many German speaking Alsacians, the German empire did win the allegiance of Saxony, Thuringia, Hanover, Hamburg and Bremen (although separatist currents persisted in Bavaria and the Rhineland).

But things were very different with many of the later developing nationalisms. As we have seen, the late arrival of capitalism meant there was rarely one predominant language or dialect among the people who were supposed to make up the new nation. The nationalists might be able to gain support from one section of the population by declaring its language the new national tongue—but only by antagonising other groups.

Even where a degree of capitalist development did take off, it did not always make things easier. For it drew new sections of the peasantry, not fluent in the national tongue, into market relationships and created a new petty bourgeoisie from among them. Intellectuals from this milieu began to codify peasant dialects into new tongues, to fight for official status for them and eventually for nation states based on them. Thus, as a continual influx of former peasants transformed Prague from a mainly German speaking city into a mainly Czech speaking one, so the demand grew to establish a new Czech state out of the Austrian provinces of Bohemia and Moravia. But at least by the late 19th century there was a clear Czech speaking majority in Prague. In many major east European, Balkan and Caucasian towns all the competing linguistic groups grew, without any one necessarily predominating: Hungarian and Romanian speakers in Transylvania; Italian and Slovene speakers in Triest; German and Polish speakers in Silesia; Lithuanian, Polish and Yiddish speakers in Vilnius; Ukrainian, Yiddish and Polish speakers in the western Ukraine; Turkish, Greek and Armenian speakers in Istanbul; Greek and Slav speakers in Macedonia; Russian, Armenian and Turkish speakers in Baku.

The capitalist world was a world organised into linguistic nation states, and so, as each ethnic group was drawn into this world, its petty bourgeoisie wanted its own language and its own state. But it had arrived too late on the scene to get this through the long drawn out, spontaneous processes that had brought linguistic homogeneity to England, Holland, France or Germany. The different nationalisms could only achieve their goals if they waged bloody wars against each other as well as—or sometimes instead of—against the old absolutisms.

What this meant was shown in all its horror with the Second Balkan War of 1913, as the rival national states of Romania, Serbia and Greece ganged up against Bulgaria and sliced Macedonia in two, causing some half a million deaths. It was shown again in 1915 when, in an effort to draw behind them the Turkish and Kurdish speaking populations of the old Ottoman Empire, nationalist 'Young Turk' officers organised the extermination of the great majority of the empire's Armenian speakers; in 1918-19 when rival Azer and Armenian nationalist groups murdered each other in Baku; in 1921-2 when the war between Turkey and Greece led to each army expelling hundreds of thousands of civilians of the other nationality. In eastern Europe, the Balkans and the Caucasus the point had been reached where nationalism came to mean 'ethnic cleansing'—pogroms, forced expulsions and even extermination camps.

Classical Marxism and the national question

Marx and Engels were part of the revolutionary movement of the 1840s. They began their political life on its extreme liberal democratic wing, but came to realise very quickly that human emancipation could only be achieved by a movement that went further and looked to working class revolution. Such a revolution would end 'national differences and antagonisms among peoples':

> *In proportion as the exploitation of one individual by another is put an end to, the exploitation of one nation by another will also be put an end to. In proportion as the antagonism between classes within the nation vanishes, the hostility of one nation to another will come to an end.*[17]

This did not mean, however, that they abstained from the struggle of bourgeois democratic forces against absolutism. They threw themselves into the revolutionary upheaval of 1848-9, criticising from the left the attempts of the bourgeois democrats to conciliate the old order. A key role in the upheaval was played by the four major national movements: the struggles to unite Germany and Italy as bourgeois national states in place of the various monarchies that divided them, the struggle to free Hungary from the Habsburg dynasty based in Vienna, and the struggle to free Poland from Tsarism, the gendarme of reaction right across

Europe. A success for any one of these movements was, in the context of 1848-9, a gain for the revolution as a whole, and a defeat for them was a victory for the counter-revolution. Marx and Engels therefore looked to revolutionary war to establish new national states in Germany, Hungary, Italy and Poland, and to inflict a final defeat on the last remnants of feudalism in Europe. Among the enemies who would have to be fought in this war were those Slav politicians in the Austro-Hungarian Empire who used the phraseology of nationalism to justify their support for absolutism. Their defeat would be part of the process of clearing the ground for the full development of bourgeois democracy and so for the struggle of the working class against the system.

Marx and Engels did not require any particularly sophisticated analysis of nationalism to see what needed to be done in such a situation. And their time was absorbed, remember, not only in engaging in revolutionary agitation, but also in elaborating a completely new view of history and society. So Engels, in particular, simply took over the terminology of Hegel's philosophy of history and distinguished between different national movements on the basis of whether they represented 'historic peoples' who had a long and dynamic history, or 'non-historic peoples' who were doomed to be marginalised by historical development. At this stage neither Marx nor Engels seem to have grasped what a new historical phenomenon the nation was,[18] how it differed from previous states or ethnic groupings, and how distant most of the movements they condemned were from sharing the characteristics of modern national movements.[19]

They began to shift their position on national movements in the 1860s, faced with a renewal of the agitation against British rule in Ireland. Previously they had opposed British repression in Ireland, but had looked to revolutionary change in Britain to bring it to an end. They now changed their views. Marx wrote to Engels:

> *I have done my best to bring about a demonstration of the English workers in favour of Fenianism... I used to think the separation of Ireland from England was impossible. Now I think it is inevitable, although after separation there may come federation*[20]

> *What the Irish need is...self government and independence from England..Agrarian revolution...Protective tariffs against England.*[21]

And to Kugelmann:

> *The English working class...will never be able to do anything decisive here in England before they separate their attitude towards Ireland quite definitely from that of the ruling classes, and not only make common cause*

with the Irish, but even take the initiative in dissolving the Union established in 1801. And this must be done not out of sympathy with the Irish, but as a demand based on the interests of the English proletariat. If not the English proletariat will for ever remain bound to the leading strings of the ruling classes, because they will be forced to make a common front with them against Ireland...[22]

In his approach to the Irish issue, Marx was making a very important point: the nationalism of workers belonging to an oppressor nation binds them to their rulers and only does harm to themselves, while the nationalism of an oppressed nation can lead them to fight back against those rulers. What is more, he was supporting the struggle of a nationality which could never be included in the list of 'the great historic nations of Europe'. However, it was not until after Marx's death that Engels began to present a new, historical materialist account of nations. An unfulfilled plan to rewrite *The Peasant War in Germany*—about popular unrest during the Reformation—led him to study the transformation of society at the end of the Middle Ages and to see material factors as giving rise to the beginnings of the nation state as a new historical phenomenon. He stressed that as the towns grew in prominence and allied with the monarchy against the rest of the feudal ruling class, 'out of the confusions of people that characterised the early middle ages, there gradually developed the new nationalisms'. But this was in a manuscript that remained unpublished until 1935.[23]

Deeper historical materialist analysis of nationalism did not begin until the end of the 19th century, when new political developments suddenly made it an urgent issue.

The growth of the socialist movement in the German empire was followed by a similar growth in Austria (which then included the present day Czech lands of Bohemia and Moravia, and present day Slovenia), and many of the best known German language Marxists came from there: Otto Bauer and Rudolf Hilferding were Austrians, and Karl Kautsky a Czech. But just as the Austrian party was enjoying its first real successes in the 1890s it was plunged into bitter arguments by the growing nationalist agitation among Austria's Slavs.

Otto Bauer tried to resolve the disputes by making a new analysis of nationalism. He argued that the nation is 'a community of culture' or 'a community of destiny', which causes all those who belong to it to experience things differently to those who belong to a different nation.[24] The nation gives all its members certain character features in common, so that an English person and a German, making, for instance, the same journey would experience it differently. This diversity of culture meant that even when people spoke the same language, as with the Danes and Norwegians or the Serbs and Croats, they remained separate nations.[25]

'It is the diversity of culture which rigorously separates nations, despite the mixing of blood.'[26]

Bauer argued that national culture went through three historic stages. It began with the period of primitive communism, when 'all the compatriots are related as much by community of blood as by culture', then went through a period of class society, in which it was bound together by the culture of the ruling class, and finally would be 'represented by the socialist society of the future'.[27] So the 'nation' can be seen in terms of the development of the productive forces, as constituting 'what is historical in us',[28] as a 'condensation of history'.[29]

He went on to attack, in the most forthright terms, those who did not see the value of the nation and instead opted for 'proletarian cosmopolitanism', 'the most primitive taking of position by the working class as against the national strife of the bourgeois world', for instance talking of 'Czech and German speaking comrades' rather than 'Czech and German comrades'. They were falling into the trap of 'rationalist, enlightenment' thinking, of 'an atomistic-individualistic conception of society' which failed to see that 'the individual man is himself a product of the nation'.

Bauer's conclusion was that socialists should embrace the idea of nation as an important social and historical factor in human existence, and tell the different nationalities that only under socialism would national culture reach its full development. 'Socialism announces to all nations the realisation of their aspiration to political unity and freedom. It does the same for the German nation.'[30] Such support for cultural nationalism, he argued, would enable socialists to prevent the fragmentation of the large states which were, in his view, necessary for economic development.

The Austrian socialists drew up an elaborate programme, based in part upon Bauer's views,[31] which promised all the different peoples of the Austro-Hungarian Empire their own national institutions within the existing imperial state structure. A national grouping in any particular locality would be given autonomy over educational and cultural affairs, and then would federate with groupings in other localities so as to form a single 'autonomous' structure right across the empire. There would be no official language, although 'whether a common language is required, a federal parliament can decide'. The whole structure was intended to encourage 'the nurturing and development of the national peculiarities of all the peoples of Austria'.[32]

The practical outcome of such a scheme was to encourage the members of the socialist movement to make continual concessions to those who stressed cultural differences within the working class, until first the socialist party and then the unions split into different national organisations—something which must have been rather gratifying to those employers, whether German or Czech speaking, who exploited linguistically mixed workforces.

The first theoretical onslaught against Bauer's position was led by Karl Kautsky. He had already begun to deepen the materialist analysis of the origins of modern nationality in the late 1880s, and went on to write numerous articles dealing in one way or another with the same issue. These were the starting point for other Marxists like Lenin. As George Haupt has noted, 'Kautsky, who formulated theories, opened parentheses and made distinctions, without engaging in systematisation, remained the indispensable reference point for a long time'.[33] His disagreement with Bauer was 'the confrontation between two conceptions of nations, to be labelled by Lenin the "psychological-cultural" and the "historical-economic".'[34]

Kautsky recognised the virtual impossibility of defining what a nation is:

'Nation' is a social formation difficult to apprehend, a product of social development, that rules have never been able to transform into a precisely defined social organism. Nationality is a social relation that transforms itself ceaselessly, which has a different signification in different conditions...[35]

But he nevertheless insisted it could be understood in relation to economic development. 'The concentration and separation of societies into nation states was one of the most powerful levers of economic development'.[36] This alone, he argued, explained why German speakers in, say, northern Bohemia regarded themselves as part of the German nation, while those in Switzerland did not.[37] Because of its role in economic development, 'The classical form of the modern state is the nation state. But classical forms exist in general only as a tendency. It is rare that they are developed in a perfectly typical fashion'.[38] What is more:

To the extent that economic antagonisms deepen, each economic region tries to develop its own urban and rural industry, but can do this less and less without hurting the industry of its neighbours. The different Austrian regions tend to separate, and the 'reconciliation' of nations becomes more difficult.[39]

He criticised Bauer for downplaying the importance of language. There was, he said, only one example of a nation that included more than one 'linguistic community', the Swiss. As for the cases where different nationalities shared the same language—he mentions the English and the Irish, the Danes and Norwegians, the Serbs and

Croats—'this does not prove that each national community is a linguistic community it simply proves that sometimes a linguistic community can comprise two nations, that linguistic community, is not the sole distinctive sign of a nation'.[40] In fact, 'the powerful role of language in social life can make us understand a good part of the force of national sentiment'.[41]

He went on to ascribe the rise of the national state to a series of factors. First, the bourgeoisie's desire to provide itself with a market for its own commodities, free from the hindrance of feudal territorial divisions or from interference by old state structures. Second, the growing importance of administration in modern society, which gives unprecedented importance to the language question: 'The bureaucracy is a structure that finds it difficult to function without a single language'. Third, the way in which the 'commercialisation of society' laid the ground for linguistic unification by increasing the frequency of intercourse between people in different localities and produced a more uniform language: 'uniformisation rarely succeeded just through the channel of education, but through the development of commercial relations at the interior of the state'.[42]

It was this, finally, which explained the rise of rival nationalities within a single state. Where the economic forces were not powerful enough to get the speakers of different tongues to learn the national language, government attempts to enforce uniformity increased the divisions between different linguistic groups. Some gained material advantages from the official status given to their language: it gave them preferential chances of promotion into and up the ranks of the state bureaucracy. But others suffered and tended to turn to national identities of their own in opposition to the official one:

> *When, in professional life or in front of a tribunal, the dominant language was spoken, the members of the other nations were at a disadvantage... Promotion of the children of artisans and peasants into the bureaucracy was made very difficult for nations which did not speak the official language.*[43]

Kautsky thus provided an account of the rise of rival nationalisms that was more historical and more materialist than Bauer's—which is perhaps why Bauer receives the praise today from those who damn Marxism for being 'reductionist' and not taking account of 'ethnicity' and 'gender'.[44] But there was an unresolved problem with Kautsky's own analysis. He saw capitalist economic development as leading to a withering away of national struggles, despite his insights into how minority groups could turn to new nationalisms. In his early writings he argued that capitalist development doomed the Czech nation to disappear. And even after he had dropped this view he still saw national conflicts as dying away as capitalist commerce became increasingly international:

> *As [social] intercourse grows with economic development, so the circle of people using the same language must grow as well. From this arises the tendency of unified languages to expand, to swallow up other nations, which lose their language and adopt the language of the dominant nation or a mixture...*
>
> *The joining of nations to the international cultural community will be reflected in the growth of universal languages among merchants and educated people...*[45]

There was an important insight here which led him to denounce Bauer for encouraging national antagonisms among socialists:

> *Never was a purely national culture less possible. Therefore it strikes us as very strange when people talk always of only a national culture, and when the goal of socialism is considered to be the endowing of the masses with national culture... When socialist society provides the masses with an education, it also gives them the ability to speak several languages, the universal languages, and therefore to take part in the entire international civilisation and not only in the separate culture of a certain linguistic community.*[46]

But the insight was buried within a wider analysis which vastly underrated the way in which capitalism provokes national antagonism at the same time as creating the possibilities of overcoming it.

Luxemburg and Lenin

Rosa Luxemburg began from a different starting point to Bauer and Kautsky. She was trying to build a revolutionary party in Poland, where the socialist movement split in the 1890s between those—like the future Polish dictator Pilsudski—who were moving increasingly in a nationalist direction and those who stood resolutely for internationalism. Yet when her party attended the congress of the International in the 1890s and of the Russian Social Democratic Labour Party in 1903, it found the majority of delegates embracing the right of Poland to independence in a way which seemed to her to give solace to her nationalist opponents at home. Right up to her death in 1918 she was to argue vehemently against any 'right' of nations to self determination and against any involvement of socialists in national uprisings.

She backed up this position with arguments that combined elements of Kautsky's view with elements of Bauer's. She located the origins of nationalism squarely in economics—in the economic needs of this or that ruling class. Her interpretation of Kautsky's account of the rise of nationalism in countries like Germany and Italy puts all the stress on the role of the big bourgeoisie.[47] She argues that its desire for domestic markets led it to promote the national movement, and gave this a realistic character. She then goes on to use this 'economistic' analysis to tear late 19th and early 20th century Polish nationalism apart:

The material base of Polish national aspirations (in the first half of the 19th century) was determined not as in central Europe by modern capitalist development, but on the contrary by the nobility's idea of its social standing, rooted in the natural feudal economy.

The national movements in Poland vanished with these feudal relations, whereas the bourgeoisie, as the historical spokesman of capitalist development, was with us, from the beginning, a clearly anti-national factor. This was due, not only to the specific origin of the 19th century bourgeoisie, alien and heterogeneous, a product of colonisation, an alien body transplanted on to Polish soil. Also decisive was the fact that Polish industry was from its beginning an export industry... Export to Russia... became the basis for the existence of and development of Polish capitalism...and the basis of the Polish bourgeoisie. As a consequence, our bourgeoisie showed political leanings...towards Russia...The class rule of the bourgeoisie in Poland not only did not demand the creation of a united nation state, but, on the contrary, it arose on the foundations of the conquest and division of Poland. The idea of unification and national independence did not draw its vital juices from capitalism: on the contrary, as capitalism developed this idea became historically outlived... In Poland there arose an opposition between the national idea and the bourgeois development, which gave the former not only a utopian but also a reactionary character.[48]

For her, if the bourgeoisie did not want a nation state somewhere, since that state was part of capitalist development, the idea was both doomed and reactionary.

Her argument arose out of the Polish context. But she extended it further. She argued, correctly, that Kautsky was wrong to see the needs of capitalism for international trade leading to a peaceful growing together of national states. Instead, she insisted, there would be increasing conflict between states, and these states would increasingly not be states with a homogeneous national population, but rather states which forcibly annexed whole peoples against their will:

> Historical development...lies...not in the tendency toward the idea of a 'national state' but rather in the deadly struggle among nations, in the tendency to create great capitalist states...The form that best serves the interests of exploitation in the contemporary world is not the 'national' state as Kautsky thinks, but a state bent on conquest. When we compare the different states from the point of view of the degree to which they approach this ideal...we look to the British and German states as models, for they are based on national oppression in Europe and the world at large—and to the United States, a state which keeps in its bosom like a gaping wound the oppression of the Negro people and seeks to conquer the Asiatic people.

This, she concluded, destroyed any possibility of a new, viable national movement emerging:

> The development of world powers, a characteristic feature of our times growing in importance along with the progress of capitalism, from the very outset condemns all small nations to political impotence... 'Self determination', the independent existence of smaller and petty nations, is an illusion, and will become even more so... Can one speak with any seriousness of the 'self-determination' of peoples which are formally independent, such as the Montenegrins, Bulgarians, Romanians, the Serbs, the Greeks...? From this point of view, the idea of 'insuring all the nations the possibility of self determination is the equivalent of reverting from great capitalist development to the small medieval states, far earlier than the 15th and 16th centuries.[49]

The characteristic feature of this part of her argument is the way in which she moves from a brilliant, dialectical account of the economic and military trends in capitalism to a completely mechanical view of the political consequences—big capital does not want national struggles and national insurrections, therefore these count for nothing.

This did not mean that her position was one of simple opposition to nationalism. For she combined her ultra-Kautskyite analysis of the roots of the nation state with a Bauerite attitude to cultural nationalism. She praised the Austrian party's Brno programme, with its scheme to divide the population into autonomous national groupings. She referred to 'national sentiments' as among 'the higher forms of psychic phenomena', and foresaw the survival of 'Polish national identity' as socialism led to 'the opening up of new vistas for the deliverance of Polish national culture'.[50] She claimed that 'the cause of nationalism in Poland is not alien to the working class—nor can it be', on the grounds that 'the working class cannot be indifferent to the most intolerable barbaric oppression, directed as it is against the intellectual and cultural heritage of society'.[51] She believed, 'The proletariat can and must fight for the defence of national identity as a cultural legacy, that has its own right to exist and flourish', but the 'national identity cannot be defended by national separatism'.[52]

By far the most theoretically sophisticated of the classic Marxist theorists of nationalism was Lenin.[53] The analysis of the new nationalisms being thrown up by the continued development of capitalism was not, for him, some academic exercise. The Russian Empire was an even more ethnically mixed state than Austro-Hungary and it was a much more explosive mixture. The revolution of 1905 was to be as much a revolution of the national minorities as of the workers, the peasants and the liberal bourgeoisie. If his party got the national question wrong its whole revolutionary strategy would be in tatters. This led him to a sharp conflict with the positions of both Bauer and Rosa Luxemburg.

Lenin's analysis of the rise of nations is based on Kautsky's materialist interpretation. Writing early in 1914, Lenin argues:

Throughout the world, the period of the final victory of feudalism over capitalism has been linked up with national movements. For the complete victory of commodity production, the bourgeoisie must capture the home market, and there must be politically unified territories whose population speak a single language, with all the obstacles to the development of that language and its consolidation in literature eliminated. Therein is the economic foundation of national movements. Language is the most important means of human intercourse. Unity and unimpeded development of language are the most important conditions for genuinely free and extensive commerce on a scale commensurate with modern capitalism, for a free and broad grouping of the population in all its various classes as, lastly, for the establishment of a close connection between the market and each and every proprietor, big or little, and between seller and buyer.

*Therefore the tendency of every national movement is towards the formation of national states, under which these requirements of modern capitalism are best satisfied... Therefore, for the whole of Western Europe, nay, for the entire civilised world, the national state is **typical** and normal for the capitalist period.*[54]

The spread of capitalist relations internationally would mean the throwing up of more and more national movements:

The greater part of Asia...consists either of colonies of the Great Powers or of states that are extremely dependent and oppressed as nations. But does this shake the undoubted fact that in Asia itself the conditions for the most complete development of commodity production and the speediest growth of capitalism have been created in Japan, ie only in an independent national state?... It remains an undoubted fact that capitalism, having awakened

Asia, has called forth national movements everywhere in that continent too; the tendency of these movements is towards the creation of national states in Asia; that it is these states that ensure the best conditions for the development of capitalism...

The national state is the rule and the norm of capitalism... From the standpoint of national relations the best conditions for the development of capitalism are created by the national state. This does not mean, of course, that such a state, which is based on bourgeois relations, can eliminate the exploitation and oppression of nations. It only means that Marxists cannot lose sight of the powerful economic factors that give rise to the urge to create national states.

By 1916 he was developing the analysis, to attack those who, in the manner of Rosa Luxemburg,[55] used the argument about the connection between the development of capitalism and the growth of the national state to draw the conclusion that national demands were 'utopian' and 'reactionary' once the most advanced capitalisms began to spread beyond their old national boundaries. This, he said, was to fall into 'imperialist economism', to try to reduce politics to a direct mechanical product of economics. Economism, he said, is the argument: 'capitalism is victorious, therefore political questions are a waste of time', the new theory was that 'imperialism is victorious, therefore political questions are a waste of time. Such an apolitical theory is extremely harmful to Marxism'.

What is more, he no longer maintained the old, Kautskyist view that the proponents of national capitalist development had to be the capitalists. He noted that the Irish uprising of 1916 had involved 'street fighting conducted by a section of the urban petty bourgeoisie and a section of the workers...' He drew the conclusion that:

To imagine that social revolution is conceivable without revolts by small nations in the colonies and in Europe, without revolutionary outbursts by sections of the petty bourgeoisie with all its prejudices, without a movement of the politically non-conscious proletarian and semi-proletarian masses against oppression by the landowners, the church and the monarchy, against national oppression, etc—to imagine all this is to repudiate social revolution.

He drew sharp practical conclusions from his analysis. He defended the slogan of the right of self determination against Rosa Luxemburg and those with similar views, like Karl Radek and Nicolai Bukharin. And he rejected the Bauerite programme of 'cultural national autonomy'.

There were two components to his defence of the self determination slogan. The first was concerned with the political consciousness of workers having the same nationality as those who ran the oppressing state:

> *If, in our political agitation, we fail to advance and advocate the right to secession, we shall play into the hands, not only of the bourgeoisie, but also of the feudal landlords and the absolutism of the oppressor nation... When, in her anxiety not to 'assist' the nationalist bourgeoisie in Poland, Rosa Luxemburg rejects the **right** to secession in the programme of the Marxists **in Russia**, she is in fact assisting the Great Russian Black Hundreds. She is in fact assisting the opportunist tolerance of the privileges of the Great Russians... The interests of the freedom of the Great Russian population require a long struggle against such oppression... The long centuries old history of the suppression of the movements of the oppressed nations and the systematic propaganda in favour of such suppression coming from the upper classes have created enormous obstacles to the cause of freedom of the Great Russian people itself, in the form of prejudice... The Great Russian proletariat cannot achieve its own aims or clear the road to its freedom without systematically countering these prejudices...*
>
> *In Russia, the creation of an independent national state remains, for the time being, the privilege of the Great Russian nation alone. We, the Great Russian proletarians, who defend no privilege whatever, do not defend this privilege either.*[56]

Against the claim that this encouraged a split in the workers' movement along national lines, Lenin replied insistently that it did the opposite. So long as the workers in the oppressed nation could see no one defending their right to national equality among the people of the oppressing nation, they would fall for the nationalist demagogy of their own bourgeoisie and petty bourgeoisie. But if they found the workers' party in the oppressing nation standing full square for the right to self determination, then they would see it as standing for their interests and turn their back on their own bourgeoisie and petty bourgeoisie. He used the example of Norway's secession from Sweden in 1905 to back up his argument. Rosa Luxemburg had argued the secession was reactionary, simply replacing one monarchy by another. Lenin acknowledged that the outcome was no great step forward for the workers. But he insisted that the attitude of the Swedish socialists, who had supported the Norwegian right to secede, ensured it was not a step backwards either:

> *The close alliance between the Norwegian and Swedish workers, their complete fraternal class solidarity, gained from the Swedish workers' recognition of the right of the Norwegians to secede. This convinced the Norwegian workers that the Swedish workers were not infected with*

Swedish nationalism, and that they placed fraternity with the Norwegian workers above the privileges of the Swedish bourgeoisie and aristocracy.[57]

By standing by the right of self determination, socialists in the oppressor country encouraged internationalism among both their own working class and that in the oppressed country: 'In reality, the recognition of the right of all nations to self determination implies the maximum of democracy and the minimum of nationalism'.[58]

Lenin's first reason for advancing the slogan of the right to self determination was, then, to do with the *principle* of fighting against reactionary ideas within the working class of the oppressing country. This did not mean he ruled out exceptional situations. He admitted there were situations in which the slogan could be misused (as Marx claimed the Czechs and South Slavs had misused it in 1848):

There is not one of these (democratic) demands which could not serve and has not served, under certain circumstances, as an instrument in the hands of the bourgeoisie for deceiving the workers... In practice the proletariat can retain its independence only by subordinating its struggle for all democratic demands to the revolutionary struggle for the overthrow of the bourgeoisie... On the other hand Marx...put the fundamental principle of internationalism and socialism in the foreground—no nation can be free if it oppresses other nations.

So Lenin's first argument was of a general, if not completely unconditional, character. But he combined with it a second argument, about the impact of the fight for self determination by the oppressed nation in certain concrete situations. This was an argument about revolutionary strategy and tactics rather than principle.

Supporting the right to self determination was not inevitably to favour the secession of a particular nation from the state. The socialists in the oppressor country could fight for the right for secession as a way of fighting against reactionary ideology, while the socialists in the oppressed country could argue for workers to oppose the practice of secession—just as the right of divorce leaves it open to the married couple to decide freely that they want to stay together:

This demand [for the right of self determination] *is not the equivalent of demand for separation, fragmentation and the formation of small states... The closer a democratic state system is to complete freedom to secede, the less frequent and the less ardent will the demand for separation be in practice...*[59]

But there were situations in which the fight of the national movement of an oppressed nation aided the international working class struggle, even if the national movement was under bourgeois or petty bourgeois leadership. For it weakened the dominant states and their ruling classes. This, Lenin believed, was the case with the Irish uprising of 1916 and with the risings among the various other peoples oppressed by the Tsarist regime and the Western imperialisms which he rightly expected the impact of world war to bring about. For this reason not only should socialists in the oppressing countries support the right to self determination in these cases, but socialists in the oppressed countries should be part of the struggle for secession. 'If we do not want to betray socialism, we must support every revolt against our chief enemy, the bourgeoisie of the big states, provided it is not the revolt of a reactionary class'.[60]

However, there were situations when socialists had to oppose nationalist agitation—as with the Polish national movement in the concrete circumstances of the First World War, when it became intricately connected with the struggle of German imperialism against British, French and Tsarist imperialism.

> *The bourgeoisie, which naturally assumes the leadership at the start of every national movement, says that support for all national aspirations is practical. However, the proletariat's policy in the national question (as in all others) only supports the bourgeoisie in a certain direction, but never coincides with the bourgeoisie's policy...*
>
> *The demand for a 'yes' or 'no' reply to the question of secession in the case of every nation may seem a very 'practical' one. In reality it is absurd...in practice it leads to subordinating the proletariat to the bourgeoisie's policy.*
>
> *The proletariat...assesses any national demand, any national separation, from the angle of the workers' class struggle.*[61]
>
> *It is impossible to estimate beforehand all the possible relations between the bourgeois liberation movements of the oppressed nations and the proletarian emancipation movement of the oppressor nation.*[62]

This point leads on to the other central feature of Lenin's position on the national question—the one which has often been forgotten by supporters of national movements who have quoted him at length in defence of the right to self determination. He condemns Otto Bauer's scheme for 'national cultural autonomy'—and Rosa Luxemburg in so far as she is favourable to it—for making concessions to bourgeois nationalism.

The argument had first arisen in the Russian socialist movement at the time of the Second (effectively the foundation) Congress of the

Russian Social Democratic Labour Party in 1903. At that point the socialist movement was still more advanced among the pockets of Jewish workers in the western Russian Empire than among the mass of other workers. Some of those involved in organising the Jewish workers had founded an exclusively Jewish socialist party, the Bund, which argued that Jewish workers had to have their own separate organisations and concentrate on agitating for separate Jewish schools and cultural organisations. They were opposed, not just by Marxists of Russian nationality, like Lenin and Plekhanov, but by many of the best known Jewish Marxists such as Martov and Trotsky. Martov, for instance, argued that to accede to the Bund's demands would be to weaken socialist organisation in every workplace and locality:

> *We cannot allow that any section of the party can represent the group, trade or national interests of any section of the proletariat. National differences play a subordinate role in relation to common class interests. What sort of organisation would we have if, for instance, in one and the same workshop workers of different nationalities thought first and foremost of the representation of their national interests.*[63]

Lenin extended these arguments into a challenge to the whole Bauerite approach, by making a sharp distinction between the fight against every element of discrimination against any group on the basis of their language or culture, and exaltation of particular national cultures.

The opposition to discrimination against and oppression of those with particular national cultures meant that socialists had to fight for the children of every group to be taught in their own language, for courts and other tribunals to hear cases in that language, and to reject any idea of the dominant language being the 'official language' to which others should bow down. 'Whoever does not recognise and champion the equality of nations and languages, and does not fight against all national oppression and inequality, is not a Marxist; he is not even a democrat.'[64]

This meant that socialists should be for any measure that would guarantee equality. They should be for 'the hiring at state expense of special teachers of Hebrew, Jewish history and the like, of the provisions of state owned premises for lectures for Jewish, Armenian, or Romanian children, or even for the one Georgian child (in one area of St Petersburg)'.[65]

At the same time socialists should not identify with *any* national culture, even that of the oppressed:

To throw off the feudal yoke, all national oppression and all privileges enjoyed by any particular nation or language, is the imperative duty of the proletariat as a democratic force, and is certainly in the interests of the proletarian struggle which is obscured and retarded by bickering on the national question. But to go beyond these strictly limited and definite historical limits in helping bourgeois nationalism means betraying the proletariat and siding with the bourgeoisie. There is a border line here which the Bundists and the Ukrainian nationalist-socialists often completely lose sight of.

Combat all national oppression? Yes, of course! Fight for any kind of national development, for 'national culture' in general? Of course not!

The development of nationality in general is the principle of bourgeois nationalism; hence the exclusiveness of bourgeois nationalism, hence the endless national bickerings. The proletariat, far from undertaking to uphold the national development of every nation, on the contrary, warns the masses against such illusions, stands for the fullest development of capitalist intercourse and welcomes every kind of assimilation of nations, except that which is founded on force or privilege.[66]

There are two nations within every modern nation—we say to all nationalist socialists. There are two national cultures within every national culture...

If the Ukrainian Marxist allows himself to be swayed by his quite legitimate and natural hatred of the Great Russian oppressors to such a degree that he transfers even a particle of this hatred...to the proletarian culture and proletarian cause of the Great Russian workers, then such a Marxist will get bogged down in bourgeois nationalism.

The Great Russian and Ukrainian workers must work together...towards a common or international culture of the proletarian movement, displaying absolute tolerance in question of language in which propaganda is conducted... All advocacy of the segregation of the workers of one nation from those of another, all attacks upon Marxist 'assimilation', or attempts where the proletariat is concerned to counterpose one national culture as a whole to another allegedly integral national culture and so forth is bourgeois nationalism, against which it is necessary to wage a ruthless struggle.[67]

The slogan of working class democracy is not 'national culture', but the international culture of democracy and the world wide working class movement.[68]

*The elements of democratic and socialist culture are present, if only in rudimentary form, in every national culture, since in every nation there are toiling masses whose conditions of life inevitably give rise to the ideology of democracy and socialism. But every nation also possesses a bourgeois culture (and most nations a reactionary and clerical culture as well) in the form not merely of 'elements', but of the **dominant** culture.*

> In advancing the slogan of the 'international culture of democracy and of the world wide working class movement', we take from each national culture only its democratic and socialist elements; we take them only and absolutely in opposition to the bourgeois culture and the bourgeois nationalism of each nation.[69]

Lenin pointed out that the socialist in an oppressor country had to be very careful how he or she saw the issue of 'assimilation':

> If a social democrat from a great, oppressing, annexing nation, while advocating the amalgamation of nations in general, were for one moment to forget that 'his' Nicholas II, 'his' Wilhelm, 'his' George, etc also stands for amalgamation by means of annexation—such a social democrat would be a ridiculous doctrinaire in theory and an aider of imperialism in practice...
> It is our duty to teach the workers to be 'indifferent' to national distinctions... But it must not be the indifference of the annexationists.[70]

It was precisely to hammer this point home that Lenin was so insistent on defending the right of self determination and secession. At the same time, however, he insisted, 'a social democrat from a small nation must emphasise in his agitation... "voluntary integration" of nations. He may, without failing in his duties as an internationalist, be in favour of both the political independence of his nation and its integration with the neighbouring state of X, Y, Z etc. But he must in all cases fight against small nation narrow mindedness, seclusion and isolation...'[71]

These considerations led Lenin to bitterly oppose talk of 'national cultural autonomy'. He argued that separate school systems for each national group would split workers one from another:

> On the boards of joint stock companies we find capitalists of different nations sitting together in complete harmony. At factories workers of different nations work side by side. In any really serious and profound political issue sides are taken according to classes, not nations. Withdrawing school education and the like from state controls and placing it under the control of the nations is in effect to attempt to separate from economics, which unites the nations, the most highly ideological sphere of social life, the sphere in which 'pure' national culture or the nationalist cultivation of clericalism and chauvinism has the freest play.[72]

Nationalism since the First World War

There can be little doubt that Lenin was right in his argument against Rosa Luxemburg and others, that the development of capitalism was leading to a proliferation of new nationalisms.

Far from these being 'utopian', nationalist movements contributed to the break up of all the great empires. The Russian Revolution of 1917, like its precursor in 1905, involved the seizure of power by nationalist movements around its periphery as well as by workers and peasants at its centre. The collapse of the Austro-Hungarian war effort in October 1918 led to rapid secession by the Czechs, the Romanians of Transylvania, the Croats and the Slovenes, leaving behind separate rump Hungarian and Austrian states. Even the victorious British Empire was shaken by a revolt in Ireland, which succeeded in gaining independence for three quarters of the country, by the first massive demonstrations in India and the first revolutionary upsurges in China. The weakening of the European colonial empires as a result of the Second World War was followed by independence for India, Pakistan, Burma and Ceylon, Indonesia and then, after a bloody war, North Vietnam, Laos and Cambodia, to be followed by Ghana, Nigeria, Malaysia, Kenya, Uganda, Morocco, Tunisia, most of French Africa, the Congo, Zambia, Malawi, and after further bloody wars, Algeria, Aden, the rest of Vietnam, Angola, Mozambique, Guinea and finally Zimbabwe. By this time virtually every member of the world's population would define themselves as a citizen of one or other of 194 national states,[73] with the USSR remaining the only sizeable multinational empire. Just as market, commodity production and capital accumulation had conquered the whole world, so had the national state as the archetypical form of organised political power.

The formation of new nations did not always throw the old empires into convulsions: Britain finally abandoned India, Holland abandoned Indonesia and Belgium abandoned the Congo without being thrown into any great domestic crisis. But on occasions it did, with the wars in Indo China and Algeria shaking metropolitan France, the war in Vietnam throwing the US into a deep political crisis, and the wars in Angola, Mozambique and Guinea leading to political revolution in Portugal. To this extent too, Lenin was vindicated.

Indeed, the vindication often went further than he himself could ever have imagined. So much has the ideal of the national state become part of the ruling ideology throughout the world system that it was taken up by movements that differed in some important respects from those he had known.

The movements which fought against the old colonial empires were usually based in the administrative divisions created by those empires themselves. These divisions ignored whatever boundaries there might once have been between groups with different languages or traditional cultures. They separated like from like, and threw like together with unlike. Yet it was within these divisions that those who took over from the colonial empires attempted to create new nations—in India and Pakistan, Burma and Ceylon, Indonesia, Malaysia and the Philippines, and throughout black Africa—without a common language for the whole country and sometimes without even a unified market.

Alongside these there have been cases of minorities reacting to their oppression by seeing themselves as a nation, even though they do not live in any defined territory or share a separate common language. This was true by the 1930s of many of Europe's Jewish minorities and by the early 1970s of very many black Americans.

Finally, precisely because the notion of nationhood was so central to the ideology of the system, people's reaction to the economic and political crisis of one existing national state was to look for a way out through the creation of a new nation, based on different criteria to the old—as with the attempts to carve a Biafran national state using the Ibo language out of Nigeria in the late 1960s, Catalan and Basque states out of post-Franco Spain, an Akali state based on the Sikh religion out of the Indian province of the Punjab, or Serb and Croat states, based on the same language but different religions, out of what used to be Yugoslavia.

In each case, those who preached the nationalist project seemed far less 'utopian' and far more 'practical' than those who turned to class politics. The nationalists were, after all, cutting with the ideology of nationhood that had come to dominate the world with capitalism.

Nationality and culture today

The profusion of nationalities has been accompanied everywhere by a stress on the differences of cultures. In the advanced Western countries the ideology of biological racism has, to some extent, given way in the last quarter of a century to what might be called cultural racism. This does not talk in terms of biological inferiority of non-whites, but of the 'cultural backwardness', or at least the 'cultural difference' of those who come from non-British, non-French, non-German—or more generally non-European or non-Western—backgrounds.

So it was that back in 1978 Margaret Thatcher played the race card shortly before an election, claiming British people were being 'swamped by people of a different culture'.

In a slightly less extreme form the arguments goes, 'everyone has their own culture, so we naturally identify with ours, and other groups with theirs'. Such thinking underlies the stress of the right wing ideologues who increasingly dominate the content of the national teaching curriculum in Britain on 'British history', 'English literature' and the Christian religion. Interestingly, these ideologues are pressing for the right of both evangelical Christians and Islamic fundamentalists to set up their own schools.[74]

The argument is, at least in part, accepted by some of those usually regarded as being on the left. Many liberal intellectuals stress that everyone must value their own culture, and even go so far as to show concern about the 'bastardisation of cultures'.[75] And many of those who react against the disguised racism of the various forms of cultural supremacism do so by asserting a cultural separatism of their own—which in a few cases becomes an inverted form of cultural supremacism. They argue that because they are of Irish, Jewish, Armenian, Asian, Arab, Muslim, African, etc ancestry, then they have to fight to preserve the purity and independence of their 'indigenous culture'. They justify their stand with references to the 'fight against cultural genocide' and 'cultural imperialism'.

Yet all these different stresses on maintaining the separation of cultures—whether from the conservative right or from those who see themselves on the anti-racist, anti-imperialist left—rest on the same fallacy. They all assume that the growing proliferation of nationalities and nationalisms rests upon a growing diversity of cultures. But the modern world is, in fact, marked by a growing together of cultures, by a trend towards a homogeneous world culture—a trend enormously more marked than when Marx and Engels noted how 'the intellectual creations of individual nations become common property, national one sidedness and narrow mindedness becomes more and more impossible, and from the numerous national and local literatures, there arises a world literature',[76] or than when Kautsky and Lenin wrote about the merging of cultures 90 or so years ago.

The word 'culture' has two different meanings, one broad and one narrow. In its broad meaning it refers to the totality of people's social practices including such things as the way they get a livelihood, their religious practices, the relations between the sexes, their moral attitudes, their sense of time, their treatment of old people and children, their cooking, and, drawing all these activities together, their language. The more restricted meaning refers to art, music and literature.

The two meanings are connected. For culture in the narrow artistic sense is an expression of culture in the wider, way of life, sense. Art grows out of the soil of the wider culture and displays certain of the elements within it in a form that can bewitch or delight, thrill or frighten. When people like a certain artistic product, they do so because they find in it something which, in one way or another, gives expression to their own lives and dilemmas.

It is this which enables 'culture' in the narrow sense to provide a sense of identity to people from a particular society, something to which they can try to cling at moments of social crisis. This is why conservatives of all sorts seek to extol what they claim is the 'traditional' national culture. They are endeavouring to appeal to past ways of living so as to oppose any challenges to the old society. It is also why those who seek to establish new nations under their own hegemony search for what they claim are radically different counter-traditions.

But culture in the narrow sense can never be more than a partial expression of people's wider way of life in a class society. For in such a society there is not one way of life, but different ways of life for each class. And art and literature tend to express the way of life of those classes who alone have the resources and the leisure to sustain artistic production—the privileged exploiting classes. Even though the best artists are those who attempt to reflect the total social experience, which includes elements of the experience of the oppressed and exploited, they do so from the point of view of those who depend on the oppressors and exploiters for sustenance, even when they are not themselves from the ruling classes.

When we talk of British art, Russian art or Chinese art, we are talking of the art of the rulers of those societies, art which may say something about the exploited classes, but only in an indirect oblique way. This is even true when we talk about Aztec art or much art from pre-colonial Africa, for specialisation in artistic production was not possible on any scale until there was at least the beginning of a polarisation into classes.

What is more, as society changes, so culture changes. It cannot be a changeless fixed thing. Any attempt to treat it as such is, in reality, a fiction, an ideological device used to bind people to certain approved patterns of behaviour. This is especially true in the modern world, a world which has been changed utterly by the development of capitalism. Everywhere on the globe people's lives have been transformed as they have been subordinated to market relations and dragged from the relative isolation of rural life into contact with vast population centres.

When people talk of 'traditional culture' of any sort, they are harking back to something which no longer fits the reality of their lives anywhere. This is true of attempts to force us to live a traditional 'English culture', most of which was historically created by and for leisured gentlemen living in a predominantly agrarian society. It is true too of those who, out of a justified revulsion against such cultural reaction, would have us turn to 'Celtic culture', 'Indian culture', 'African culture', 'Islamic culture', or any other.

In fact, the forms of culture that dominate in every part of the world are products of very recent history, even when the conservatives claim an ancient lineage for them. It was, for instance, only a century ago that Celtic literature was reborn at the hands of modern, bourgeois—and usually Anglo-Irish—intellectuals like Lady Gregory and Yeats, or that modern petty bourgeois nationalists sought to create a Hindi speaking culture in opposition to that of the plebeian market language of the Delhi region, Hindustani, and the courtly version of it, Urdu.

The contemporary 'national' forms of both high art and popular art are very much the products of the recent, capitalist, period of human existence—thus with the different forms of popular music that tend to dominate different regions of the globe. As an authoritative study, of non-Western popular music tells, these are all relatively recent products, based on the drawing together of elements from different cultures:

> *The most conspicuous form of acculturation involves Western influence— especially the adoption of Western musical elements (such as instruments, harmony and vocal style) by non-Western musical cultures... The Western disco, rock and slow ballad have become international styles, promoted by a network of multinational corporations.*[77]

But, of course, Western music itself was not a product of the European peoples alone. A central component of it came into being as 'descendants of African slaves in the Americas developed dynamic, hybrid musics synthesising African-derived rhythms and Western melodic and harmonic patterns.'[78]

Similarly, in parts of the globe new regional styles have been based on a synthesis of traditional and Western forms. Thus Indian film music—which today has a multinational audience stretching from Vietnam and Indonesia to the former Yugoslavia,[79] is formed by a merging of local styles from south and north India, using 'Western harmony in its own distinctive way',[80] while modern African popular music arose as 'some...Caribbean...styles—especially the Cuban rumba—became widely popular in the Congo and other parts of Africa from the 1950s on, and generated new hybrids of native African and Afro-Caribbean music'.[81]

The example of popular music shows how advanced the tendency towards the fusion of cultures can be. There may not yet be a single world popular music, but there are a relatively small number of interacting regional styles, with the trend being towards fusion and the conquest of worldwide audiences, not towards separation and narrow national traditions. That is why its impact is resented by the cultural conservatives in every country. Yet popular music is probably the form of artistic culture that most penetrates the life of the great mass of people: its closest rival in terms of popularity, spectator sport, although hardly an 'artistic product', is even more a uniform worldwide phenomenon.

Such cultural growing together should really surprise no one. The dynamic of capitalist accumulation is creating, in fact, a worldwide way of life (or rather contrasting worldwide ways of life for the opposing classes). Significantly, the creators of modern popular cultures are those thrown together in the great cities by the spread of capitalism:

> *One of the most remarkable features of the evolution of popular music is its association in numerous cultures world-wide with an unassimilated, disenfranchised, impoverished, socially marginalised class, the lumpenproletariat of hoodlums, pimps, prostitutes, vagrants, sidewalk vendors, drug addicts, musicians, miscellaneous street people and assorted unemployed migrants... It was such groups...that gave birth to such diverse and vital forms as rebetika, modern kroncong, reggae, steel band, the tango and jazz... The lumpenproletariat are city dwellers... They are inherently predisposed to new forms of cultural expression.*[82]

But it is not only the creators of an art form who determine its popularity, and therefore who determine what will flourish and what will die out. It is also the consumers, those for whom they perform. And for the mass of workers and the urban middle class (as well as the lumpens, tempos of work) patterns of consumption, styles of dress, forms of recreation, forms of sexual relations and the rest increasingly cut across the old cultural barriers. Languages remain different, but what they say is increasingly the same.

If there is, in this broad sense, increasingly a world culture, it is not surprising that art—both in its popular and its 'highbrow' forms—is increasingly international, with a world audience for films and TV programmes, rock bands and symphony orchestras, for novels and operas.

Just as in popular art there is increasing interaction between regional styles, each the product of capitalist development, so in high art the pre-capitalist forms have been replaced by international, capitalist forms. Thus the novel, which was a literary form created as the bourgeoisie fought for power in Western Europe, has been adopted and mastered by writers from the non-Western world like Ngugi, Achebe, Rushdie, Ben Ochre, Marquez and so on.

Cultural imperialism occurred when dominating powers forced conquered peoples to adopt their language and their view of world history—as the British and French did in various parts of their empires, or as the Russians did first under the Tsar and then under Stalin. It was a by-product of imperialism proper—the bloody and barbaric process by which empires were carved out and whole peoples exterminated.

But the fusion of cultures today cannot be dismissed as simply a product of enforced subjection. Rather, it flows from the irreversible changes wrought by the spread of capitalism. It occurs because throughout the world people are trying to come to terms with living in societies which are moulded by the same world system, which are subject to the same tempos of accumulation. As the forms of exploitation undertaken by ruling classes get more and more alike, so do their lifestyles and their culture. By the same token, as the humdrum everyday lives of the mass of people become ever more dependent on their ability to sell their labour power and to fit into the tempo of work in the factory, mine or office, so their forms of recreation, culture and even dress converge. Rhythms of modern pop, for instance, reflect— even if only by trying to provide an escape from—the reality of urban life and the compulsion to paid labour. The novel form dominates in literature everywhere because it gives expression to the way bourgeois and petty bourgeois intellectuals experience a present day worldwide reality.

Nothing brings home the fact of an increasingly international culture more than the television images of the civil wars between rival nationalities that have broken out in the former Yugoslavia and the former USSR. For the mass of fighters on either side wear the same jeans and the same trainers, listen to the same Walkmans or ghetto blasters, follow the same sports and quite likely watch the same soap operas. This is because, if they were not fighting, they would be living essentially similar lives, working at near identical jobs.

The process of transformation is not of course complete. A large portion of the world's population are still peasants rather than wage labourers. Among the wage labourers there are those who live on the brink of starvation, unable to get anything more than the occasional day's work, and those who are in full time employment in large industry. In many cities there is a very large petty bourgeoisie, often merging at its lower reaches with a mass of still barely urbanised former peasants, which can still mobilise behind the demand for a return to tradition—as with the Islamic movements in many middle eastern countries or the Hindu supremacist movements in India. Yet the trend towards fusion of cultures is still overwhelming, simply because the pressures of the world system on the lives of everyone within it are overwhelming. That is why the returns to tradition are always phoney:

the traditions are manufactured, with the most modern techniques being used to recast the meaning of the oldest texts.

The culture created by modern capitalism is of course a deficient distorted culture. It is the culture of a class society which drains meaning from the lives of millions of people. It is a culture which has condoned slavery while preaching freedom, producing Belsen as well as Beethoven. The point is not to worship this culture in the manner of so many post modernists, but to recognise it as the only terrain people have to fight on, since the system which created it has made obsolete and destroyed all others.

Modern theories of nationality and nationalism

The two great tendencies of the last 75 years—the proliferation of nations, with many created among groupings that did not fit into the classic 19th century model, and the growing homogeneity of culture worldwide in every respect except language—has led to confusion among certain recent writers on nationalism. They see that, although there no longer seems to be any fixed, objective criteria for saying what is a nation and what is not, an identification with 'your own' nation is taken for granted by virtually the whole of humanity.

The result has been a tendency to see nationalisms as arbitrary constructs, detached from the economic development of capitalism. This is the tenor of Nigel Harris's recent book, *National Liberation*. For Nigel, capitalism is by its very nature an international system, based on the free movement of commodities and finance. It grew up within a system of national states, which were being constructed by pressures—the competition between rival absolutisms—other than itself, but today has an innate tendency to break through the boundaries between these states and to establish a new multinational order. All that holds it back is the continuing ability of political forces to get people to identify with the ideology of nation.

Benedict Anderson's very influential book, *Imagined Communities*, makes a greater effort to locate the growth of rival national consciousness in material reality. What he calls 'print capitalism' plays a very important role in his account. And he sees the rising bourgeoisie as playing a vital role in the creation of the first European nations: 'The coalition between Protestantism and print capitalism quickly created large new reading publics—not least among merchants and women who typically knew no Latin—and mobilised them for politico-religious purposes'.[83] The growth of new national consciousness in the 18th and 19th centuries was possible because of 'a half fortuitous but explosive interaction between a system of production and productive relations (capitalism), a technology of communication (print) and the fatality of human linguistic diversity'.[84]

Once some nations were already established, individuals from certain social groups could imagine establishing new ones, based on giving a printed form to languages, 'The "nation" thus becomes something capable of being consciously aspired to...rather than a slowly sharpening frame of vision'.[85] 'A model of the independent nation was available for pirating'.[86]

The audience for the new printed languages came, by and large, from 'families of ruling classes of nobility and landed gentry, courtiers and ecclesiastics, rising middle strata of plebeian lay officials, professionals, and commercial and industrial bourgeoisies'.[87] So 'in world historical terms bourgeoisies were the first class to achieve solidarities on an essentially imagined basis... In Europe these solidarities had an outmost stretch limited by vernacular legibilities'.[88]

But once the model was established along linguistic lines in Europe, it could operate if necessary without them. The European powers established administrations in the colonies that cut across old linguistic divisions. The indigenous middle class that was recruited to fill many lower and middle administrative positions began to imagine themselves taking charge and copying the European model: 'Is Indian nationalism not inseparable from the colonial administrative-market unification, after the Mutiny, by the formidable and advanced of the imperial powers?'[89]

However, Anderson does not succeed in combining these elements into a coherent, total, materialist analysis. For, instead of recognising the nation state as the typical form of capitalist rule, he puts the emphasis on subjective factors that led people to want to 'imagine' new forms of community. These factors first emerged, he argues, when social and economic changes in the late medieval period led to the breakdown of 'cultural concepts of great antiquity' which gave 'a certain meaning to the everyday fatalities of existence (above all, death, loss and servitude)'. From that point, 'the search was on for a new way of linking fraternity, power and time meaningfully together'.[90]

The roots of the nationalist ideology, then, are finally located in existential yearning, not capitalist development, despite the promise of much of Anderson's argument. This becomes clearer in his more recent 'New World Disorder'[91] in which the strength of nationalism is ascribed, not to capitalism as such, but to 'two significant factors' linked to 'the rise of capitalism...mass communications and mass migrations'. 'Print capitalism brought into being mass publics who began to imagine through the media a new type of community: the nation', while 'the mass appearance in settled communities of thousands of immigrants did not, and will not, fail to produce its own ethnicisations...Le Pen's neofascist movement in France...the National

Front in Britain..."White Power" extremists in the United States....'
This is to repeat the old fallacy that immigration is to blame for racism—despite the very powerful evidence that racism is often strongest where there are fewest members of ethnic minorities (as with anti-semitism in Poland today, or with anti-black racism in virtually all white towns and suburbs in Britain).

The weakness in Anderson's otherwise powerful argument is undoubtedly connected with the starting point of his book. He began to write it, he explains, in the late 1970s under the impact of the first war between what he saw as socialist states—China and Vietnam. His whole aim was to understand what it was about nationalism that made it a central feature of socialist as well as capitalist societies. By refusing to see China and Vietnam as societies dominated by the dynamic of competitive accumulation—as a state organised variant of capitalism—he was driven to look outside capitalist society for the roots of nationalism, to see these instead in the satisfaction of innate psychological needs.

The result, paradoxically, is that Anderson is blind to something which the non-Marxist, Ernest Gellner, does grasp. Gellner sees the development of history not in terms of primitive communism, slavery, feudalism, capitalism and socialism, but rather of 'primitive' society, agrarian society and industrial societies. Despite the innumerable faults with this approach, it does provide him with one advantage over Anderson when looking at the so called socialist societies of the mid-20th century. He does not expect them to be any different in their essentials to capitalist societies, and looks for material explanations for those shared features which differentiate both from previous societies. Thus he is absolutely scathing about attempts to see nations as eternal: 'Nations as a natural God-given way of classifying men are a myth; nationalism which sometimes takes pre-existing cultures and turns them into nations, sometimes invents them and often obliterates pre-existing cultures—that is the reality'.[92]

He argues it is the need of each 'industrial society' for a 'homogeneous' population, literate in a single tongue, that gives rise to the nation:

> *It is not the case that nationalism imposes homogeneity... It is the objective need for homogeneity that is reflected in nationalism... A modern industrial state can only function with a culturally standardised, interchangeable population... Nationalism is not the awakening of an old, latent, dormant force, though that is how it does present itself. It is, in reality, the consequence of a new form of social organisation, based on deeply internalised education-dependent high cultures, each protected by its own state.*[93]

Just as the nation is a result of objective material realities, so too is the striving after nationhood among the masses. With industrialisation:

> The illiterate, half starved populations from their erstwhile cultural ghettos who are pulled into the melting pots of shanty towns yearn for incorporation into one of those cultural pools which already has, or looks as if it might acquire, a state of its own, with the subsequent promise of full cultural citizenship, access to primary schools, employment, and all.[94]

When entry into the perks of nationhood is easy, he argues, they will forget their old culture and assimilate—thus explaining the reality that there are around ten times more potential languages in the world than there are nations or aspiring nations. But when they are 'spurned' they will seek some other way to define themselves. 'Nationalism as such is fated to prevail, but not any particular nationalism'.[95]

Gellner can therefore go beyond both Anderson and Harris in seeing why the drive to identify with a nation—and if necessary to try to create new nations—is such a central feature of the modern world:

> Nations can be defined only in terms of the age of nationalism, rather than the other way round... When general social conditions make for standardised, homogeneous, centrally sustained high calderas, pervading whole populations and not just elite minorities, a situation arises in which well defined educationally sanctioned and unified cultures constitute very nearly the only kind of unit which men willingly and ardently identify... Only then does it appear that any defiance of their boundaries by political units constitutes a scandal... Under these conditions, and these conditions only, can nations be defined in terms of both will and culture.[96]

But Gellner has a vast blind area of his own. He does not conceive it possible that industrial society could be organised in a way other than it is. To this extent his much more materialist analysis leads to a conclusion very like Anderson's: the nation dominates all existing societies, and we have to like it or lump it. Gellner, who was involved in protests against the descent into rival barbaric nationalisms in Yugoslavia in the summer of 1991, clearly does not like it all that much. But he can point to no other way forward.

Eric Hobsbawm's work *Nations and Nationalism since 1780* takes for granted a framework very similar to Gellner's,[97] although with far more references to the Marxist tradition which, Hobsbawm points out, was the first to grasp that nations are not timeless entities but constructed with the rise of 'modern society'. Most of the work is concerned with fixing a mass of historical material into the framework—so much at times that the reader is in danger of getting lost amidst a mass of fascinating facts, unable to see the wood for the trees. But Hobsbawm departs from Gellner at a number of points.

First, he insists the views of those who align with national movements or national states may not be as clear cut as the nationalist leaders claim:

> If I have a major criticism of Gellner's work it is that his preferred perspective of modernisation from above makes it difficult to pay adequate attention to the view from below.
>
> The view from below, ie the nation as seen not by governments and spokesmen and activists of nationalist (and non-nationalist) movements, but by the ordinary persons who are the objects of their action and propaganda, is exceedingly difficult to discover...
>
> We cannot assume that national identification—when it exists— excludes or is always or ever superior to the remainder of the sets of identifications which constitute the social being...
>
> National identification and what it is believed to imply can change and shift in time, even in the course of quite short periods.[98]

Later he elaborates the argument further:

> Men and women did not choose collective identification as they chose shoes, knowing that one could only put on one pair at a time. They had, and still have, several attachments and loyalties simultaneously, including nationality, and are simultaneously concerned with various aspects of life, any one of which may at any moment in time be foremost in their minds, as occasion suggests. For long periods of time these different attachments would not make incompatible demands on a person... It was only when one of these loyalties conflicted directly with another that problems of choosing between them arose.

He provides a graphic example of how social concerns and national loyalties have interacted by quoting Peter Hanak's research on letters from soldiers from different ethnic backgrounds serving in the Austro-Hungarian army during the First World War:

> During the first years there was not much nationalism or anti-monarchism among the correspondents... The years of war, but especially the first Russian revolution, raised the political content of the intercepted correspondence dramatically. Indeed, the censors' reports on public opinions unanimously observed that the Russian revolution was the first political event since the outbreak of war whose shock waves penetrated to the lowest levels of the people. Among the activists of some of the oppressed nationalities such as the Poles and Ukrainians, it even raised hopes of

*reform—perhaps even of independence. However, the dominant mood was for peace and **social** transformation.*

The political opinions which now begin to appear even in the letters of labourers, peasants and working class women, is best analysed in terms of three interlocking binary opposites: rich-poor (or lord-peasant, boss-worker), war-peace, and order-disorder. The links, at least in the letters, are obvious: the rich live well and don't serve in the army, the poor people are at the mercy of the rich and powerful, the authorities of state and army, and so on. The novelty lies not only in the greater frequency of complaints...but in the sense that a revolutionary expectation of fundamental change was available as an alternative to passive acceptance of destiny.

National feeling comes into the arguments only indirectly, chiefly because, to cite Hanak, 'until 1918 national sentiment had not yet crystalised out, among the broad masses of the people, into a stable component of consciousness...' Nationality appears most often as an aspect of the conflict between rich and poor, especially where the two belong to different nationalities. But even where we find the strongest national tone— as among the Czech, Serbian and Italian letters—we also find an overwhelming wish for social transformation... The period when the October revolution made its first impact was the one in which the social element in the public mood was at its strongest...

It was only when the wave of strikes in Austro-Hungary and Germany in January 1918 failed to bring down the regime and force an end to the war that people began to look away from social revolution and to look for their salvation through nationalism: 'But even when, in the course of 1918, the national theme finally became dominant in popular consciousness, it was not separate from or opposed to the social theme. For most poor people the two went together, as the monarchy crashed...' Hobsbawm argues that 'nationalism was victorious...to the extent that the movements which reflected the real concerns of the poor people of Europe failed in 1918. When this happened, the middle and lower strata of the oppressed nationalities were in position to become the ruling elites of the new independent...petty states'.[99]

The second novelty in Hobsbawm's account is that he claims the hold of nationalism is declining, despite the widespread belief to the contrary. He bases his claim on a number of arguments.

First, he denies that most of the new states that have emerged in the ex-colonial world since 1945 can really be counted as national states, since confined within the old colonial administrative boundaries they cannot achieve linguistic homogeneity or gain any real loyalty from the mass of their subjects. Yet this only proves they are unsuccessful—

because late coming—national states. All aspire to become the focus of identity of their subjects, and some are successful, even if the identification is not total (but then, Hobsbawm's own analysis shows we should not expect it to be): despite the state's failure to impose a common language, very many Indian citizens do identify with 'their country', even if they also identify themselves as Hindus or Muslims, workers or employers, Brahmins or untouchables. In Africa and the middle east the fact that state boundaries cross cut linguistic boundaries does not always stop the state becoming a focus of loyalty for the middle classes who depend on it for a livelihood and look to it to 'modernise' society, and who in turn exert ideological influence on the workers, the lumpenproletariat and the peasantry.

At the time of writing he had a second, even more dubious, argument, concerning the 'socialist' countries:

> *Inasmuch as such regimes do not, at least in theory, identify with any of their constituent nationalities and regard the interests of each of them as secondary to higher common purpose, they are non-national... It was the great achievement of the communist regimes in multinational countries to limit the disastrous effects of nationalism within them... The 'discrimination' or even 'oppression' against which the champions of various Soviet nationalities abroad protest, is far less than the expected consequences of the withdrawal of Soviet power.*[100]

One only wishes at this point that Hobsbawm would take seriously his own injunction to look things 'from below' and not just in terms of how official spokespersons present them. He might have asked himself what it meant to be a Tatar or Caucasian temporary worker living in a hostel in Moscow, a Turkic speaking conscript into a Russian speaking army, or a Kazakh speaking child in Alma Ata, a city without a single nursery using the native language. As it is, the realities of oppression are confined to two footnotes, one mentioning the Romanisation of Ceausescu's Romania (but not persecution of the Turks in Bulgaria, still less the ethnic cleansing which drove Hungarian speakers from Slovakia and German speakers from Bohemia, Moravia and western Poland after 1945) and 'the mass transfer of entire populations on the grounds of their nationality which took place after the war' in the USSR (but not the glorification of Tsarist Russia's conquest of the non-Russian peoples that became the official ideology from that time on).

Whether Hobsbawm likes it or not, all the Eastern European regimes were seen by everyone who lived in them as regimes dominated by single nationalities.[101] It is hardly surprising that, since people have been able to express themselves freely, there have been revolts of minority nationalities, and attempts—often orchestrated by remnants of the old ruling parties—to mobilise the dominating nationalities against them.

But Hobsbawm makes two other points that have rather more going for them. He argues:

> Nationalism...is no longer a major vector in historical development. In the 'developed' world of the 19th century, the building of a number of 'nations' which combined nation state and national economy was plainly a central fact of historical transformation... In the 'dependent' world of the first half of the 20th century...movements for national liberation and independence were the main agents for the political emancipation of most of the globe... Both were typically unificatory as well as emancipatory...
>
> The characteristic nationalist movements of the late 20th century are essentially negative, or rather divisive.

There is a correct element in this argument. Capitalism today finds even the biggest existing states too small for its operations. The idea that smaller states will make it easier for people to cope with the vagaries of the system is absurd. But this was already true 80 years ago when Rosa Luxemburg used this argument against Lenin. And in economic terms she was right: the successor states to the Austro-Hungarian Empire, for instance, failed abysmally to advance their economies in the inter-war years,[102] cut off as they were by state boundaries from their old raw materials and markets. But politically she was wrong, because millions of people flocked to nationalist movements, tore the old empires apart and created new states anyway.

The fact that nationalism is a blind alley does not automatically stop people going down it, even if it does mean at some point they are likely to do a U-turn and start coming out again.

Hobsbawm's final point is that much that is loosely called nationalism is not concerned with building new states at all, but rather with mobilising people from certain linguistic or ethnic backgrounds to exercise political pressure on existing states. This, he says, is a product of the way in which economic development has pulled vast numbers of migrants from many different backgrounds into the great cities of the world. The degree of ethnic mixing makes any idea of establishing a new mono-ethnic state impossible. But it also creates powerful constituencies for those who want to make political careers by promising favours to one linguistic, ethnic or religious group rather than another. In extreme cases the result will be horrendous communal bloodbaths. But even if these groups are organised around nationalist identification with a distant land of origin, they cannot be considered nationalist in the way the term is usually used.

His case here is very strong. Yet he still overstates it. In conditions of economic collapse, movements demanding the driving out of other ethnic groups can fight for control even of modern, multinational cities—as we have seen in Bosnia in recent months. Ethnicity can go beyond communalism and aspire to impose new ethnic state boundaries using the most barbaric means.

Some of Hobsbawm's arguments show that the potential exists for resisting nationalism, that it is not the unstoppable juggernaut many people believe. But they do not show how that potentiality can become a reality. To do that Hobsbawm would have to break with his own watered down Eurocommunism, with its residual admixture of nostalgia for Stalinism, and look to the class alternatives he mentions when writing of the First World War.

Social crises and nationalism today

The central contention of this article so far is that the mystery of the nation state disappears when it is seen as the typical form of political administration associated with the advance of capitalism, from its beginnings in the western fringe of Europe to its present day conquest of the whole world. At each stage those who have striven to share in the gains of this advance, whether they themselves have been capitalists, state bureaucrats or members of the literate middle class, have wanted to have a local national state of their own. The fact that in order to gain such a state they have sometimes had to bend the definition of 'national' almost beyond belief is irrelevant, as is the failure of many of the new states to deliver the economic gains expected from them.

The system of nation states, then, is the political correlate of the full blown capitalist mode of production. It is the political form which, having aided capitalism in its conquest of the world in its youth, persists into its maturity and old age.

The strength of the ideology of nationalism under capitalism is not, then, surprising. It is part of the reflection in people's consciousnesses of the experience of living in a capitalist world. Just as living under capitalism makes the great mass of people take for granted that commodity production, alienated wage labour and competition are more common than co-operation, so it makes them take for granted the necessity of the nation state. And nationalist consciousness makes sense so long as they do not challenge the system as a whole: within it the individual capitalist is in a very weak situation unless he has a state to enforce his interests on others;[103] the individual peasant family hopes the state will protect it against the inevitable ups and downs of the market in foodstuffs; the individual worker knows he or she has to belong to a state to be allowed to work and live freely, and to apply for welfare benefits when necessary.

Marx made the point nearly 150 years ago that the ruling ideas are always the ideas of the ruling class. And one of those ideas is the idea of the nation as a 'natural unit' for grouping together a section of humanity into its 'own' cordoned off part of the planet.

The ruling ideas are not immutable. On this at least Hobsbawm is absolutely right. Great social crises create situations in which ideas and realities move in opposite directions, in which social turmoil and human suffering conflict with old allegiances, in which people find it literally impossible to continue to live according to the old ways, in which the outbreak of sudden confrontations creates new antagonisms and new loyalties.

In such periods people's consciousness is not monolithic, but contradictory, to use Gramsci's description.[104] Old ways of seeing things co-exist with new ways of seeing things. People continue to express themselves using concepts while taking actions which imply completely new ones. In the end the contradiction can only be resolved by breaking with the old or abandoning the new. But the end can sometimes be a very long time in coming.

Thus the development of capitalism in the 16th and 17th centuries created forms of social behaviour that challenged the whole ideology of medieval Christianity. The logic of this challenge led to the complete rejection of religious ways of thinking by the Enlightenment. But this rejection did not permeate right through into popular consciousness for centuries. In the interim people who identified with the new ways of living tried to reconcile themselves partially to the old ways of thinking by continuing to accept Christianity, but in new reformed versions.

The speed of the onset of crises and the degree of social turmoil is much greater under capitalism than under any previous mode of production, and the stresses besetting old forms of consciousness accordingly that much more acute. Nevertheless, contradictory, hybrid forms of consciousness are an inevitable feature of mentality for the great mass of people at the first stage of any great convulsion: the mass of workers who overthrew the Tsar and established soviets in February 1917 did allow Prince Lvov to head the Provisional Government; the German workers who got rid of the Kaiser and ended the war did, disastrously, allow Ebert, Scheidermann and 'the bloodhound' Noske to maintain the power of the bourgeoisie and the officer corps; the Polish workers who created a huge independent trade union and inflicted the first major defeat on Stalinism in the summer of 1980 did bow down to the Pope and accept the advice of those who preached compromise with their rulers.

It is in this context that we have to explain the sudden rise of new nationalisms. The idea of the division of humanity into nations is etched into people's consciousness under capitalism. If one national state fails them, the easiest thing is to turn to the idea of creating a different national state. It seems so much more 'practical' to rearrange the pieces on the board than to invent a totally new game.

This can be encouraged by the material interests of wide sections of the middle class—especially where a large part of a region's population are fluent in a language other than the official one of the old state. For some of them a separate state—or at least a grant of national autonomy—means improved access to bureaucratic posts. Hence the flourishing of Catalan nationalism in the last couple of years of the fascist regime in Spain, as wide sections of the Catalan speaking middle class joined and exercised influence on a struggle that had previously been spearheaded by mainly Spanish speaking workers. But language is not an indispensable factor: in any formation of a new state identification with the struggle for it can enhance many career prospects.

The directing of discontent into nationalist demands can also be of benefit to important sections of the capitalist or state capitalist ruling class. The most powerful rarely promote nationalism themselves, and they sometimes do their best to resist it as detrimental to their own powerfully established links with the old state. But even then they can come to regard it as the lesser evil compared with the growth of a movement for social revolution. And less powerful elements within the ruling class can see sponsorship of a secessionist state as a very good way of accelerating their own accumulation of wealth. Thus it was not the small Bengali speaking big bourgeoisie who initiated the movement to separate eastern Pakistan from the central state apparatus in western Pakistan in 1971, but some of them managed to profit enormously when separation finally led to the formation of the new national state of Bangladesh.

A final factor is also of immense importance in helping to trigger identification with nationalist slogans—the extent to which the old state carries through policies that can be seen as involving oppression along national lines. The classic form this takes is discrimination against those who speak a certain language—as with the Turkish government's attempts in the 1980s to ban Kurdish or the Sri Lankan government's insistence that Sinhalese, not Tamil, is the official language. Although the middle classes suffer most, workers too face problems every time they come in contact with the state—with its police, its courts, or even its post offices. But discrimination does not have to be formal, as black people in Europe and North America are all too aware. A particular linguistic or religious group can find they are treated as second or third class citizens every time they come into contact with police officers, officials or employers. This was always the experience of the Irish (especially, but not only, the Catholics) under British rule, of the Bengalis under Pakistani rule, and of Kurds under Iraqi rule. The logic of the situation leads to a vicious circle of oppression: the minority protest at the discrimination against them, the state regards them as disloyal, arrests their spokespeople, disbands any representative institutions they possess, censors their press, encourages further discrimination against them, and thus heightens their feeling of alienation from it. What begin as mild protests aimed at securing a better place within the existing state often end up as irreconcilable demands for secession.

But the element of real oppression is not always necessary for a movement to gain mass support. Just as there is usually support of a fairly passive nature for the official nationalism of the state among the majority of its population, so great social and political crises can see that support transferred by a section of the population to its secessionist rival. Indeed, because secession offers change and any change seems like improvement, the loyalty to the new nationalism can be stronger than that to the old— although this increased strength need not last long.

Scotland provides an example of how the nationalism of the non-oppressed[105] can fluctuate wildly. Independence, or at least devolved government, seems on occasions to offer a quick way for people to break from the hold of a Tory government and the grim effects of Britain's long drawn out economic decline. Support for nationalism, and for the Scottish National Party in particular, grows very quickly. Identification with the superficial symbols of British nationalism—the 'national' sports teams, the 'national' flag, 'national' culture and 'national' celebrities—becomes overwhelmingly an identification with Scottish symbols. But the support remains passive for the great mass of people and when no breakthrough to independence occurs, can die down as quickly as it arose. And then people see no contradiction in identifying with Scottish symbols (the football team) and British symbols (the monarchy, the armed forces, and even the Olympic team,[106] an identification that the Scottish National Party does not challenge!).

This does not mean that the nationalism of the non-oppressed cannot occasionally present problems for the existing state. Fortuitous conditions can turn it into a focus for much wider discontents of a social nature, and the state can react by trying to crush it, so creating oppressive conditions that did not exist before. It is worth remembering that until the mid-1930s Basque nationalism was a right wing force in Spanish politics; it was the actions of the state itself which forced it to align itself with the left and to take up a position of irreconcilable hostility to fascism.[107]

More recently the nationalisms of peoples who are not subject to oppression on the basis of any national characteristics, but who live on different sides of state boundaries drawn by great powers in the past, have had considerable political impact. The movement against the Stalinism of the East German state machine in 1989 transformed itself into a movement for incorporation into the Federal German Republic, while in South Korea much of the reformist left has seen national reunification as the central slogan—even though parties of the conservative right also call themselves 'unification' parties.

In any case, the turn towards nationalism among workers must be regarded as one of the ways the ideas of the ruling class continue to exercise an influence, even when the crisis of the system begins to break people from a conservative attachment to the old order. The extent of this influence depends here, as in other cases, on two factors: the level of collective struggle against the system, and the degree to which socialist organisations exist on the ground, capable of taking up political and ideological arguments in each workplace and locality. Where nationalist influence is greatest is where the crisis results in defeat and demoralisation rather than struggle among workers, and where the ideological crisis of most of the left since the collapse of Stalinism has done most damage.

For the rise of nationalism cannot be separated from the crisis of the left internationally which has accompanied the crisis of the system. There is an enormous vacuum on the left, which often leaves those who preach nationalism (or in large areas of the world, religious fundamentalism) with little socialist competition.

Nationalism since the collapse of Stalinism

The vacuum on the left is greatest and the crisis of the system reaping more havoc than anywhere else outside sub-Saharan Africa in the countries that used to be called Communist. It should be no surprise that these have experienced the greatest growth of rival nationalisms in the last few years.

The fate of the former USSR shows how economic crisis—the 'stagnation' that began in the last Brezhnev years giving way to contraction and mass impoverishment in the last Gorbachev years—can create political crises, and political crises find expression in the growth of national movements. It shows how members of the middle class intelligentsia create movements which make the national question the focus through which all other discontents are meant to be focused—the popular fronts in the Baltic states, Moldavia, Armenia and Azerbaijan, Rukh in the Ukraine, and the Round Table in Georgia. It shows how the very real oppression suffered by very large numbers of ordinary people could allow these movements to gain enormous mass followings (a much larger and more active following than the various democratic movements among the Russians). And it shows how at a time of major political crisis important figures within the ruling class itself could switch to nationalism as a way of maintaining their control over part at least the old state—Kravchuk in the Ukraine, Nazarbayev in Kazakhstan and, most amazingly of all, Yeltsin in Russia beats the nationalist drum and claims the dominant nationality has been exploited by the others.

But it is the Yugoslav case which is the most revealing—if also so far the most horrific.

The state had been carefully reconstructed after the defeat of the German occupation in the Second World War to balance its main Slav constituents—Slovenes, Serbs and Croats—against each other, so preventing political disruption caused by Croats and Slovenes feeling they were being dominated by Serbs (as in the pre-war monarchy) or Serbs feeling they were dominated by Croats (as under German occupation). To this end the Serbs of Montenegro, the Macedonians (regarded by the Serbs previously as 'southern Serbs') and the mixed Serbian-Croat-Muslim population of Bosnia were all given their own republics separate from Serbia proper, while the mixed Serb and Hungarian speaking area of Vojvodina in northern Serbia were given an autonomous status. All Slavs had an equal chance of rising in the state bureaucracy; the only oppressed nationality was the Albanian speakers of Kosovo, who were denied their own republic and subject to systematic discrimination at the hands of everyone else. But it is important to understand that the structure was not based on any systematic attempt to undermine national allegiances, rather on using each to neutralise the others. Divide and rule was always present.

The structure worked well for its rulers until the late 1960s. The state's cohesion was such that it survived unscathed through the various serious external political crises of 1948, when it split from the Russian bloc, and the economy grew rapidly for the next 20 years. When a loss of economic dynamism led to another political crisis in the late 1960s, with the purging of the interior minister, the weakening of police control allowed discontent to express itself through student demonstrations in Belgrade and a rise of Croat nationalism within the ruling party itself in Croatia. A clampdown succeeded in breaking both movements, but only because it was followed by a growing institutionalisation of the rival Slav nationalisms at the governmental level. The heads of each of the republics were able, to some extent, to head off discontent by giving the impression they were fighting for 'national' interests within the federal government.

Then in the 1980s an economic crisis broke out with a vengeance. There was growing unemployment, growing inflation and a drop in living standards until they were no higher than they had been in the 1930s. There was an explosion of discontent—and much of it on a class basis. The number of strikes leapt from 100 in 1983 to 1,530 in 1987, when there were powerful calls for a general strike as workers broke into the federal parliament. But at this point powerful political figures set out to protect themselves against the growing anger from below and to advance their own careers by deliberately inflaming national hatreds.

The first to do so was Slobodan Milosevic, a rising figure in the Serbian party leadership. He launched a massive campaign against the alleged persecution of Serbs in Kosovo and used huge demonstrations of all the classes in Serbia—industrial managers gave workers time off to attend, where they were joined by student organisations, veterans, members of the academy of science and so on—to take over control of the Serbian leadership and then to impose his nominees on Vojvodina and Montenegro. His efforts were soon matched by others. In Croatia a Titoist general who had fallen from grace, Franjo Tudjman, began courting supporters of the wartime Ustashe regime that had butchered Serbs and demanded that Croats police the Serbian inhabited areas of Croatia. In Slovenia leaders of the old ruling party threw in their lot with what had been the leadership of the liberal opposition throughout Yugoslavia to join together to press for secession.[108]

The rival nationalist campaigns of Milosevic and Tudjman reinforced each other. By bringing down the Vojvodina and Montenegro governments, Milosevic frightened Croats with the spectre of Serbian hegemony over the whole of Yugoslavia. By attacking the rights of the Croatian Serbs, Tudjman drove them into the hands of Milosevic and forces even further to the right. By supporting the Yugoslav armies onslaught on Slovenia and then parts of Croatia, Milosevic encouraged Croats to rely on Tudjman and the paramilitary groups to his right. The horrific logic of what they were both up to was shown when they agreed secretly to partition Bosnia between them and to destroy the harmony that had existed between Serbs, Croats and Muslims in its capital, Sarajevo. 'Uniting the divided nation' became a slogan which authoritarian right wing parties in both Serbia and Croatia could use to draw support behind them.

What Milosevic and Tudjman had discovered was that in a declining economy nationalist slogans could draw sections of the middle class into a fight for rival state machines and the careers available within them, could divert workers from fighting to defend living standards and could give sudden popularity to individual members of the old ruling class. Because nationalism has always been part of the ruling ideology, it always presents a possible safety valve for sections of ruling classes in moments of acute crisis.

But that is not the end of the matter. For if the movement to form new national states cannot open up new economic possibilities for society as a whole, then it cannot provide more than temporary relief for ruling classes. Here the difference between national movements in capitalism's youth, when they advanced the forces of production, and their role today, when they constrain any such advance, is important. Having gained power, the nationalists still have to confront the crisis of the national economy, and this at a time when pressure to placate the nationalist desires of their own supporters exerts pressures on them to seize fresh territory and enlarge 'the nation'. So long as the nationalist frenzy continues its upward path, the economic problems get greater. The moment the nationalist frenzy fades, the economic problems—and with them the class struggle—suddenly move back to the centre of the stage. The very discontents sidetracked by the nationalist agitation then return to haunt those who used it to hoist themselves into power.

As so often in history, war is used to head off class struggle, but the cost of war then heightens the class bitterness in society, and threatens to end in the overthrow of those who promoted it. At the time of writing, nobody can tell what is going to emerge from the bloody morass in former Yugoslavia—or for that matter in Moldova, Azerbaijan and Armenia, or Georgia. But what is very clear is that there is no stable political outcome to a situation in which nationalism can tear states apart but has no economic programme for carrying society forward. Just as general social discontent switched into nationalist hatreds, so national hatred can suddenly switch back into social struggles, particularly as the violence and cost of inter-ethnic struggles produces war weariness and bitterness against those who run the governments.

A war like that in former Yugoslavia necessarily gives rise to vague desires for peace among vast numbers of people and to anti-government demonstrations. If these feelings can be fused with the struggles of workers against the cost of the war and the effects of the economic crisis, then the wave of nationalism can be beaten back. But class politics does not arise automatically. It has to be argued for. Here an enormous responsibility lies with those small groups, who alone of the genuine left have survived the crisis of Stalinism.

Socialists and nationalism

The left cannot fulfil its responsibilities unless it is clear on the relation between nation and class. Its starting point has to be a clear understanding that nationalism is about the organisation of capitalist society. On this Kautsky and Lenin were absolutely right against Otto Bauer. Internationalism cannot be achieved by the arithmetic addition of different nationalisms, but by a conscious opposition to them all. There are not Serbian or Croat, English or Irish, Russian or Ukrainian socialists, but socialists who happen to live in one or other of these states. Socialists are not proud of their nationality. They are proud of the denial of their nationality. By the same token, socialists do not stand for the maintenance of 'their own' national culture, but for the integration of all that is best in every culture into a new, cosmopolitan, human culture. This is important for those who have been brought up to identify with the culture of oppressor nations—but not for them alone. As Lenin stressed repeatedly, any defence of the separation of cultures ends up in a defence of the separating off of workers from one another, just as the capitalist production process pulls them together. It plays into the hands of reactionaries among both the oppressor and the oppressed nationalities.

At same time, however, socialists have to understand the only way to bring workers of different nationalities together is to insist on free association. Internationalism does not mean identification with existing states. Workers who regard themselves as having a certain nationality cannot unite freely with other workers within the same state unless they know those workers defend their right to secede if they so wish. Croat workers will not unite with Serb workers unless the Serb workers defend their rights—including the right to secession. Serb workers will not unite with Croat workers unless Croat workers oppose every attempt to discriminate against and oppress the Serb minority within Croatia. Only by the workers of different nationalities defending each others' rights can they create circumstances in which nationality ceases to be of significance to any of them.

There is a difference between oppressor and oppressed nationalities that socialists have to understand. We can fight on the same side, temporarily, as the bourgeois or petty bourgeois leaders of the oppressed nations against the oppressor. We can never be on the same side as the oppressors against the oppressed. And internationalism can never mean simply balancing between one and the other.

But even when we find ourselves on the same side of the barricades as the leaders of a national movement, we have to understand their goals are not our goals, their methods not our methods. They are out to establish new capitalist or state capitalist states, and that will mean them turning against their own workers and if necessary turning their guns on us. We are out to develop the international struggle of workers, to unite workers of the oppressed nationalities with workers who have mistakenly identified with the oppressor in the past.

We are for the right of secession—and, in certain concrete situations for the struggle for secession—because we are for the unity of workers. Nationalists who are for the same goals are out to break this unity, to put nation before class.

One of the reasons the left is in such poor shape to deal with nationalist challenges like that in former Yugoslavia or the former USSR is that it has not understood these things in the past. It has flipped between wrapping itself in the flags of small 'progressive' nationalisms and identifying with the great oppressor states like the USSR—or even, in the present war in former Yugoslavia, calling for the intervention of the major Western imperialisms. It will indeed be tragic if the left does not learn how to fight for internationalism as people become sickened by the nationalist delirium.

Notes

1 E Hobsbawm, *Nations and Nationalism since 1780* (Cambridge, 1990).
2 B Anderson, *Imagined Communities* (London, 1991).
3 E Gellner, *Nations and Nationalism* (Oxford, 1983).
4 N Harris, *National Liberation* (London, 1990).
5 A typical example is S Pacu, *A History of Transylvania* (New York, 1990).
6 E A Wrigley, 'London's importance 1650-1750', in J Patten (ed), *Pre-industrial England*, pp196-197.
7 A point made by Gramsci, see A Gramsci, 'The Renaissance', *Selections from Cultural Writings* (London, 1985), pp222-234.
8 Which was why Gramsci could see Machiavelli as a theorist of a rising bourgeoisie, even though he looked to a feudal prince to achieve his goals.
9 The key part in this decision is said to have been played by Alessandro Manzoni, who first wrote his enormously influential novel *I promessi sposi (The Betrothed)* in the Lombard dialect, and then spent 15 years changing it into Tuscan, see for instance D M Smith, *Italy: A modern history* (Michigan, 1959).
10 I Banac, *The National Question in Yugoslavia: Origins, History, Politics* (London, 1984), p81. See also, E Hobsbawm, *Nations and Nationalism since 1780*, op cit.
11 G Brennan, *The Spanish Labyrinth* (London, 1960) p29.
12 The expression was actually invented by a critic of Griffith, but nevertheless was an accurate summary of his economic nationalism, which was modelled on that of the German Friedrich List. See N Mansergh, *The Irish Question* (London, 1965) p238.
13 See B Fitch and M Oppenheimer, *Ghana, The End of an Illusion*, pp33 and 182-183.
14 'The Counter-Revolution in Berlin', *Neue Rheinische Zeitung*, 12 November 1848, in Marx Engels *Collected Works*, vol 8 (Moscow, 1977) p17.
15 O Bauer, *Die Nationalitaetfrage und die Sozialdemokratie*, p271, quoted in R Rosdolsky, *Engels and 'non-historic' Peoples* (1987) *Critique* p35.
16 B Anderson, op cit, p87.
17 K Marx and F Engels, *Manifesto of the Communist Party*, in Marx, Engels and Lenin, *The Essential Left* (London, 1960) p33.
18 This has escaped some writers on the approach of Marx and Engels to the national question. Thus Ephraim Nimni, a follower of the anti-Marxist Laclau, ascribes to them a sophisticated materialist analysis which they did not, in reality, hold at this time. See his *Marxism and Nationalism* (London 1991).

19 The Czech movement was closer to a modern national movement that those of the Ruthenians and the South Slavs. Even as early as 1848 an incipient Czech bourgeoisie and petty bourgeoisie was attempting to unit the Bohemian and Moravian peasantry behind its programme for 'national' capitalist development, in a way which certainly was not true for the Highlanders, the Bretons, and the Carlists. Marx's *Neue Rheinische Zeitung* did show some sympathy for the Czechs, until their leaders threw their weight behind the Austrian monarchy's attacks on the democratic movement.
20 Letter of 2 November 1867, *Marx-Engels Collected Works* (Moscow, 1987) pp460-461.
21 Letter of 30 November 1867, in *Marx-Engels Collected Works*, vol 42, op cit, pp486-487.
22 Marx to Kugelmann, 29 November 1869, in ibid, vol 43, pp390-391.
23 See 'On the Decline of Feudalism and the Emergence of the National States', written at the end of 1884 and now available in *Marx-Engels Collected Works*, vol 26 (Moscow, 1990), pp556-565. Only two years earlier, in his manuscript 'On the Early History of the Germans' Engels was still speaking of 'the German nation' as existing at the time of Julius Caesar, see *Collected Works*, vol 26, p30.
24 O Bauer, 'The Concept of Nation', from *Die Nationalitaetfrage und die Sozialdemocratie*, available in French translation in G Haupt, M Lowy and C Weill (eds), *Les Marxistes et la question nationale* (Paris, 1974), p235.
25 O Bauer, ibid, p238.
26 Ibid, p239.
27 Ibid, pp241-242.
28 Ibid, p 243.
29 Ibid, p249.
30 Ibid, p264.
31 Although he was critial of certain aspects of it, according to E Nimni, *Marxism and Nationalism*, op cit, p145.
32 The programme, adopted at the Austrian party congress in Brno (Bruenn) in 1899 is contained in Rosa Luxemburg, *The National Question* (New York, 1976) pp104-105.
33 G Haupt, 'Les Marxistes face a la question nationale: l'histoire du problem', in G Haupt et al, op cit.
34 Ibid, p49.
35 'Nationality and internationalism', *Neue Zeit*, January 1908, translated in French, ibid, p129.
36 K Kautsky, 'La nationalité moderne', *Neue Zeit* 1887, translated into French, ibid, p119.
37 Ibid, pp114-127.
38 Ibid, p114.
39 Ibid, p116.
40 Ibid, p35.
41 Ibid, p136.
42 K Kautsky, 'Nationality and internationalism', *Neue Zeit*, 1908, ibid, p136.
43 Ibid, pp137-138.
44 For a typical example, see E Nimni, *Marxism and Nationalism*, op cit.
45 K Kautsky, 'Nationality and internationalism', quoted in R Luxemburg, *The National Question*, op cit, pp126-127.
46 Ibid, p127.
47 See 'The National Question and Autonomy', written in 1908-9, available in ibid, p159.
48 Ibid, p177.
49 Ibid, pp129-131.

50 Ibid, p93.
51 Ibid, p97.
52 Ibid, p96.
53 Although on this, as on so many other issues, Trotsky—who had already written brilliantly on the Balkans during the wars of 1912 and 1913—took up Lenin's legacy after he joined the Bolsheviks in 1917 and deepened some aspects of it. Stalin's 'Marxism and the National Question', written in 1913, used to be quoted by many on the left as a classical exposition of the Bolshevik position. Much of it is a straightforward regurgitation of Kautsky's account of the origins of the nation state and of Lenin's argument for self determination and against cultural national autonomy. But it also attempts to define what a nation is using a list of factors. The attempt has been very influential, but in fact breaks with the general approach of Lenin and gives a lot of attention to psychological and 'national character' factors in a manner that is closer to Bauer than Kautsky and Lenin.
54 V I Lenin, 'The Right of Nations to Self Determination', in *Critical Remarks on the National Question and the Right of Nations to Self-determination* (Moscow, 1971), pp40-41.
55 Although most of his polemic was not directed against Luxemburg but against Radek.
56 V I Lenin, 'On the Right of Nations to Self Determination', op cit, pp56-57.
57 Ibid, p70.
58 Ibid, p77.
59 Ibid, p101.
60 V I Lenin, the discussion of self determination summed up, in *Critical Remarks*, op cit, p124.
61 Ibid, p83.
62 Ibid, p83.
63 *Minutes of the Second Congress of the RSDLP* (London, 1978), p81.
64 V I Lenin, 'Critical Remarks on the National Question', in *Critical Remarks*, op cit, p16.
65 Ibid, p31.
66 Ibid, pp22-23.
67 Ibid, p21.
68 Ibid, p10.
69 Ibid, p13.
70 Ibid, p137.
71 Ibid, p138.
72 Ibid, p24.
73 Figures for 1984, from M Kidron and R Segal, *The New State of the World Atlas* (London, 1984).
74 See *Independent on Sunday*, 2 August 1992, p5.
75 In a recent televised discussion between Stuart Hall, former guru of *Marxism Today*, a French new philosopher and Salman Rushdie, only Rushdie showed any sign of understanding that there could be something *good* about a fusion of cultures.
76 Marx and Engels, *The Manifesto of the Communist Party*, in Marx, Engels, Lenin, *The Essential Left* (London, 1960), p18.
77 P Manuel, *Popular Music of the non-Western World* (Oxford, 1988) p20.
78 Ibid, p20.
79 Ibid, p20.
80 Ibid, p21.
81 Ibid, p20.
82 Ibid, pp18-19.
83 B Anderson, op cit, p40.
84 Ibid, pp42-43.

85　Ibid, p67.
86　Ibid, p81.
87　Ibid, p76.
88　Ibid, p77.
89　Ibid, p63, see also, for an elaboration of his argument, pp119-121.
90　Ibid, p30.
91　A talk for the Australian Broadcasting Corporation, printed in *New Left Review* 193, March/June 1992.
92　E Gellner, op cit, p48.
93　Ibid, pp46-48.
94　Ibid, p46.
95　Ibid, p47.
96　Ibid, p55.
97　It was written after both Gellner's and Anderson's.
98　E Hobsbawm, *Nations and Nationalism since 1780*, op cit, pp10-11.
99　Ibid, pp127-130.
100　Ibid, p172-173.
101　With the partial exception of Yugoslavia, where the domination was in the hands of the two nationalities who spoke Serbo-Croat and the third Slav speaking nationality, the Slovenes all of whom united against the non-Slavs, Albanian speakers.
102　The only, partial, exception was the Czech part of Czechoslovakia.
103　Both Nigel Harris and to a lesser extent, Eric Hobsbawm, make great play of the existence of capitals today that are not tied to national states or are tied to very small ones, like Singapore or Hong Kong. But these capitals are overwhelmingly the exception, not the rule. The great corporations that dominate world production may operate across national frontiers, but they all make sure they have at least one national state to fall back on in emergencies. Even Hong Kong's capitalists are not really an exception: they have relied on the British state in the past, and are now much keener on the statelet merging into the giant Chinese state than are the great mass of Hong Kong people. For the more general arguments against Nigel Harris's view, see my 'The State and Capital', *International Socialism* 2:51.
104　*Il Materialismo storico e la filosofia di Benedetto Croce* (Turin, 1948) p38.
105　For the arguments showing the lack of national oppression in Scotland, see C Bambery, 'Scotland's National Question' (SWP, 1990).
106　Thus the *Glasgow Herald*, 10 August 1992, could emphasise the 'achievements' of the British team at the 1992 Olympics and print a list of medals under the title 'Britain's Role of Honour', even if some of the emphasis was on the performance of Scottish competitors. At the same Olympics thousands of spectators in the audience showed their double national identity by waving the Catalan flag when a Castillian athlete won a major event.
107　G Brennan, *The Spanish Labyrinth*, op cit, pp268, 279-280.
108　For a detailed account of developments up to the end of 1991, see D Blackie, 'The Road to Hell', *International Socialism* 53, Winter 1991.

New from Bookmarks

The case of Comrade Tulayev

By Victor Serge

Serge's classic novel, in print for the first time in 20 years, is set against the backdrop of Stalin's purges and the Spanish civil war. An invaluable insight into a world now collapsed, but whose legacy lives on.

£8.95

Available from Bookmarks, 265 Seven Sisters Road, London N4 2DE, or PO Box 16085, Chicago, Il 60616, US, add 10 % postage.

Why the Earth Summit failed

DAVID TREECE

Introduction

We are in our third decade of a series of developmental and environmental conference binges, each of which is first said to herald salvation and then derided for its impotence. There is one difference today: the 'Cold War' can no longer serve as a pretext to set aside the real issues. Far from history having ended, its real contours are only now becoming clear. It is not socialism which has failed but...modernity as a whole, including the very economic model which the North has urged—and continues to urge—upon the disadvantaged South. The Earth Summit will see divergent objectives. The North wishes to talk about the environment while the South wants to talk first about development. A new world outlook has to begin with the interconnection of these goals. Tragically, there is no reason to believe that it will start in Rio.[1]

The inability of capitalism even to begin to solve the social and environmental problems it has created was demonstrated to the world with breathtaking clarity in June 1992 at the United Nations Conference on Environment and Development, or Earth Summit. Just a month earlier, the mass rebellion in Los Angeles had exposed the bankruptcy of George Bush's claim to have instituted a New World Order out of the human and ecological devastation of a Gulf War which, in order to guarantee US control over the region's petroleum resources, took the lives of 200,000 and condemned hundreds of thousands more to medieval conditions of disease, material deprivation and continuing political tyranny. Millions then witnessed the unabashed contempt displayed by the world's most powerful leader for the hopes and expectations of so many who saw in the Earth Summit the last opportunity to embark on a commonly agreed global programme of 'sustainable development'; first, in his reluctance even to attend the Summit, and then in his refusal to sign key, binding agreements on biodiversity protection and atmospheric emissions involving significant financial commitments and compliance with specific timetables.

There is an enormous gap between the widespread sense of urgency aroused by the current environmental and developmental crisis and the outrageously cynical and inadequate response offered by Western leaders. This gap mirrors the almost instantaneous disillusionment that has greeted the redemptive promises of market capitalism in the New World Order, both East and West, since the collapse of Stalinism. The *Guardian* editorial which prefaces this article, with its talk of the 'failure of modernity' and of the Northern 'economic model', is symptomatic of the current political and ideological vacuum at the centre of this crisis, which so urgently demands a revolutionary Marxist intervention.

The first responsibility of such an intervention must clearly be to identify with the genuine concerns and fears that the environmental crisis has generated, while arguing against that brand of 'ecocatastrophism' which interprets each successive disaster as the warning eruption of an imminent apocalypse, whose cause and outcome lie beyond the rational control of human beings. The public sense of catastrophism, if it exists, has real roots in the history of the last decade, which has seen the greatest concentration of social and environmental disasters not otherwise accounted for by military conflict—the leakage of poisonous dioxin gas from the Union Carbide plant at Bhopal in 1984, the explosion of the nuclear reactor at Chernobyl in 1986, the 1988 floods in Bangladesh and the increasing levels of rainforest destruction in South East Asia, equatorial Africa and Amazonia, to name just a few examples.

The challenge to the revolutionary Marxist tradition goes beyond merely identifying the 1980s as a 'decade of disasters' however, and poses the need, which this article seeks to address, for an analysis of the crisis within the wider context of the specific character of recent capitalist development at a regional and global level.

Some of the representatives of developing nations and nongovernmental organisations at the Earth Summit attempted unsuccessfully to prioritise the link between the environmental crisis and the impact of debt, the world recession and the structures of trade and aid on the Third World economies. For many observers sceptical of the possibilities for genuine international co-operation, the deadlock reached on every key item after the 15 solid weeks of preparatory negotiations leading up to the Summit had revealed two irreconcilable agendas dividing the issues of environment and development between North and South: the North's determination to offload its responsibility for the global environmental mess onto the South, and the South's concern, first and foremost, with its own economic development.[2] As the Summit itself unfolded, that North-South polarisation was increasingly expressed through two counterposed arguments over the responsibility for the crisis: on the one hand, the North's over consumptive industrial 'model' of development and, on the other, the South's inability to manage its 'population explosion'.

Any serious attempt to explain the failure of the Earth Summit must first acknowledge the central role played by imperialism in sacrificing the interests of the world's dispossessed majority to the destructive dynamic of global capital accumulation and market competition. The only significant decisions to emerge from the UN Conference, as shown below, actually served to strengthen the ability of institutions already dominated by the major advanced economies, such as the World Bank, to dictate the priorities of development within the societies of the Third World. The link between political leadership in environment policy and the imperialist struggle for control over the resources of the developing world was exposed when Japan offered to assume the role of ecological superpower apparently left vacant by the US. A major polluter and consumer of tropical timber via its logging activities in the Pacific rim countries, Japan has decided to boost its international economic profile by committing 7.7 billion US dollars, far more than any other Northern contribution, to overseas environmental aid.[3]

But such an analysis must also challenge the 'third worldism' of those who implicitly or explicitly accept that imperialist exploitation imposes a contradictory set of interests between, on the one hand, the peasants and workers of the developing world and their own agricultural and industrial bourgeoisie and, on the other, their counterparts in the imperialist countries. If the last ten years have simultaneously been the decade of environmental disasters, East and West, North and South, of international debt crisis and of unprecedented economic turmoil, then these are symptoms of both the deepening integration of the global system and its consequent instability.

The incorporation of the newly industrialising economies, in particular, into the doubly exploitative structures of that imperialist system has depended on the collaboration of local ruling bourgeoisies, who have pursued conscious and deliberate strategies of capitalist modernisation in order to guarantee the integration of once peripheral territories, resources and populations into their own national markets. This is merely the latest, most intensely concentrated and violent phase of a process of regional and global integration which began with Europe's colonial expansionism in the 15th century.

The environmental disasters of the 1980s and early 1990s cannot be viewed, then, simply as the wounds inflicted on a marginalised Third World by a predatory, extractive imperialism, for all that this has often defined its character historically. Neither, therefore, can the environmental crisis be resolved through the regulation of consumption patterns or controls on population growth, were they even desirable, or by piecemeal reforms or adjustments to the conditions of international trade and debt, even if the bankers and business community were open to persuasion. The world's resources, environments and peoples are locked into a globally integrated system of exploitation, whose defenders and representatives, gathered together at the Earth Summit, inhabit not only the cities of New York, Tokyo and London, but Sao Paulo, Jakarta and Bombay, too. The struggle to rescue the planet's environment from destruction and set it on a path of genuinely sustainable, rational development is inseparable from the battle between contending classes for the organisation of society in the interests of either profit or need, a battle that is being waged in the forests of tropical Latin America and Asia, in the mines and oil fields of eastern Europe and the Gulf, and in the factories and shanty towns of the industrialised world, both North and South. Its outcome will be decided by our ability, the ability of a united, international working class movement, to challenge the conditions of our present, global exploitation in their entirety, and ultimately abolish them.

Winners and losers at Rio

There is general agreement that the single most serious threat to the global environment is the impact of toxic emissions on climate patterns. The pollution of the atmosphere with carbon dioxide, released by the burning of fossil fuels and the destruction of trees, is producing a cumulative 'greenhouse effect' whereby the sun's heat is trapped after being radiated back from the Earth. Even the apparently minimal increases in global temperatures caused by this process will be sufficient to melt the polar ice sheets, flooding low lying land and literally drowning entire nations. Other greenhouse gases, such as methane, nitrous oxide and chlorofluorocarbons (CFCs), are destroying the vital stratospheric ozone layer which protects living organisms from the effects of ultraviolet radiation. The discovery of a hole in this ozone layer over the Antarctic has heightened fears of increased rates of skin cancers, damage to crops and fisheries and further disturbances to temperature levels.[4]

Yet while the scientific community is calling for a 60 percent reduction in atmospheric emissions immediately, the most that was agreed at Rio was an open ended, non legally binding statement of 'intent' to hold emissions at 1990 levels. With the help of Britain's environment secretary, Michael Howard, the US, whose industries are responsible for 25 percent of global emissions, managed to delete the specific target date of 2000 from the treaty, previously agreed by 110 countries.[5]

A biodiversity agreement aimed at protecting the world's stocks of plant and animal species was similarly undermined by the US's refusal to sign or commit significant resources to aiding developing countries in this task.[6] If, as a result, current rates of tropical deforestation continue, 'some 15 to 20 percent of the world's estimated 3.5 to 10 million plant and animal species may become extinct by the year 2000... [though they have] tremendous future potential as renewable sources of energy, industrial products, medications, genetic inputs to agriculture and applied biological research, if they are not eliminated first.'[7] This will gravely jeopardise our capacity to meet future global needs for the diversification and substitution of food crops, given that 90 percent of the world's current food production is dependent on just 16 of the planet's 80,000 edible plant species, all of which are located in the tropics.[8] At the same time, a wealth of medicinal resources and expertise, much of it accumulated by the forests' indigenous inhabitants, will be sacrificed, and with it the potential to combat diseases such as the HIV viruses and various forms of cancer.

According to the 1992 World Development Report, developing countries will need to spend between 75 and 100 billion US dollars annually by the end of the 1990s to stabilise and reduce pollution and environmental damage. This is equivalent to between 1.5 and 2.5 percent of these countries' GDP. By contrast, most donor governments attending the Summit failed even to honour their long-standing UN commitment to raise Official Development Assistance aid to 0.7 percent of GDP. Compare this to the 6 billion US dollars in military aid transferred from the US and the Soviet Union to the Third World in 1972 alone, at the height of the Vietnam War,[9] or the 950 billion US dollars earmarked for worldwide arms spending in 1993. The paltry 3 to 4 billion dollars that are to be pledged by the rich nations will be channelled through the Global Environmental Facility (GEF), a scheme first devised behind the closed doors of a G-7 summit meeting, ensuring the exclusion of Southern governments from the discussions.[10]

As a recent *Ecologist* magazine editorial argues, the GEF will in fact serve to further impose the economic priorities of the dominant powers on the developing nations, under the guise of 'helping' those countries 'to contribute towards solving global environmental problems':

> By designating the atmosphere and biodiversity as 'global commons', the GEF implicitly suggests that everyone has a right of access and that local people have no more claim to them than a corporation based on the other side of the globe. Pressing problems with a direct impact on local peoples—desertification, toxic waste pollution, landlessness, pesticide pollution and the like, all of which occur throughout the globe and could therefore be judged as being of 'global concern'—are pushed to one side whilst the local environment is sized up for its potential benefit to the North and its allies in the South.[11]

By framing environmental problems in terms of solutions which can only be provided by the input of capital, technology, managerial expertise and economic policies under the control of the imperialist powers, the GEF will effectively tighten its grip on those aspects of the environment—the seas, forests, the atmosphere and biodiversity—that are essential to the profitability of the global capitalist economy.

In the furtherance of these interests, the GEF is ironically already being used to subsidise environmentally damaging projects under the cloak of financing 'suitable mitigatory measures' and so 'internalising' ecological costs. Thus the Arun Hydro-Project in Nepal is being indirectly funded by GEF biodiversity conservation money.[12] It should be of no surprise to learn that the administration of the GEF is being entrusted to the World Bank, whose intimate association with Third World mega-disasters is now notorious.[13] The Bank's powers have been additionally strengthened by the creation of an 'Earth Increment' fund and a 15 percent budget increase for its affiliate, the International Development Association, which makes loans or grants of up to 6 billion US dollars a year to developing countries.[14]

In 1987, following successive exposures of the World Bank's support for hydroelectric, roadbuilding and colonisation schemes in the Philippines, Amazonia and India, which violated even its own guidelines on environmental and social protection, it announced a review of its policies and the appointment of a new staff of specialised environmentalists. But within days of the close of the Earth Summit, a hitherto suppressed independent report revealed how the same policies had been flouted in the implementation of the Sardar Sarovar dam and irrigation project on India's Narmada river. Flooding devastated the lands of 240,000 mainly tribal people, at the same time damaging downstream fisheries; fewer than half of those displaced will receive compensation, and fewer still will benefit from irrigation.[15] Their future is likely to repeat that of the 20,000 Amazonian peasants and Indians deprived of their land and livelihoods in the 1970s by another Bank financed project, the Tucuruí hydroelectric scheme. Many of them still lack domestic electricity supplies and are plagued by the malaria carrying mosquitoes which infest the stagnant water surrounding their homes.[16]

The Earth Summit has therefore reinforced the collective strategic influence of the dominant capitalist states over development in the Third World. 'In the GEF, the World Bank is judge, jury and executioner'[17] of an agenda set by its majority shareholders, and presided over by its US chairman. The Bank's role, as defined by the Bretton Woods Charter in 1944, is that of promoting 'private foreign investment by means of guarantees or loans'; that is to say, its financial commitments to the infrastructural sectors of energy and transport serve as a catalyst to attract private capital investment in projects oriented towards the external market. In this sense it has complemented the broader function of its sister organisation, the International Monetary Fund, whose lending policies, exercised during the last decade through Structural Adjustment programmes, have been designed to maximise the export of capital and goods from the developing economies, and 'to seek the elimination of exchange restrictions that hinder the growth of world trade.'[18] In other words, the precarious nuclear power programmes of Brazil and the Philippines, and the devastating roadbuilding and hydroelectric schemes of Amazonia, Indonesia and India are the price paid by local people for being obliged to participate as vulnerable and unwilling junior partners in the global 'free' market.

At the same time, the Summit gave a clear go-ahead for the private sector to take full advantage of the free trade conditions fostered by these multilateral state institutions. The 800 page *Agenda 21*, the conference's non-binding action plan for sustainable development, leaves the GATT (General Agreement on Tariffs and Trade) free to ignore environmental issues altogether. The UN Conference on Trade and Development (UNCTAD), the poor countries' response to GATT, has meanwhile ceased to have any meaningful role at all. Earlier in the year the UN Secretary General, Boutros Boutros-Ghalli, axed the Centre on Transnational Corporations (UNCTC), the only world body to monitor the activities of multinational corporations.[19] Intensive lobbying at the Summit by the Business Council for Sustainable Development (BCSD) ensured that these corporations were absolved of any legal responsibilities for environmental degradation, in exchange for a promise of self regulation.

Among the 600 or so transnational conglomerates belonging to the BCSD, which account for a third of global GDP and 70 percent of world trade, are such pioneers of ecological stewardship as Shell, Unilever, Rio Tinto Zinc and Du Pont.[20] Du Pont is just the latest to have embarked on a publicity campaign of self promotion as the environmentally enlightened visionary of the business world. Yet as a recent report argues, 'If any one company can be held accountable for the hole in the ozone layer, it is Du Pont.'[21] As the single largest corporate polluter in the United States, Du Pont produced more chemical pollution in 1989 than Allied-Signal, Ford Motor Company and Union Carbide combined. Its total reported pollution was 14 times that of Dow Chemical, 20 times that of Chrysler and 30 times that of Mobil—all companies that are themselves among the top 100 US polluters.

If Du Pont is a pioneer, it is in the development and production of CFCs. Since the company first marketed them in 1931, it has enjoyed a near monopoly of the trade in many of the compounds used in aerosol sprays, insulating foams, cleaning agents, chillers and automobile air conditioners, controlling as much as a quarter of the global market. In March 1988 it won media admiration and praise from environmentalists by announcing that it would unilaterally halt the production of CFCs. In fact, when the impact of these compounds on ozone depletion was first revealed in 1974, the company vigorously fought a US ban on aerosol sprays and argued for non-regulation of the industry. In the 1980s, Reagan's anti-regulatory policies removed any incentive to research into alternatives, and Du Pont instead expanded its CFC production facilities in Japan in response to increased world demand for non-aerosol products. The company's decision to now shift to 'CFC-Lite' substitutes (HCFCs and HFCs, which will themselves continue to contribute to global warming and ozone degradation, if at lower levels) is therefore a strategic move to ensure its monopoly of a new market in advance of its competitors. Part of this strategy is to buy time for itself, convincing the Bush administration that its products are the only viable alternatives to CFCs, and ensuring that the 1990 US Clean Air Act amendments postponed the phasing out of HCFCs and HFCs to the year 2040. In the meantime it is busy securing major commitments from industrial customers, such as General Motors.[22]

Du Pont's corporate environmental image must also be set against its record in falsifying information concerning its toxic emissions and failing to uphold safety standards. In April 1991 a mining subsidiary of the company, Consolidation Coal, was found guilty on six counts of tampering with coal dust samples used in monitoring permissible dust levels in underground mines, and was fined 20,000 dollars. In the previous year, its oil subsidiary Conoco was forced to pay the residents of Ponca City, Oklahoma, 23 million dollars in compensation for the contamination of homes and property by seepage from its refinery and tank farm. Since June 1990 the company has been fined on at least six occasions for the mishandling and dumping of toxic materials, chemical leakages and the distribution of damaging pesticides.[23] This gives the lie to the 'polluter pays' principle, the notion defended by some environmentalists that the market can be used as a mechanism to control the destructive activities of big business. In reality, 'internalising' environmental costs by attributing a monetary value to them in this way simply commercialises and legitimises the right of capital to degrade the environment, while passing on the real costs to the consumer.

The 'alternative' Summit agenda: population, consumption, limits to growth and debt

It is against this background, the subjugation of the environment to the destructive forces of a market dominated by multinational capital and administered by multilateral financial institutions, that we must assess the alternative explanations for the environmental crisis advanced by the Greens and others.[24] The related arguments about the need for controls on world population growth, Western consumption levels and industrial growth have been addressed previously in this journal and elsewhere.[25] Without rehearsing them again in detail, it is worth identifying the underlying assumption which unites them—that the capitalist status quo, in particular the dynamic of the market, is natural and inescapable.

The Malthusian theory that the Earth's resources can only sustain a finite population was first used in 19th century England precisely in support of the logic of the free market, which dictated that the unemployed should be denied 'outdoor relief' through the Poor Laws, and condemned instead to choose between the workhouse or starvation. Its modern equivalent, as set out in *The Limits of Growth* (1972) and its recently published update, *Beyond the Limits*, effectively imposes a double sacrifice on the world's exploited majority in the name of 'natural' limits, which are in reality the product of the private monopoly of resources and their squandering in the competitive drive for profit. When the Greens say that a slowdown in Third World population growth must be matched by the contraction of industrial output in the West, they are offering nothing more than a mirror image of existing capitalist society, whose recessions, wars and famines regularly guarantee the destruction of whole sectors of industry, the slashing of consumption levels for millions through mass unemployment and the decimation of entire populations. Frederick Engels provided what remains the Marxist response to this 'Green' Malthusian legitimation of the market system a century and a half ago, in his *Outlines of a Critique of Political Economy* (1844):

> *The productive power at mankind's disposal is immeasurable... Capital increases daily; labour power grows with population; and day by day science increasingly makes the forces of nature subject to man. This immeasurable productive capacity, handled consciously and in the interest of all, would*

soon reduce to a minimum the labour falling to the share of mankind. Left to competition, it does the same, but within a context of antitheses. One part of the land is cultivated in the best possible manner, whilst another part... lies barren. One part of capital circulates with colossal speed; another lies dead in the chest. One part of the workers works 14 or 16 hours a day, whilst another part stands idle and inactive, and starves. Or the partition leaves this realm of simultaneity: today trade is good; demand is very considerable; everyone works; capital is turned over with miraculous speed; farming flourishes; the workers work themselves sick. Tomorrow stagnation sets in. The cultivation of the land is not worth the effort; entire stretches of land remain untilled; the flow of capital suddenly freezes; the workers have no employment, and the whole country labours under surplus wealth and surplus population.[26]

One example will suffice to illustrate the remarkably contemporary ring of Engels's description. In a world where just 44 percent of potential arable land is actually exploited, while 950 million people are chronically undernourished, Brazil occupies eleventh place in the league of economies but fifty-ninth in the table of human development.[27] Forests are cleared and US banned pesticides are poured into the soil to guarantee Brazil's place as the second largest global exporter of soya beans. Meanwhile 20 million peasant farmers are prevented from supplying domestic food needs by the ranchers' and plantation owners' monopoly of agricultural land, which ensures that just 18 landowners control an area equivalent to that of the Netherlands, Portugal and Switzerland combined, much of it lying idle. As a result, 40 percent of the country's 150 million population live in endemic hunger, the world's fourth worst record, whose latest symptom is a new form of dwarfism amongst the inhabitants of the impoverished north east.

To claim in these circumstances that the relationship between population, resources and environment is thus shown to have reached the breaking point of sustainability means two things: leaving unquestioned the system of private monopoly and global market competition which lies at the heart of this misery and destruction; while at the same time condemning the victims of that system, North and South, to pay three times over for its preservation—first, as exploited wage labourers and peasants, second, through the degradation of environments which are often also the very source of their livelihood, and third, by suffering the artificial scarcities upon which profits depend. As Engels said of Malthusianism:

Through this theory we have come to know the deepest degradation of mankind, their dependence on the conditions of competition. It has shown us how in the last instance private property has turned man into a commodity whose production and destruction also depend solely on demand; how the system of competition has thus slaughtered, and daily continues to slaughter, millions of men. All this we have seen, and all this drives us to the abolition of this degradation of mankind through the abolition of private property, competition and the opposing interests.[28]

There is one further factor, specific to late 20th century capitalism, which is widely accepted as playing a major role in pressurising Third World governments to promote socially and environmentally damaging projects: the burden of debt repayments to Western creditors. Certainly even a fractional reduction in the 1.3 trillion US dollars owed by the developing countries would be sufficient to pay for the 100 or so billion US dollars needed annually to clean up the world's environment. It is true, as Susan George and others have noted,[29] that the five countries with the largest areas of tropical forest threatened with destruction— Brazil, Indonesia, Zaire, Peru and Colombia—are also all among the top debtor nations. The 1991 floods and mudslides in the Philippines, which killed 6,000 and made 43,000 homeless, can be traced to a 4 billion US dollars agricultural project aimed at generating exports to service the country's 26 billion US dollars worth of debt. The clearing of irreplaceable tracts of rainforest left the local populations and soils deprived of the vegetation which would otherwise have protected them against the impact of the typhoon that swept across the country.

In the 1980s some environmentalists suggested that it was possible to kill two birds with one stone, exploiting the relationship between debt and environment to their mutual benefit. This they would do by means of 'debt-for-nature swaps', through which organisations in the creditor nations would buy up and cancel some of the loans owed by developing countries in return for grants to local non-governmental organisations for conservation projects, in particular national parks. By mid-1991, 19 such swaps had been completed, most of them in Costa Rica, the Philippines, Ecuador and Madagascar.

In reality, however, these deals, besides failing to address the wider economic forces which threaten the survival of fragile ecosystems, have in fact served to reinforce the imperialist structures tying the debtor nations to their creditors. What effectively happens is that environmental groups in the developed world give money to commercial banks in the developed world, while a Third World country promises to give money to its own environmental groups. The transfer of resources from South to North is left unaffected, indeed the swaps actually legitimise the debt in the face of campaigns by local trade unions and popular organisations which argue that the loans have already been repaid many times over through extortionate interest rates. The struggle for local democratic control over the environment and over development priorities is thus undermined, enabling the dominant economies to further their strategy for appropriating and merchandising resources in the Third World.[30]

In any case, the notion of a simple causal relationship between debt and environmental disaster is itself questionable. Far from being the desperate response of indebted governments to the pressure to keep up interest repayments, many of the mega-projects in the energy and transport sectors of the Latin American and Asian economies were initiated in the 1970s by way of loans which themselves contributed to the debt crisis of the following decade. The Bataan nuclear power plant in the Philippines, for example, was ordered in 1976 from Westinghouse on a design rejected in the US for safety reasons. The 2.1 billion US dollars debt incurred for the plant—which was built just 60 miles from Manila, on three earthquake faults and near two active volcanoes—has been costing the Filipino people 500,000 US dollars a day in interest payments since 1987.[31] The most ambitious agro-industrial development scheme in Amazonia, the Grande Carajás Programme, was launched in 1980, when Brazil's debt stood at 60 billion US dollars. Yet total borrowing for Carajás was itself projected at 62 billion US dollars, hardly the cautious response of a weak, peripheral economy to financial crisis.[32] What this and similar projects instead force us to confront is the role played by national states in Latin America and Asia, allied to indigenous and multinational capital, in integrating previously marginal economies, populations, resources and environments into the global system.

Industrial revolution in the tropics

The last quarter century has seen the emergence of new centres of capitalist production, in particular in Mexico, Brazil, South Korea, Taiwan, Hong Kong and Singapore, which have rendered the term 'Third World' obsolete as a description of the major economies of Latin America and South East Asia.[33] Like others before them in the post-war period, such as India, these Newly Industrialising Countries managed, through massive state intervention, to raise their export of manufactured goods above that of raw materials, often evolving regional, sub-imperialist spheres of influence in the process.

This phenomenon is most obviously identified with the urban industrial centres, such as the São Paulo conurbation with its Ford and Volkswagen automobile plants, or the shipyards of Seoul. What is less readily acknowledged is the extent to which these development strategies have often included the incorporation of the most remote rural regions and their populations into the national market structure and into the process of industrialisation. Thus the tropical hinterlands of Brazilian Amazonia and the outer islands of Indonesia are suffering the effects of late capitalist modernisation whose classic features, completed over a period of two centuries during Europe's industrial revolution, have here been compressed into the space of a generation. These are permanent, irrevocable economic and social transformations, not merely sporadic cases of extractive plunder, and it is their swiftness and intensity which explain much of the environmental upheaval currently being experienced.

The first of these processes is the appropriation of vast areas of land and their natural resources as private capital under monopoly control. Private and state enterprises, ranchers and plantation owners employ legal means and force of arms to carry out mass evictions in what, in the Amazon, has been described as 'one of the most rapid and large-scale enclosure movements in history as more than 100 million acres pass from public to private ownership.'[34] This is the source of the current, unofficial war between rural labour and the agrarian bourgeoisie which has claimed the lives of some 1,700 peasant farmers since 1964, as the state provides tax incentives for banks and industrialists to speculate on idle, deforested land, while the landowners' organisation, the UDR, holds cattle auctions to finance its private armies.[35]

A major consequence of these latter day clearances is the enormous shift of population, not only via migration to the established urban centres of the South, but also into the newer cities of the Amazon, such as Manaus, Belém and Marabá, and further west along the state built highways which function as bleeding arteries draining the forests of their timber and other resources. Parallel to the urbanisation of Brazil's population at a national level, which has reduced the rural sector from 70 percent to less than 30 percent over the last quarter century, the Amazon has seen its own proletarianisation of the peasantry, many of whom are directly involved in environmentally destructive industries, such as the burning of charcoal for the production of pig iron. One migrant from Bahia put his predicament starkly and simply, as he recognised that, like it or not, he was now an industrial worker: 'We're in the saw-mills because we've got no option. If we try and work on the land, the gunmen will stick their guns down our throats.'[36]

In many cases, population movement has been a matter of systematic state policy, involving the ethnocidal repression of communities whose peasant and tribal economies pose an obstacle to the integration of the national capitalist market. Indonesia's Transmigration programme, which absorbs 6 percent of national spending, initially aimed to move 65 million people from the central islands of Java, Lombo, Bali and Madura to the outer islands in order to replace the rainforest with cash crop plantations. By 1984, 3.6 million had already been resettled, thousands of them facing starvation on disastrous colonisation schemes, while the local tribal inhabitants have been swept aside.[37]

The Indonesian government is already notorious for its savage repression of the indigenous inhabitants of East Timor, where a peaceful nationalist demonstration was massacred late in 1991. But it has long since pursued quasi-fascist policies of forcible racial assimilation through its implementation of the Transmigration Programme, in the interests of promoting 'national security' and crushing potential dissent. In 1985, the minister for transmigration recalled a youth congress of 1928, where it was concluded that:

we are one nation, the Indonesian nation; we have one native country, Indonesia; one language, the Indonesian language. By way of Transmigration, we will try to realize what has been pledged, to integrate all the ethnic groups into one nation, the Indonesian nation... The different ethnic groups will in the long run disappear because of integration...and... there will be one kind of man...[38]

Similarly, the geo-political strategy of Brazil's military planners has used the language of integration to conceal ethnocidal policies whose aim has been to eliminate the collectivist, non-accumulative and non-market based economies of the region's Indians. 'We do not want a marginalised Indian, what we want is a producing Indian, one integrated into the process of national development', said the president of the state Indian agency in 1969.[39] The state colonisation programmes of the 1970s sought to deny the existence of any indigenous Amazonian population, describing the region as 'a land without people for a people without land', a familiar slogan to anyone acquainted with the history of the Israeli state's occupation of the Palestinian territories. Despite Brazil's official return to civilian rule in 1985, military force continues to play a key role in the state's efforts to integrate Amazonia into the national economy. Since late 1986, under the Northern Watershed Project, 6,500 km of the region's northern frontier, representing 14 percent of the entire Brazilian territory, has been under military occupation. The aim is to guarantee access for state and private capital to the region's sizeable mineral and fossil fuel reserves, many of them concentrated on Indian lands.[40]

Such measures have laid the basis for the industrialisation of Amazonia, whose centrepiece is the Grande Carajás programme. Financed with private and state capital, and loans from the World Bank, the EEC's Coal and Steel Community, and Japanese, European and US private banks, the scheme's central purpose is the exploitation of the world's largest iron ore reserves. A 900 km railway was constructed to export the iron to these countries, and to provide an outlet for the further complex of industries spawned by the project, including pig iron smelting, charcoal burning, aluminium smelting and sawmill processing. As well as the threat to 2.4 million hectares of rainforest, this has resulted in the chemical pollution of rivers and the atmosphere, the wholesale eviction of peasant and Indian communities and the shattering of their lifestyles.[41] Above all, it demonstrates how, through the integration of indigenous and multinational capital, and the intervention of national state and multilateral institutions, resources, populations and ecosystems once at the distant margins of the world economy are now fully locked into a global system of exploitation.

The class struggle and the environment

At the same time, Carajás is a powerful illustration of the fundamental contradiction within capitalism, the way in which it generates both the processes by which the world's environment is systematically degraded and the force, the only force, which is capable of exploiting that environment creatively, rationally and in the interests of the majority—the working class.

The struggle of one small sector of labour, the rubbertappers of western Amazonia, to defend their forest environment and livelihood, was brought to light by the murder of the trade unionist and revolutionary socialist, Chico Mendes, in December 1988. Some of the few instances where the rainforest has been saved from the ranchers' chainsaws and bulldozers have been the results of mass pickets involving the rubbertappers and their families, who have confronted and appealed to the ranchers' employees as fellow workers. The movement culminated in the mid-1980s in the creation of a Forest Peoples' Alliance uniting the rubbertappers and their traditional rivals and enemies, the Union of Indian Nations, and in the first successful expropriation of a rubber estate and its conversion into an extractive reserve under workers' control.[42] For some this offers a model for a sustainable alternative to the industrial exploitation of the region.

But a partial and local reform such as this must inevitably confront the isolation and vulnerability of such a small sector of workers in the face of a ruling class which has not hesitated to use the police and army to maintain its control over the region's resources. It must also address the problem of its vulnerability to the forces of the international market. Even allowing for some diversification, what degree of economic security can be guaranteed by a dependence on the commercialisation of a limited number of extractive commodities in the context of a world market notorious for its instability and price fluctuations? By way of an indication, in March 1991, the Rubbertappers' Council protested that its members' livelihood was threatened by the current price of rubber in

Brazil, which is fixed at rock bottom levels under the influence of multinational tyre companies such as Goodyear and Firestone.

As Júlio Barbosa, Chico Mendes' successor in the leadership of the Rubbertappers' Union, has argued, the local struggle for improved conditions must be linked to the wider, and ultimately international struggle against capitalism as a whole.[43]

Among those companies active in the exploitation of the Amazon region's mineral resources are subsidiaries of multinationals such as Rio Tinto Zinc, Shell, BP and Anglo-American, familiar protagonists in the worldwide battle between capital and labour as it is being fought in Europe, the Americas, Asia and the Middle East.

The first step in building that united working class movement is to make the connection with the vibrant and increasingly organised industrial proletariat that has grown up around the Carajás project, in the east of the region. Workers here in the construction industry, the power plants, mines, iron smelters, sawmills, in the Brazil nut processing factories, in education and urban transport, are fighting over health and safety issues, wages and for the basic right to trade union organisation. But they are also placing environmental questions at the centre of their demands; a united campaign in the city of Marabá succeeded in shutting down the charcoal burners which had been polluting local homes and schools.[44] Urban and rural trade unionists have united in the defence of forest peasants attacked and arrested by police working hand in glove with a local landowner.

In many cases skilled workers brought into the region by the mining and smelting companies based in the urban centres of the south have taken traditions of organisation and socialist politics with them. The writer and journalist Arthur Ransome recorded how, in revolutionary Russia, the lateness of industrialisation meant that many factory workers retained their connection with their native villages through annual migrations backwards and forwards from the towns, carrying with them the ideas of the revolution.[45] In many ways, the swiftness of the social and economic transformations in late 20th century Brazil means that, despite the often enormous physical distances involved, the proximity between the experiences of urban and rural workers is even greater, and therefore the possibilities for building a united political movement even more promising. Chico Mendes' trade union and political career would be incomprehensible without his chance friendship with a revolutionary veteran of the 1920s and his involvement in the construction of the nationwide independent trade union federation, the CUT, and the Workers' Party.[46]

Thousands of miles away, in India, the recently murdered revolutionary workers' leader, Shankar Niyogi, helped to forge similarly extraordinary links between the experiences of workers in Asia's largest steel company and the tribal workers of the Chattisgarh forests.[47] Elsewhere in India, too, the power of collective organisation has achieved tangible, if minor, victories in the struggle against destructive development projects. Construction of the Sardar Sarovar dam led to clashes between police and thousands of local demonstrators protesting because they were not consulted about the project. As a result, Japan, which had originally agreed to co-fund the scheme, pulled out in 1990.[48]

The Bhopal disaster in December 1984 offers an inspiring and at the same time tragic reminder of how the collective identity of workers gives them a unique interest in fighting for solidarity with the rest of their class, not least in the struggle over the environment. A leak of the highly toxic MIC gas spread from the Union Carbide chemical plant over 40 square kilometres, killing thousands and affecting hundreds of thousands more with eye and respiratory complaints. Yet it was the self sacrifice and organisation of transport workers which ensured the evacuation and survival of many others. Staff at the railway station close to the factory remained at their jobs, waving incoming trains through and alerting neighbouring stations to stop trains entering the city. Many of these workers subsequently died from the effects of the gas themselves.[49]

The Earth Summit demonstrated that those who hypocritically claim to speak of 'our common future', while upholding an exploitative, destructive market system, cannot be relied upon to abolish the conditions which endanger our well being and survival. Paradoxically, though, the same capitalist system which devours resources and environments from the furthest reaches of the globe in its drive to accumulate and compete, has also created its own gravedigger. The integration of capital brings with it the integration of labour, the development of a world working class that is forced to engage in a common struggle against the international bourgeoisie, whether in the forests of Amazonia and Indonesia or the factories and oilfields of North America, Europe and the Middle East. Nearly a century and a half ago, in the *Communist Manifesto*, Marx and Engels wrote:

The bourgeoisie has through its exploitation of the world market given a cosmopolitan character to production and consumption in every country... But not only has the bourgeoisie forged the weapons that bring death to itself; it has also called into existence the men who are to wield those weapons—the modern working class—the proletarians.

Today the necessity and potential for an international revolutionary movement to complete that task has never been greater. In all possible senses, we have a world to win.

Notes

1 *Guardian*, 1 June 1992.
2 K Thompson and J Vidal, 'History Goes on Hold', *Guardian* 3 April 1992.
3 'Japan Set to Take World Lead on Aid', *Guardian*, 25 April 1992, and 'Environment superpower role for Japan', *Guardian*, 5 June 1992.
4 See F Pearce, *Turning up the Heat* (London 1989), introduction and ch 1.
5 J Vidal, 'Good Intentions Doomed by Gulf Between Rich and Poor', *Guardian*, 15 June 1992.
6 Ibid.
7 W C Baum and S Tolbert, 'Development projects', draft chapter for the World Bank on 'The Role of Environmental Management in Sustainable Economic Development', World Bank, Office of Environmental Affairs, Projects Advisory Staff (September 1983) p8, cited in S George, *A Fate Worse Than Debt* (London, 1990), p167.
8 S George, ibid, pp166-167.
9 Ibid, p23.
10 J Vidal, 'Good Intentions Doomed...' op cit.
11 O Tickell and N Hildyard, 'Green Dollars, Green Menace', *The Ecologist*, vol 22, no 3, (May/June 1992), pp82-83.
12 Ibid.
13 See, for example, *The Ecologist*, vol 15, nos 1/2 and 5/6 (1985), vol 16, no 2/3 (1986) and vol 17, no 2/3 (1987), all of them special issues devoted to bank financed projects.
14 J Vidal, 'Good Intentions Doomed...' op cit.
15 J Erlichman, 'World Bank Dam Draws Censure', *Guardian*, 19 June 1992.
16 See D Treece, *Bound in Misery and Iron: the impact of the Grande Carajás Programme on the Indians of Brazil* (London, 1987), pp82 and 102-108.
17 I Johnson, administrator of the GEF, cited in O Tickell and N Hildyard, op cit.
18 S George, op cit, p50.
19 J Vidal, 'Good Intentions Doomed...' op cit.
20 K Watkins, 'The Foxes Take Over the Hen House', *Guardian*, 17 July 1992.
21 J Doyle, 'Hold the Applause: a Case Study of Corporate Environmentalism', *The Ecologist*, vol 22, no 3, (May/June 1992), p87.
22 Ibid, pp88-89.
23 Ibid, p86.
24 See, for example, Earthscan's *Beyond the Limits* (1992) and the contributions by P Harrison and S George to the *Guardian*/Oxfam Earth supplement (June 1992).
25 See M Simons, 'The Red and the Green—Socialists and the Ecology Movement', *International Socialism* 2:37 (Winter 1988), pp51-58, and D Blackie, *Environment in crisis: the socialist answer* (London, 1990), pp17-27.
26 F Engels, 'Outlines of a Critique of Political Economy', appendix to K Marx, *Economic and Philosophic Manuscripts of 1844* (London, 1977), pp171-172.
27 See the United Nations Human Development Report 192.
28 F Engels, op cit, p176.
29 N Guppy, 'Tropical deforestation: a Global View', *Foreign Affairs*, vol 62, no 4 (Spring 1984), note 13, table 1, p930, cited in S George, op cit, p166.
30 See R Mahony, 'Debt-for-Nature Swaps: Who Really Benefits?', *The Ecologist*, vol 22, no 3 (May/June 1992), pp97-103.

31 S George, op cit, p18.
32 D Treece, op cit, pp12-20.
33 See N Harris, *The End of the Third World: Newly Industrializing Countries and the Decline of an Ideology* (London, 1986).
34 S Hecht and A Cockburn, *The Fate of the Forest: developers, destroyers and defenders of the Amazon* (London, 1990), p107.
35 See S Branford and O Glock, *The Last Frontier: Fighting over Land in the Amazon* (London, 1985).
36 N MacDonald, 'From Peasants to Workers', *Brazil: a mask called progress: an Oxfam report* (Oxford, 1991), p79.
37 See 'Indonesia's Transmigration Programme: a Special Report in collaboration with Survival International and Tapol', The *Ecologist* vol 16, no 2/3, 1986, pp58-117.
38 Cited in M Colchester, 'Unity and diversity: Indonesian Policy Towards Tribal Peoples', The *Ecologist*, vol 16, no 2/3, 1986, p89.
39 L Beltrão, *O índio, um mito brasileiro* (Rio de Janeiro, 1977), p26.
40 See E Allen, *Calha Norte: Military Development in Brazilian Amazonia* (University of Glasgow Institute of Latin American Studies Occasional Paper no 52, 1990).
41 See D Treece, op cit.
42 See C Mendes, *Fight for the Forest: Chico Mendes in his own words* (London, 1989).
43 Interview with *Socialist Worker*, 28 October 1989.
44 See the video documentary *Amazon Sisters* (Pinpoint Productions, 1992).
45 A Ransome, *Six weeks in Russia 1919* (London, 1992), p65.
46 C Mendes, op cit, pp16-17, 24-27.
47 J Rose, 'Death of a Fighter', *Socialist Review* (July/August 1992), p17.
48 J Erlichman, op cit.
49 A Gupta, *Ecology and development in the Third World* (London, 1988), pp53-55.

Advocates for Animals

Steven Rose's 'Do animals have rights?' in issue 54 of *International Socialism* described a number of organisations within the animal rights movement, some of whom advocate the liberation of laboratory animals. The organisation Advocates for Animals was mentioned in this context. Steven Rose was wrong to make such a false and misleading statement about Advocates for Animals, which does not participate in or support any illegal activities. Its director has written to us and pointed out that Advocates for Animals does not advocate illegal activities or the 'liberation' of animals from laboratories. The editors of *International Socialism* are happy to accept his assurance and apologise for misrepresenting the position of Advocates for Animals.

2 volume special boxed set.

Arthur Ransome in Revolutionary Russia

with an introductory essay by Paul Foot

ARTHUR RANSOME, author of Swallows and Amazons, and a score of other famous and successful children's stories, wrote perhaps the best account of the Russian Revolution in the English language.
He was a journalist in Russia when the revolution broke out in 1917. An educated, cultured English gentleman in his early thirties, he was thrilled and inspired by the tumultuous events which shook the world all around him.
Here for the first time since the 1920s are the two books Arthur Ransome wrote about the Russian Revolution. The first describes six weeks in Russia 1919; the second the deep economic and political crisis which devastated the revolution — but did not destroy it — in 1920. The books are introduced by *The truth about Russia*, a short, strong lyrical appeal to the American people to understand and support it. This appeal has never before been published in this country.
Arthur Ransome was committed to the Bolshevik revolution. But these books are neither sentimental nor extravagant. They are at once sober, well-argued and passionate reports by the best foreign correspondent of his day. They are indispensable to anyone interested either in the Russian Revolution or in Arthur Ransome, or both.

'I have been trying for years to get the revolutionary pamphlets printed, and it delights me to know that someone has succeeded at last. I hope they sell in vast quantities. I am also glad you take the line that you do: I absolutely agree that the collapse of Stalinism should not mean the end of socialism, or even of revolutionary socialism'. *Hugh Brogan* biographer of Arthur Ransome.

£12.95

Available from Bookmarks, 265 Seven Sisters Road, London N4 2DF

REDWORDS

Can Castro survive?

MIKE GONZALEZ

After years of indifference, it seems that attention is focusing once again on Cuba. The gleeful ideologues of the right, particularly in the United States, sit waiting for the demise of Fidel Castro. For some on the left, his survival seems the last hope for the concept of a socialism that can be successfully built within the frontiers of a single state. In a world where the collapse of the eastern European regimes has exposed the degree of integration of the world economy in the last decade of the 20th century, there is something incongruous about a global theory of social change that rests on the defence of a single weak island economy. Even more poignant is the fact that such a defence so often originates in a stubborn refusal to recognise that more than 30 years after the 1959 revolution, Cuba remains under siege and imprisoned in its economic weakness—an unfulfilled promise.

As the capitalist market wreaks its havoc across eastern Europe, Russia and beyond, Cuba appears to be one of the very few pockets of resistance to its global imposition. Fidel Castro has repeatedly announced that his government will not tolerate the introduction of the market, and the most recent Congress of the Cuban Communist Party (in October 1991) was emphatic in its denunciation of multi-party democracy. At the same time the fulsome articles offering Cuba as a tourist paradise for 1992 make clear how desperate it needs foreign trade and hard currency.[1] The advocates of the market point to that contradiction and assume that it is only a matter of time before Cuba echoes eastern Europe in a full assimilation of the market and the introduction of bourgeois democracy. As the US election approaches, however, the right expresses a growing impatience with the obdurate Cuban regime. Among North American conservatives the test of candidates' credentials may well be their readiness to hasten the process of change in Cuba.

The response on the left has been to reverse the formula. But the principle that my enemy's enemy is my friend is a dangerously simplistic one, whose weaknesses have been exposed over the years in the defence of one East European tyranny after another in the name of socialism. Is Cuba materially different from those regimes? Has it been an advocate of an alternative path to socialist transformation? Has its post-revolutionary history provided a record of democracy and participation which might provide a different foundation for socialist ideas? The analysis that follows shows that the answer to these questions can only be a firm negative. What then has brought together former champions of the Stalinist regimes on the one hand, and erstwhile spokespeople for Trotsky's theory of permanent revolution on the other, in a new campaign for an uncritical and urgent defence of Cuba?

Since 1959 Cuba has symbolised the possibility of a successful resistance against US aggression. It still retains that significance; the conservative anti-Castro lobby still murmurs about invasion and Bush still regards Cuba as the one block to a domesticated and pliant network of states in the backyard. After Grenada, Nicaragua and Panama, the fall of Castro would undoubtedly be celebrated in Washington as a much needed imperial victory; and that is certainly how it would be experienced in Latin America too. That is why all socialists will unequivocally mobilise against any such imperialist victory, and expose the real purposes that underlie the talk of human rights and the democracy of the market.

The fall of the Stalinist regimes has provided an opportunity to reclaim the authentic revolutionary tradition founded on the self-emancipation of the working class, on socialism from below. It would be absurd to exempt some regimes from the exhaustive analysis that this implies. Yet many argue that we must do precisely that in the case of Cuba.

It is our starting point that Cuba does not represent a fundamentally different idea or practice which can serve as a point of departure in the post-Stalinist world. On the contrary, Cuba under Castro is not a challenger but a defender of the same ideas and strategies that have been exposed in the last two years. The sacrifices of its population, the subordination of all other considerations to the urgent tasks of economic survival, have generated deepening conflicts between the state and the mass of the people. And while imperialism seeks every means to exploit those conflicts for its purposes, that does not absolve us from the need to understand and explain them from the perspective of socialism. It certainly cannot lead to the absurd contention that, in Brecht's powerful parody, the government faced with a dissident people 'should dissolve the people and elect another'. The suggestion that the Cuban state is a defender of socialism against its own misguided population by sleight of hand provides new clothes for an idea of socialism without workers' power or workers' democracy, of socialism which addresses only questions of accumulation—in other words, of Stalinism.

An active imperialist victory in Cuba would be a disaster. It would be equally tragic, however, if at this crucial crossroad, revolutionaries suspended the honest accounting of the history of class struggle or set aside the Marxist analysis of the class nature of society in particular cases. While Cuba has mounted a stalwart resistance to the physical assaults of imperialism over the past three decades, it has not resisted the imposition of the priorities of the capitalist system. The Cuban state has pursued a strategy for national survival in the context of a hostile world capitalism; the costs of that survival have been met by a Cuban working class which will now again be asked to accept new and deeper levels of exploitation. Further, that exploitation will be organised by the state. Now more than at any other time it is imperative that socialists argue not merely that capitalist priorities can be administered in a more or less humane manner, but that the wholly different priorities of socialism remain on the historical agenda for the Cuban working class. The struggle for a different society will be conducted at the national level against the state, and it is a matter of urgency that workers reappropriate the long tradition of independent working class organisation as an essential instrument in that struggle. The context of change, however, is the international reality of capitalism. In Cuba, as elsewhere, the task of socialists is to prepare the working class for its own emancipation. That preparation begins with a rigorously honest appraisal of the present reality, and an understanding of its historical roots.

Origins of revolution

Cuba was the last Spanish colony in Latin America to win its liberty. It became independent in 1898 after a three year war. But it was a short lived freedom—for this was the era of United States expansion into the region. Cuba had an important role—strategic and economic—in North American plans; it was to be one element in a chain of military bases across the Caribbean and Central America from which the new imperialists could oversee their area of interest to the south. Furthermore, American capital already had interests in Cuba.[2]

Using a spurious excuse that was to become very familiar, the United States immediately moved on the newly independent country claiming that its citizens were in danger. The Marines were sent to the island, directly to protect the capitalists and owners who had investments in the expanding sugar industry. By 1902, the United States controlled the national bank, the customs service, the police and the presidency and had inserted into the Cuban constitution a clause (the Platt amendment) allowing the US to intervene directly in Cuban affairs whenever the interests of their citizens were threatened.

Cuba therefore never experienced a period of political independence nor a possibility of economic development. Consonant with US interests, it was sugar that absorbed the bulk of new investments in the decades to come, and it was sugar production that dominated the economy from that moment on. Between 1900 and 1920, US investment in sugar rose from $80 million to $1,525.9 million, and production from 309,000 to 5,347,000 metric tons.[3] But it was not only the scale of production that was significant; the bulk of the land it took place on was also directly owned by North Americans—by 1926, 63 percent of sugar production was in US hands. The Cuban agrarian capitalist class had by then become incorporated into the North American economy, its room for manoeuvre destroyed in the wake of what was called the Dance of the Millions. During the First World War the consumption of sugar in the US had risen steadily, and new mills were opened in Camaguey and Oriente provinces to cater for the demand. In 1919 world prices hit a new high. All available cultivable land, and all capital for investment, went into planting for the 1920 sugar harvest. Then world prices fell dramatically. The ensuing bankruptcies delivered cheap sugar land into North American hands.

On the eve of the 1929 crash, then, it was clear that 'Cuba was a protectorate of the United States, that its government functioned in a realm of political unreality, that the final resort was US banking interests and the State Department'.[4] In the countryside a small peasantry coexisted with a huge, largely black, cane cutting labour force which could anticipate four months of work each year. For the rest of the time they were buried in abject poverty. Much of the rural population drifted towards the cities, particularly Havana, where the service industries served those who administered the state or the system of trade. They oversaw the export of sugar, overwhelmingly to North America, and the import of the 75 percent of goods imported directly from the United States in return.

Washington also controlled Cuban political life, and the new dictator Gerardo Machado, who came to power in 1927, was their creature. His main opposition came from a student movement dominated by nationalist ideas whose radical wing, the Directorio, led by Antonio

Guiteras, organised for direct confrontation with the state. The Communist Party, newly formed around the charismatic Julio Antonio Mella, was still small, and its growth undoubtedly affected by Mella's assassination at the hands of Machado's hoods in 1929.

But Machado could do nothing about the catastrophic impact of the crash on this one-product economy so closely interwoven with the United States. The value of exports fell from $200 million in 1929 to $78 million in 1931 and $42 million in 1932.[5] This was the context of a rising popular struggle—among workers and students in particular; the Directorio led demonstrations and prepared direct action against the dictatorship, and the trade unions acted with increasing militancy as the living conditions of workers grew steadily more intolerable. This was especially true for those workers on the plantations, many of whom were now experiencing full unemployment and deepening misery as sugar production collapsed. It was their trade union, the CNOC, whose strikes in 1933 ushered in the year of struggle.[6]

The CNOC was led by members of a growing Communist Party; and the party was influential too among the bus drivers of Havana who launched a strike later that year. The impact was dramatic—workers occupied the sugar mills and defended them with arms in hand, soviets were briefly formed in a few areas, and students were active in the movement of protest and opposition. The Machado dictatorship fell on 23 August and between then and 9 September, Cuba was effectively ruled from below. On 24 September the Directorio issued its manifesto, demanding national independence, economic development, and a social revolution. Ten days later, a group of sergeants led by a clerk called Fulgencio Batista, took control of the army—their rhetoric too was radical nationalist and attempted to embrace the demands of the strikers. Their political purposes, of course, were very unclear—after all Batista still only enjoyed power and influence to the extent that he spoke with the voice of the mass movement. For the moment, he spoke its language and bided his time. On 9 September, Grau San Martin was nominated to the presidency, 'appointed in effect by a revolutionary assembly of students meeting in continuous session on the second floor of the National Palace.'[7] His cabinet included Guiteras, leader of the Directorio—a key organisation in the heady days of 1933.

This was clearly a revolutionary moment—yet it was squandered. Within four months Grau resigned and Batista took his place. The Directorio dissolved itself because it could not agree on a programme —but in any event it shared with the clandestine ABC organisation a commitment to creating a tight cadre organisation which would 'impose a revolutionary programme from power by means of a dictatorship'. Later, in the struggle against Batista, the Directorio would be reformed and again provide a political framework for the struggle against the dictatorship, drawing in Fidel Castro among others.

But where was the Cuban Communist Party? It had grown rapidly in the course of the battles against Batista, it led the main trade unions, and it was the bearer of a political tradition that provided the workers of 1933 with their models for an alternative power. While it had originally supported the strikes, 'the leaders of the CP called on the workers to stop the general strike at a time when it had already grown into spontaneous armed insurrection'.[8] Later they condemned Grau and the Directorio, and stood aside from the struggle, for it was the general line of Stalin that Communist Parties should have no truck with social democracy.[9]

Without a political direction, the great social movement stepped back from the historical possibility of social transformation that it had enshrined and fought for. Within months (in January 1935) Batista came to power, dedicated to rooting out the memory and organisation of those months. He had Guiteras killed (the CP denounced Guiteras in November 1933 for suggesting that Batista was an enemy of the movement and should be arrested) and moved quickly to proscribing the Communist Party and destroying the trade union leadership. Later, towards the end of the decade, Batista, with the support of the Communist Party, rebuilt the unions *from the state*. With the Nazis in power in Germany, Stalin saw that the Soviet interest lay in forging alliances with the Western imperialisms—he moved rapidly therefore to abandon the ultra-left policies of the so called 'Third Period' and instructed Communists to forge the broadest 'popular fronts' with all and any democratic forces. The result was that the Cuban Communist Party now entered an alliance with its erstwhile persecutor Batista. As Blas Roca, general secretary of the party, put it

> *We must impress upon the people the need for a positive attitude toward Batista, and do our utmost to support his progressive endeavours... The first task of the revolutionary movement is to struggle for national unity based on a democratic programme...*[10]

It was the Communist Party who now built the state trade union federation, the CTC, and who provided its secretary, Lazaro Peña. In exchange for these and two ministerial posts, the Communists gave Batista their support and acted as the instrument of his control over the trade unions—'class struggle was now subsumed as a state activity'.

The nationalist current

For the radical nationalists growing up under the Batista dictatorship, therefore, certain realities were incontestable. Opposition to the dictatorship came from the liberal nationalists, the Autenticos, led by Grau San Martin. The search for a revolutionary tradition led them back to the armed struggle theories of the Directorio and the ABC. The Communist Party, on the other hand, represented a tradition that had stood aside from the struggles of 1933 and had collaborated actively with Batista ever since. While US domination and control of Cuban economy and society remained the central and defining reality, the Communists had no consistent record of denouncing or exposing it— and indeed had actively collaborated with its Cuban surrogate. In the eyes of a new generation of radical nationalists emerging in the 1940s, the CP was totally discredited and they turned instead, as Castro did, to the uncorrupted nationalism of Eduardo Chibas's Ortodoxo Party and to the tradition of direct confrontation which he, as an ex-leader of the student Directorio, represented.

In 1952 elections were announced; the new generation of election candidates included Fidel Castro, standing for the Ortodoxos—formed in 1947 to represent what they saw as a genuine nationalist tradition betrayed by the Autenticos. In the event Batista staged a coup and the poll never took place. For Castro and those around him, this served only to confirm that there was no electoral method that would get rid of Batista. There was, after all, no convincing alternative. The Autenticos of Grau had entered government in 1946, with Batista's acquiescence. In their six year period of office they had launched a bitter and largely successful attack on the Communist Party, ousted its members from the leadership of the trade unions and installed in their place a corrupt anti-communist trade union bureaucracy identified with the new CTC general secretary Mujal. The corruption in high places was common knowledge, and it was the Autenticos, after all, who oversaw the conversion of Havana into a weekend gambling and prostitution centre for North Americans controlled by organised crime—hand in hand with 'respectable' business.[11]

For the United States, Batista was a perfectly acceptable substitute for Grau; he was in any event the power behind the throne and had always served US interests well. After 1952, Batista adopted a policy of 'Cubanising' sugar, which meant that by 1958, 50 percent of sugar cultivation was in Cuban hands; yet it threatened neither the scale nor the nature of sugar trading, nor American control of sugar refining. More importantly, the fact that sugar land was Cuban property in no sense led to a diversification of economic activity nor to a retention of capital within Cuba for purposes of investment. The Cuban capitalist class invested its profits abroad—largely on the Miami seaboard—or spent them in luxury consumption. In 1953, 41 percent of the labour force was in agriculture and 17 percent in manufacturing—but the bulk in small scale industry or service related manufacture. Cuba's mineral deposits were barely developed (and what plant there was was wholly US owned), and the rising levels of state expenditure affected services only. Indeed it was hardly surprising that public expenditure affected the economy so little—since 25 percent of the total went on graft and bribes in an expanding and corrupt bureaucracy.[12]

What is surprising, given the level of contempt for Batista and the visible corruption of his regime, was that the level of public resistance should have been so low. While the better unionised sections of the Cuban working class continued to receive under the new trade union bureaucracy the benefits and privileges they had grown accustomed to under Communist leadership, the rest—the nearly 500,000 seasonal sugar workers for example—experienced deepening misery. The economy remained in thrall to the US. In 1952 US interests owned 48 percent of sugar production, 90 percent of electricity production, 70 percent of oil, 100 percent of nickel production, 25 percent of the hotels and so on. In 1958, on the eve of the revolution, Cuba remained a sugar dependent economy tied to the US—sugar employed 25 percent of the labour force, represented 80 percent of Cuban exports, occupied 80 percent of industrial investment and half of the cultivable land. Of 170,000 farms, 150,000 were less than 48 acres, and 600 over 1,500 acres. The structure of the Cuban economy had changed little in the previous five decades—and sugar had brought little benefit to the bulk of Cuban workers.

Yet when Batista did fall under the weight of his own unpopularity and corruption, it did not produce another 1933, a general rising of the working class under a revolutionary leadership. Indeed throughout the 1950s, the working class remained demoralised and disoriented. The Communists were so completely discredited by their collaboration with Batista that they had little or no influence; the right wing trade union leaders provided goods and services for their members and remorselessly persecuted the left. Resistance to Batista therefore came from outside the organisations of the working class under the leadership of discontented sectors of the middle class.

The 26ists

Fidel Castro was one of them. Like the Directorio Estudiantil, inheritors of the organisation led by Guiteras which had played such a key, if confused role in 1933, he now saw armed confrontation with the state as the key to the dictator's overthrow. The first such action, the assault on the Moncada barracks on 26 July 1953, was a failure; several were killed and Castro was arrested and imprisoned. Released two years later under a general amnesty, Castro went to Mexico and began to organise an armed guerilla group. Trained by a veteran of the Spanish Civil War, the 80 or so rebels landed from the motor boat Granma late in 1956. They were met by Batista's troops and many of the group were killed instantly. About 12 of them survived, including the Argentine doctor Ernesto Che Guevara who would later share the symbolic representation of the Cuban revolution before the world.

This tiny group then set about building a guerilla campaign against the corrupt and stagnant Batista regime. There is no doubt that Batista had very few supporters in rural Cuba, and the guerillas enjoyed the support of the workers and peasants in the Cuban countryside. It is crucial to acknowledge the nature of that support, however—for the argument about support and popularity has played a key role in Cuban political debate ever since. Passive support is a quite different thing from active involvement. The guerilla band remained small until the last—in mid-1958 it consisted of some 180 people, and even at the point of Batista's fall it claimed 800 or so combatants. The reality is that the social composition of the guerilla army in Cuba—and the experience was later to be reproduced elsewhere—was fundamentally middle class. Its leadership certainly came from that social sector. And that composition was reflected in the character of its urban support—with fundamental repercussions for the political strategies of the 26th July Movement both before and after the revolution of 1959.

The first urban movement in support of the guerillas was led by Frank Pais. The growing civil resistance against Batista was fertile ground for propaganda by the 26th July Movement. Direct action was combined with support activity—finding provisions and support for the guerillas. When, in February 1957, Pais was captured and killed, there was an immediate response among workers in and around Santiago. But their actions were not co-ordinated and linked to the civic resistance groups on the one hand and liberal opposition on the other. The *organisations* of the working class took no part. Nonetheless, the debate within the 26th July Movement centred on the potential urban movement that these events had revealed. Despite Guevara's insistence that the leadership of the movement must remain in the mountains, a second general strike was organised for 1958. But it was organised with the methods born of the general strategy of armed struggle—from a command centre in the mountains and through a network of clandestine cells. The workers who were to be the actors in this drama were given no opportunity to develop their own organs of struggle or resistance—that did not figure in the political strategies of the 26th July Movement.

And the Communist Party exploited that contradiction to denounce the Movement as a group of 'petit bourgeois putschists'. When Batista's repression came, the workers offered no response, for 'the 26th July Movement was neither the party nor the political leadership of the Cuban working class.'[13] From now on, the military struggle took absolute priority over the political, and the command structures of the organisation were reinforced.

In the event Batista's corrupt and repressive regime was an inefficient defender of American interests, and the US government grew increasingly cool towards him—as his loyal friend and supporter, the US Ambassador Earl T Smith, complained. When arms shipments to Batista were suspended, Smith argued that liberals like Herbert Matthews, who published a sympathetic interview with Castro in *Life* magazine in 1957, had taken over the Latin American desk at the State Department.

The guerilla movement played its part in hastening the collapse of the Batista regime, but he was not quite the enemy represented in subsequent histories of the period. On 1 January 1959 his regime was overthrown; no one rose to defend him. No alternative power existed and the guerilla armies marched into Havana under the leadership of Fidel Castro and Che Guevara.

In the speech he delivered after the Moncada assault, 'History will absolve me', Castro set out the framework of his future politics.[14] It was a programme of democratic and economic reforms, embracing industrialisation and a redistribution of some land, principally the plantations owned by foreign firms and their Cuban agents. In the years that followed Castro was at pains to underline the moderation of the strategy—its purpose to develop his programme for capitalist economic development as quickly as possible:

> *I personally have come to feel that nationalisation is, at best, a cumbersome instrument. It does not seem to make the state any stronger, yet it enfeebles private enterprise.*[15]

Or

> *Never has the 26th of July Movement talked about socialising or nationalising the industries. This is simply stupid fear of our revolution.*[16]

Yet for the first months Castro held back as various bourgeois politicians tried and failed to exert control over the situation. Effectively power belonged to the 26th July Movement, though on what basis they would organise that power was far less clear. Their popularity, however, was undisputed. The dictator was gone, and the new leaders were manifestly very different from the venal bureaucrats who had dominated the state machine of the dictatorship. As if to underline the point, Castro quickly introduced severe measures against state corruption. Immediate moves were made to introduce programmes for educational reform and health care. Early in the year a number of strikes reinforced wage demands which were quickly accepted, though Castro appealed to other workers to restrain further such demands. Initially, unemployment fell as wage rises fuelled consumption. The strikes ended as quickly as they had begun. There were no further demands for more far reaching social change, no spontaneous expressions of popular power—as there had been for example in 1933. There was none of that collective confidence and creativity, no sign of the 'festival of the oppressed' that usually accompanies a general rising of the working class.[17] Power had not been *seized* by the workers or the landless peasants; they seemed rather to be watching and responding to the decisions of the new command. It was the bearded men in olive green, the *barbudos*, who now assumed control and set out to carry through *from above* the changes envisaged in the general programme for social reform described by Castro.

The guerillas in power

What Cuba revealed so clearly was that:

> *While the conservative cowardly nature of a late-developing bourgeoisie is an **absolute law** the revolutionary character of a young working class is neither absolute nor inevitable.*[18]

On the contrary Cliff has shown that under such conditions the trade unions grow under the aegis of the state and are overshadowed by the political compromises which limit them to economic demands. In the Cuban case such compromises were enacted and defended by the Communist Party—and the consequence was 'a labour movement that was conservative, bereft of idealism'.[19] It was that very weakness that created the conditions for the emergence of the movement led by Castro.

The ravages and corruptions of imperialism were open and arrogant; the entrapment of the economy in imperialist purposes was not challenged by Batista's 'Cubanisation' measures nor by the *relatively* better conditions of life of some organised sectors of workers. For the bulk of the population, the realities of everyday life were grim—and all the more so when a tiny section of the population, a sycophantic and unproductive bourgeoisie, conspicuously displayed its life of luxury. Yet the Cuban working class offered no *organised collective resistance* to the state, and its self proclaimed political leadership offered no alternative strategies. Into this vacuum stepped the group of disaffected intellectuals around the 26th July Movement, offering themselves as the representatives of the 'nation's interest' above the contending classes, and expressing an absolute determination to carry through *from the state* a programme for economic modernisation and development. 'They embodied the drive for industrialisation, for capital accumulation, for national resurgence'[20]—in other words the unfulfilled tasks of a disabled national capitalist class.

For the Communists, the *barbudos* in power represented a serious problem. They had played no part in the overthrow of Batista—indeed in the eyes of Castro they were hopelessly compromised with him. They had repeatedly denounced the 26th July Movement for its opportunism and its petit bourgeois origins. Within the Cuban Workers Congress (CTC), which they still dominated, the Communists found themselves facing an internal battle for the leadership which they lost; the first congress after the fall of Batista elected a leadership in which six Communists (PSP members) were set against 15 supporters of the 26th July Movement, who, like the new general secretary David Salvador, were often virulently *anti*-communist. But the Movement had no roots in the working class movement, no organisation at the base to carry through a revolutionary transformation from below. It became clear very quickly that Castro needed the Communist Party's trade union machine for his own purposes. While he had changed the leadership, it was a move conducted from above and did not represent a major shift on the ground, where the old trade union leadership retained control. After the initial concessions, the key issue—and an urgent one—was to control wages and link them to productivity, to the purposes of economic development. In this the Communist Party was a key ally. Already emphasis was increasingly placed on the need for sacrifice on the part of the better paid workers, on the exchange of individual for social wages. Winning these arguments required a structure of local organisation which was controlled by the Communists. That was the basis on which a pragmatic reconciliation began.

The other key element of Castro's programme was enacted in May 1959, with the agrarian reform decree which redistributed land previously owned by foreign capital among the poor peasants.[21] Only estates of over 1,000 acres (402 hectares) were expropriated—representing about 25 percent of cultivable land. Even the larger Cuban owned farms were for the most part left untouched. It was hardly a revolutionary land reform, as many liberal commentators in the United States pointed out; its primary intention was to give land to the landless and to draw into effective use land hitherto unemployed or underemployed. In the first place, this could raise food production for domestic consumption; in the second, it might raise cane production in the non-plantation sector—for sugar remained the key to the whole economic programme.[22]

It became obvious, however, that the problem was not just using the land but using it more productively—and that required large scale investment in technology and new production methods in every area of agriculture. In fact, Cuban capitalists withdrew much of their investment and were reluctant to replant; their allies in the United States were even quicker to react. The US government, which had maintained a certain ambiguity in the first few months of the new regime (even allowing Bell Telephone to negotiate terms for the takeover of the Cuban telephone service), now denounced the Cuban land expropriations and immediately threatened to withdraw the sugar quota. US interests had $1 billion invested in Cuba, much of it in the sugar and sugar related activities on which the Cuban economy depended. And 95 percent of the sugar went to the US under the quota agreement. Ending the quota, therefore, was a devastating blow.

The Cuban response was immediate and unavoidable. By September 1959 the Cuban state assumed a more interventionist role; the land of known collaborators of Batista was confiscated, the National Institute for Agrarian Reform (INRA) was established with Fidel Castro at its head, and people's stores were set up to prevent speculation. By early 1960 the US had cut the sugar quota and oil was to provide the excuse for abolishing it altogether. When Cuba announced it was to receive a limited quantity of Russian oil (after the Mikoyan delegation in February that year), the US oil companies refused to refine it in the Cuban installations. In response Cuba seized the refineries and in June President Eisenhower cut the remaining quota. Cuba seized more US assets and the United States imposed a total economic embargo which persists to the present. The impact of the embargo was dramatic; before 1959, not only was the bulk of Cuban exports destined for the United States but it was also the source of 80 percent of Cuban imports.

In the war that the United States mounted against Cuba in the subsequent months, the responses of the Castro government were essentially pragmatic reactions. After June 1960, the US government gave increasingly open and active support to ex-Batista supporters preparing armed counter-revolution in Cuba. At the same time, the US was rapidly calling its other allies in Latin America to heel to isolate Cuba politically as well as economically. One arm of that policy was the Alliance for Progress, whose programmes for guided reform under American tutelage were a specific alternative to the radical nationalist reforms exemplified by Cuba.[23] The other arm of US strategy was the notion of 'collective security' (that is the common security interest of the US and

Latin America) that was enshrined in the 1961 Punta del Este Treaty, whose object was the military and political encirclement of Cuba.[24]

Cuba responded by creating internal organs of vigilance against the counter-revolution—the Committees for the Defence of the Revolution (CDRs)—and popular militias to guard key installations. When, in April 1961, right wing mercenaries supported and financed by the Kennedy administration and directly assisted by several Central American military tyrants, invaded Cuba, they were immediately and devastatingly repulsed by the militias. This incident, called the Bay of Pigs invasion after the area where the counter-revolutionaries landed (called Playa Giron in Spanish), gave a massive boost of popular support to Castro.

At the same time, the defenders of the old order were leaving Cuba in droves (half a million in the first eighteen months or so). There were no more tourists visiting the brothels and casinos of Havana, and the parasites were calling in their debts and going home to Miami. The businessmen followed. The Cuban private capitalist class had gone, but the task of developing the economy remained. It fell to the new state whose directive role had become more and more central as the United States imposed absolute economic isolation and industry and agriculture fell increasingly under its control.

Who now ran the state? By mid-1959, the state was without question in the hands of Castro, though the battle for absolute control continued. The old state functionaries, Batista's immediate circle, and the higher echelons of the military and the police left Cuba within that first year. But the key sectors of the bureaucracy, the Communist trade union leaders, were incorporated into the new state machine replacing the right wing bureaucrats. The first expression of the new state, the ORI (Integrated Revolutionary Organisations), drew under the hegemony of Castro the Directorio and other groups. While it began by waging a battle against the Communists inside the trade unions, it very rapidly became clear that the 26th July Movement did not have an independent base in any sector of the population. It was not the pinnacle of a mass movement. The forging of a new ruling group at the top would permit the creation of *the mass organs of state power* from above. The army, for example, was formed from a *merging* of the rebel army and elements of the existing military. The army was not *replaced* by the popular militia—on the contrary, they remained under the control of a command structure of sharp and rigid hierarchy.

Every visitor to Cuba was impressed by what Huberman and Sweezy called 'direct democracy'[25]—the running dialogue between Fidel Castro and the population of Cuba, usually assembled in vast crowds in the main square of Havana. Exhilarating though they were, it is now clear that these public spectacles were not part of a transition to the devolution of power to the workers, but rather a substitute for such power. The militia were answerable to the army command and not vice versa; the trade unions were answerable to those in control of the state.

This is not in any way to deny the popularity of the new regime or the enormous significance of the new government. Indeed the major changes that followed the flight of Batista were only possible because of that popularity. The initial measures raised living standards overall and the wages of workers in particular. The commitment to health care and education were acted upon immediately. Nothing so clearly represents the hope and optimism with which socialists as well as liberals and democrats invested Cuba as the education campaign of 1960 which virtually eliminated illiteracy in Cuba in a single year. The teachers were largely the educated urban young who took themselves and their dreams into the countryside to teach the people to read. The old palaces of corruption in Havana were now filled with people in beards and dressed in olive green who had not enriched themselves. From the tribune in the square or from his jeep, Fidel spoke with everyone. But nothing gave as much pleasure as to see the American empire tremble under the impact of such a small country. In an era when the dominant Stalinism had abandoned the revolutionary role of the workers, the colonial revolutions seemed to fill that role.

The commitment to building an independent state capable of carrying through economic development was clearly present. But this was not to be confused with a commitment to socialism, to the self activity of the producers. The immediate expansion of the economy created a short term response; but the task that the new regime set itself was rapid accumulation,[26] a shift of resources to industry, success in an environment of competitive accumulation. Even during this period that Maspero calls 'the Cuban fiesta'[27], power was concentrated in the new state, and in the figure of Fidel himself. The mass organisations were not subject to direct democracy from below; their tasks were set by the new state. The army mobilised the militia as a defence force—but the command structures were reinforced in the early years of the revolution.

If the real conditions of emergence of the new Cuban state, and the relationship between those controlling it and the mass organisations from the outset is not addressed, then all subsequent analysis becomes impossible. Either we simply deny the concentration of power in the state and the absolute priority given to the tasks of accumulation, or we seek (in vain) some dramatic break in the symbiosis of state and people. In fact there is a continuity imposed by the class dynamics of capitalism—the pursuits of competitive accumulation.

From the outset, Castro and Guevara saw industrialisation and diversification as the keys to growth and to breaking the cycle of dependency on the United States. They were right, of course, but how was that to be organised in a country without capital or technology? In the first few months, the Cubans used every means to convince the United States. But despite appeals from a range of liberals and intellectuals, the US administration was unyielding. The Cuban leaders then turned to the Cuban Communist Party, whose increasingly central role arose from the growing influence of the Soviet Union on Cuban thinking. Its economic methods, and their attendant political structures, provided Castro with a model of centralised planning which Guevara, as the Director of the National Bank, enthusiastically endorsed. Guevara added, too, a recognition that economic expansion would require considerable sacrifice from the Cuban workers, that the promise of immediate benefit was illusory, and that the method of achieving that generalised austerity was *political*—convincing the workers that the new state was a *workers'* state. The adoption of these ideas coincided with a growing economic commitment by Russia to Cuba ($1 million a day is the figure usually quoted). The announcement by Castro late in 1961 that the revolution 'had become Marxist-Leninist' represented more than anything else an acknowledgement of that deepening interdependence. He did not mean that the revolution was committed to the self-emancipation of the working class, nor that it had adopted proletarian internationalism. Instead it harnessed popular and workers' organisations directly to the implementation of the plan—in factories, for example, joint worker-management technical commissions increasingly took the place of workplace trade unions. The emphasis on the collective, on egalitarianism and on sacrifice, were replaced now by stress on material incentives, linked to the imperious need to raise productivity. And the stress was reinforced by the introduction of stringent rules on absenteeism, identity cards etc. At the same time, resources were diverted massively away from consumption and into investment in machinery that was now only available from Eastern Europe and paid for with sugar. The contradiction, of course, was that the diversion of resources into industry and away from agriculture brought a *fall* in the production of sugar, the only means Cuba had of earning abroad.

Between 1961 and 1963, therefore, Cuba under Castro was implementing a highly bureaucratic, centralised command economy. The mass organisations were part of the structure of implementation, rather than control or accountability. And the lack of independent organisation in the revolution itself or in the aftermath made the task of imposing this new direction easier.

Yet this hardly corresponds to the reputation that Cuba has enjoyed in the past, nor to the image that its champions present today. In fact

Cuba's image on the left derives from a brief period in its history (1963-69) which was wholly uncharacteristic of the last thirty years of Cuban history. In any event, appearances can be deceptive, especially when the spectator is such a willing participant in the delusion.

Avoiding the Russian embrace

The US economic embargo closed the avenue of a renegotiated relationship with the mainland. But it did not end there. The US government, under Eisenhower and Kennedy, was committed to the encirclement of Cuba. In mid-1960, the US government approved the setting up of an anti-Castro guerilla front in Escambray province and there was a great deal of talk of direct invasion. The CDRs and the militias were responses to the threat of invasion—and they proved their efficacy when 1,400 right wing Cubans landed on the Bay of Pigs. The force was easily and rapidly destroyed and the anticipated general uprising throughout Cuba never occurred—it is hard to imagine it was ever anything other than a right wing paranoid dream.

What the Bay of Pigs did, however, was finally sever the links with the United States. In the two years since the revolution the Castro government had responded to each new assault by further radicalisation. The agrarian reform of 1961 was more far reaching and thorough than the first reform decree; the commitment to rapid industrialisation was now, in Guevara and Castro's view, the overwhelming priority. Lacking resources and cut off from American capital, Cuba turned to the USSR—not only for resources but also in search of administrative and political methods with which to achieve the rapid development they envisaged. Clearly a close relationship with the Soviet Union was a condition of the strategy; so too was the incorporation into the state bureaucracy of those closest to Soviet thinking—the members of the PSP, the Cuban Communist Party. It was their inclusion which was signalled by the formation of the ORI; it was their leading role in the political economy that was acknowledged, in the wake of the Bay of Pigs invasion, when Castro declared the revolution to be 'Marxist-Leninist' in April 1961.

In an immediate sense, this signalled an end of the idealism of Che Guevara's earliest writings; socialist emulation and collective solidarity were not efficient weapons in the race to accumulate. Soviet advice was clear—and reflected in the introduction of material incentives, productivity norms, and stringent systems of labour discipline including the imposition of obligatory identity cards for workers. The adoption of a Soviet model of economic planning changed the direction of agricultural reforms too, with an emphasis on collectivisation and state farms.

Ultimately the whole programme rested on an exchange of machinery, technology etc for sugar exports. Payment in non-convertible roubles necessarily obliged Cuba to buy Russian machinery—indeed to wholly restock at a time of scarce resources. In 1962, living standards were still rising compared to 1958—though the rate of increase was slowing as surplus was directed towards industry. Yet the dilemma was that more land was required to produce the rising quantities of sugar envisaged in the economic plans while a growing population expected to consume more and better food. Even by 1963-64, it was becoming clear to the Cubans that their dependency on sugar was growing, that diversification of the economy was receding, and material incentives had little impact where there were so few available consumer goods. A disastrous sugar harvest in 1963 forced Cuba to call on Russia for assistance, and then to undertake significantly raising sugar production. The circle of sugar was closing again. And without a strategy, changing and shifting direction in response to events, the Cuban rulers could see no escape.

The need to seek out other avenues of development grew urgent after the events of October 1962—the Cuban Missile Crisis. A US spy plane photographed Russian missile bases on Cuba. Kennedy announced that Cuba would be blockaded until the missiles were removed. A Russian fleet sailed towards the Caribbean and most observers, including myself, counted out the final minutes on the Armageddon clock. Then the Russian ships turned back, agreement was reached and in exchange for public assurances that Cuba would not be invaded, the removal of missiles began.

For the Cubans, what emerged very clearly from the episode was the nature of Soviet support for Cuba—that Cuba was a pawn in its global geopolitical strategies. Castro angrily refuted the Russian leader Krushchev's assertion that Cuba had asked for missiles to be located there to protect Cuba against invasion.[28] Faced with the blockade, however, the Cubans raised their slogan of 'Patria o Muerte' (Fatherland or Death). The Russians were happy to sacrifice the Cubans to the greater demands of US-Soviet detente. Castro was enraged by this cynical betrayal—but he could and did say nothing. Internally, the state bureaucracy was well established with the Communist Party at its core.[29] While Castro did carefully reopen a debate on alternative economic strategies, Cuba remained a firm advocate of the Russian position in the split with China, signed new trade agreements in 1963, and acknowledged the political role of the Communist parties in Latin America.

Then in 1965, the Cubans sought a new direction; the context was the disillusionment with Russia and the search for an alternative road to economic development. Castro turned on the Communist Party's old guard, jailing several of them; he made contact with China and began to seek relations with other Third World countries. Then in 1965 Che Guevara published his seminal essay *Man and socialism in Cuba*[30], in which he argued for a 'great leap forward' on a Chinese model,[31] based on the sacrifice of the workers, a period of austerity and scarcity, whose compensations would come not from material but from 'moral' incentives, recognition by the collective and revolutionary selflessness. It was a return to the voluntarism of the first year of the revolution, in which the principal actor would again be the state engaged in a struggle for rapid, forced accumulation with the support of the workers.

As Guevara described it, production based on 'socialist emulation' would be:

voluntary labour in which man sees himself portrayed in his own works and understands its human magnitude...thus man truly achieves his full human condition when he produces without being compelled by the physical necessity of selling himself as a commodity.[32]

The problem is that words exist in a material reality, in this case circumstances in which the labour was to be a contribution to a process of forced rapid accumulation in which the compulsion upon Cuban workers to sell their labour power was redoubled. The context was a situation of scarcity in which the consumption needs of workers had to be systematically subordinated to the accumulation of a surplus in an economy which did not have any untapped resources at its command other than labour itself. Workers were here being asked to accept an intensified exploitation, a voluntary renunciation of the fruits of their labour in order to fuel a state fighting for its survival according to the laws of the market and administering those laws. The state completed the task of capitalist accumulation through exploitation; to describe that as non-alienated labour was absurd.

At the same time Guevara spoke increasingly of the need to break Cuba's isolation, the need to challenge imperialism in 'one, two, three, many Vietnams'. It is possible that he was coming round to an understanding of the impossibility of achieving socialism, or even development, in one country—and that this was the real basis of his disagreement with Castro.[33] He was certainly by now openly critical of Soviet planning methods and indeed of the role of the Soviet Union on the world stage.[34]

The decision to spread the revolution, however, corresponded to the search for alternative markets and sources of imported goods, to a wider economic foundation outside the strait jacket of the deepening dependency on the Soviet Union. In a larger sense it may have rested on a notion of development on a Latin American scale—but that was never articulated. Crucially, it served an internal function—to mobilise the Cuban working class behind its own exploitation, to emphasise the moral rewards of sacrifice and self denial. The material reality of Cuba was that the 'great leap' required a large scale shift of wealth away from consumption and into investment in development. And with all its emphasis on its voluntary character, the reality was that the drive was coercive. It was conceived and conducted from above, led from the state. For behind the talk of popular power and revolutionary democracy there was an increasingly direct control from the centre over political life; the already tied organisations of democracy were set aside in favour of a direct relationship between Castro and the people without the benefit of democratic control or accounting. The state, 'personified' in Castro (a concept which then, as now, seems to mesmerise Western supporters of Cuba,[35]) was the actor in history—political life became the activity of the state among the masses.

It was not scarcity that drew Western intellectuals to Cuba, not its internal accumulation strategies that won the hearts of a whole generation of the left. It was, significantly, Cuban internationalism which gave it such a heady reputation. Against the grey and mechanical versions of Marxism that prevailed among the old left in Europe, Cuba's ideology promised a concentration on the will, spurned the obstacles that material conditions represented and adopted the politics of the guerillero symbolised in Che Guevara. It was not the material force of workers that could turn the tide of class struggle, but the will of the revolutionary and his example. It fitted perfectly into the political method of the Cuban state, and it echoed the general *disillusionment* with the politics of class that now prevailed among a new generation of revolutionary youth. In part it was a healthy reaction against Stalinism—in part it was an impatient idealism that could not wait to carry through the slow construction of revolutionary organisation capable of leading a workers' revolution.

There was no doubt that the new atmosphere of internationalism and revolution was healthy—but it was not proletarian internationalism. Indeed it *assumed*, generalising from the specific experience of Cuba, the absence of the working class from the revolutionary process. It took Cuba as its model, and Guevara's descriptions of the mechanics of guerilla war as its political text. The guerilleros *substituted* themselves for the absent revolutionary class.

It was that very absence that drew to Cuba the wave of support and enthusiasm of many Western intellectuals and students seeking revolutionary potentials elsewhere. They found the revolutionary subject in those who stood outside the established political traditions, in the marginals and the alienated of the inner metropolis, in youth, but above all in the Third World—as if that Third World was not itself already the scene of an industrial production shaped by the powerful metropolitan countries, and which was transforming more and more Third World inhabitants into workers. Instead of connecting with the growing trade union movements of Latin America, the guerilleros saw their natural allies among the peasants and the poorest rural populations.[36] Revolution in this sense became a matter of alienation and moral purity; what made a revolutionary was the degree of sacrifice and suffering rather than the successful identification and mobilisation of the *power* to change the world. In this perspective, the chief instrument for change was not the organs of working class struggle but the national state.

The death of Che Guevara in Bolivia in October 1967 exemplified the courage and self sacrifice of a generation of genuine and committed revolutionaries whom he inspired and represented. It also made manifest the consequence of a revolutionary strategy developed in isolation from a working class which at that very moment was occupying a central role on the political stage of Latin America—yet which merited no recognition in the strategy of guerilla warfare.[37] The generalisation of the Cuban experience really came to grief here, though the support for guerilla groups still continued for a brief period. Yet for Cuba the figure of Guevara continued to serve an internal purpose; to legitimise a continuing demand for sacrifice. What the demand concealed was declining production, falling living standards for the bulk of workers[38], and an increasingly desperate reaction by the leadership. It was Castro's obsession with the 10 million ton sugar harvest for 1970 which was most revealing.

The pursuit of a sugar harvest unprecedented in Cuban history represented a final drive to accumulate sufficient resources from export revenues to launch an industrialisation programme. Like so many other measures, it was adopted without thought or planning, as an act of desperation. The irony is that the subordination of all other considerations to the achievement of this notionally crucial target led to extraordinary distortions, a diversion of both investment and labour *away* from industry, but—since most of the factory and voluntary labour was highly inefficient compared with the professional cane cutters—it did not yield a consequential rise in productivity. Cuba's obligation to Russia was to deliver 8.5 million tons—any excess could be sold on the world market. In fact, of course, the bulk of sugar was traded through mutual trade agreements; the sudden arrival of an extra 1.5 million tons on a limited open market would almost certainly have reduced the price further and undermined the very purpose of *la Gran Zafra*—the Great Harvest. In the event, the 8.5 million ton result was the biggest on record, but nowhere near enough to achieve its stated aims.

In fact, Castro himself clearly realised this far earlier; for neither the first nor the last time, he managed to sustain a rhetoric of unyielding principle while acting with considerable pragmatism. The Russian invasion of Czechoslovakia in August 1968 provided the opportunity for Castro to set down his marker for the changes to come and to open a new rapprochement with Russia.

Analysts are fond of stressing the double edged nature of Castro's famous speech.[39] He certainly did underline the point that Warsaw Pact troops had been less ready to defend other countries—a backhanded reference to the Missile Crisis of 1962—and reiterated the need to be prepared to commit such troops in the event of any future confrontation. Nonetheless the overall tenor of the speech is clear and consistent. Castro gave his support to Russia at a moment when it was universally condemned for its intervention against the proponents of the Prague Spring. Even before the outcome of the Great Harvest was known, and in the midst of the Great Revolutionary Offensive,[40] Castro implicitly acknowledged the failure of an economic project. While even at this late hour Castro was anxious to retain some room for manoeuvre in his relations with Russia and other states, the central thrust of the speech was to accept the identity of Cuban and Soviet interests.

The cause, as ever, was primarily economic. In the first place it was an implicit recognition that austerity had failed to guarantee the economic leap forward that Castro had anticipated. On the contrary, a growing disaffection among workers and increasing absenteeism were a constant preoccupation for the Cuban government throughout 1969, and culminated in the stringent labour laws of 1970. While the exploitation of labour was the task of the Cuban state in its race for accumulation through the 1960s, it was still insufficient to provide economic independence. The Czechoslovakia speech marked a recognition of that reality and a political and economic reconciliation with the USSR. By 1970 it was the Joint Soviet-Cuban Economic Council (JUCEPLAN) which was the supreme economic decision making body. The Communist Party of Cuba was again given a central place, after its marginalisation during the 'Guevarist' phase, and Soviet planning expertise was reinforced by a strengthening of the state relative to the rest of the social system.[41]

There could be no mistaking what the Cuban regime was doing. The bid for the 10 million ton sugar harvest—a figure that was extravagant from the beginning—gave absolute priority to the production of an investable surplus. Everything was sacrificed to it—social spending, working class consumption, long term projects for diversification. All rhetoric apart, for Cuba it represented the acceptance of its role in the world market as a commodity producer. The 10 million ton figure was important precisely because it would allow Cuba to cover her 8.5 million ton obligation to the USSR and leave 1.5 million tons for sale on the world market. Aside from whether the 10 million tons were ever a realistic possibility, or whether the arrival of so much extra Cuban sugar would have undermined the world market price; the immediate impact of the campaign was far reaching in every sphere of Cuban life.

All resources were diverted to sugar; industrial projects were abandoned. Everything now rested on raising sugar production, and *everything* was subordinated to the project. Other economic areas were abandoned, labour was taken to the cane fields, even though it was often inefficient. The ideological pressure on workers to accept a diversion of resources from social spending and consumption grew more intense by the day. Of a list of 20 areas of consumer production, output fell between 1965 and 1970 in all but three, and both absolute and per capita growth fell in this period.[42] As living standards fell, increasingly severe disciplinary measures were enacted. The language of internationalism, of democracy and participation in fact veiled an extraordinary level of centralisation of power in Castro himself—a centralisation that would be formalised after the event in the 1976 constitution, confirmed at the *first* congress of the Cuban Communist Party. The army took an increasingly central position in the command structure.

It was hardly surprising that in this situation low labour productivity and absenteeism came to figure as central concerns in political speeches. By 1970 material incentives were reintroduced, as well as growing wage differentials. The internal differentiation within the working class was formalised in the existence of an Advanced Workers Movement, membership of which was a precondition for membership of the Communist Party. Elected at the factory level from a list drawn up by the government, the advanced worker was defined by his or her work discipline, punctuality, productivity etc. Dissent or criticism were disqualifications. But inclusion brought significant material privileges—rationing, put in place during the previous four years, was abolished in 1970. While consumer goods were not universally accessible, they were available to those who could earn bonuses and increments; indeed the advanced worker could even save money and earn interest on savings accounts.

There was already a clearly defined layer of privilege within Cuban society which could now embrace a group of privileged workers. Irrespective of material possessions (though it was visibly the case that some people were far better endowed with them than others), the concentration of power gave a shrinking group at the cusp of the society an incontestable power. The much vaunted mass organisations—the Committees for the Defence of the Revolution chief among them—were always conduits for the implementation of state decisions or organs of state vigilance. There was no sense in which their government appointed leadership was subject to control from below. When trade union elections were held in 1970, turnout was low and public debate was not permitted—in any event there were no means of expressing public criticism. Canvassing was not allowed and only government media existed. The disinterest in the processes of election was hardly evidence of an involved or interested population. Against the background of all the other expressions of discontent—absenteeism, cynicism, shoddy work, drunkenness—to which public speeches made continuous reference, the picture was one of growing but unorganised disaffection.

The turning point came in 1970. What is described by analysts through the anodyne term 'the institutionalisation' of the revolution, was the abandonment of a project for independent economic development, the recognition that Cuba would survive in a world economic system on the same terms as any other weak national capital. Internally, the emphasis was expressed in new work norms, sanctions for low productivity and tightening controls on any form of dissent.[43]

All this represented the conditions for survival in a world economy and the full integration of Cuba into the Soviet economic sphere. Not only had Cuba now effectively abandoned its aspiration to develop its own industry or diversify its economy; it now became a sugar producer within an integrated economic system. In 1972 Cuba joined Comecon, but in 1970 the Cuban-Soviet Commission for Economic Scientific and Technical Cooperation had already become the central decision making body, charged among other things with drawing up the 1976-80 Five Year Plan. In 1971 Castro acknowledged that 'you cannot jump stages of growth' (how far he had come from the politics of the revolutionary will; little wonder that he never mentioned Guevara any more!).[44] Inexorably, Soviet planning methods took over; material incentives, enterprise profitability, one man management, five year plans. By 1973 prices were decontrolled, and three years later profit sharing was introduced for managers. These were symptoms of the general integration of the economy into the Soviet ambit. By 1973, 67.5 percent of all Cuban trade was with the USSR; its machinery and manufactures were bought in Eastern Europe using non-convertible currencies, and the proportion rose steadily throughout the next decade and a half. All other areas of economic activity were now subordinated to the central drive to produce sugar.[45] The nearly $7 billion of Soviet investment that reached Cuba between 1970 and 1986 served not to break that circle but to reinforce it.

These changes were accompanied by an increasing militarisation of labour, and indeed of government—by the mid-1970s ten of the 20 ministries were under military control. The 1971 Anti-Loafing Laws were draconian in the extreme, and the means of collective self defence or even self expression simply did not exist. As one trade union leader put it:

> *[the role of the unions] is to reconcile our interests as the working class with those of our revolutionary state. Our main role is as a harmonious not an antagonistic counterpart to management.*[46]

The tone had already been set by the 1973 CTC Congress where Lazaro Peña, the old CP General Secretary, scornfully denounced 'petit bourgeois egalitarianism'.

The reality of Cuban society was perhaps best expressed in the first congress of the Cuban Communist Party meeting in 1975 to ratify the new 'socialist' constitution. The congress confirmed Fidel as General Secretary of the CP, head of the armed forces and President of the Council of Ministers. His brother Raul was named as his deputy in all functions and his natural successor. And in all the leading organs of the state, power rested with 18 individuals fulfilling overlapping functions. None of these individuals were subject to election, recall or account. Against that background the acclaimed experiment in popular power, one year earlier, is exposed for the sham that it was—for while delegates to the bodies of this new form of 'local power' could be elected at the lowest local level, the superior bodies were composed of government nominees. And the Communist Party itself spoke for the privileged layer of Cuban society; over 50 percent of its members were managers or bureaucrats.

Cuba in the world

It is against that background that we should set an examination of Cuba's role in the world. In 1970, over the protests of those who had fully absorbed the Guevarist message of the 1960s,[47] Castro abandoned the armed road with scarcely a second glance, and threw his considerable weight behind the electoral road to socialism represented by Allende in Chile.[48] Cuba now sought relationships with bourgeois nationalist governments like those of Velasco in Peru or Torrijos in Panama on the basis of their common anti-imperialism and irrespective of their treatment of their own working class. Cuba was building an alliance of like minded *states* and not an international movement of struggle.

In this sense, Cuban strategies corresponded closely to Soviet interests, having diverged briefly from it in the late 1960s. Speaking at Algiers in 1970, Castro threw the authority of Cuba behind the Soviet role at the conference of the Non-Aligned Movement and denounced those who accused the USSR of imperialism. Castro's visit to Chile gave new legitimacy to the Latin American Communist parties whose previous role had left them in such discredit. In a real sense, Cuba acted on behalf of a Soviet Union seeking zones of influence in Latin America and played a leading role in the formation of a non-aligned bloc.

There are those who claim that Cuba's high profile in international matters, and particularly in Angola, indicated a return to the old internationalism. On the one hand, the internationalism of the 1960s was part of a general strategy for transformation which had now been explicitly abandoned; on the other, the wider context was of a search for a network of relationships with bourgeois states in the context of a nonaligned movement. Most significantly, Cuba's economic and political dependence on the USSR was the over-arching reality, and while there were tensions and disagreements at times, Cuba continued to be a stout defender of the general strategy of the USSR. The Angola case illustrates the point precisely.

Cuban troops were first sent to Angola in 1975; the Cuban government is emphatic that it did so in response to specific requests from Agostinho Neto, leader of the embattled MPLA government. In the course of its armed struggle against the Portuguese, the MPLA had created a number of liberated zones, giving it control of some 40 percent of the country. The collapse of Portuguese colonialism in 1974, however, found it without equivalent strength in the cities, where the right wing nationalist organisations FNLA and UNITA had a significant base. The agreement for Portuguese withdrawal, signed at the beginning of 1975, was therefore a compromise between the three organisations, and gave a series of additional guarantees to the Portuguese ex-colonists. By mid-1975 it was clear that despite the agreements, the struggle for domination of Angola was far from settled, and that moves to ban mass rallies and demonstrations in the cities were winning supporters for the right. In July Neto launched a military assault against the right.

The South African government, however, was also watching events in the region. In response to decolonisation, and in order to pre-empt the formation of a block of ex-colonial states, it moved to a policy of destabilisation, using its economic and military hegemony in the region to mount a series of assaults against Angola and Mozambique.[49] It responded to the MPLA's offensive by moving troops across the Angolan border, guarding the Namibian border and throwing its strength behind the UNITA forces located largely in the south of the country. These were the circumstances in which Neto called for Cuban help.

The call was directed specifically to Cuba; Neto and Castro had a long standing relationship stemming from the 'solidarity' period of the

1960s. But the implication drawn by some commentators that the Cuban response, sending some 35,000 troops, was in some way an act of defiance against Russia and a manifestation of Cuban political independence, is disingenuous. Decolonisation provided an opportunity for the Soviets to win regional influence in South Africa, a policy later enshrined in the Brezhnev doctrine. The Soviets provided a massive airlift of military equipment without which the Cuban troops could not have mobilised in such strength. And there is no doubt that it was the speed of their response that enabled them to decisively tip the military balance and ensure the defeat of the South African invasion. Yet it is curious that these analyses of the Cuban role systematically underestimate the high level of mass activity in the towns, and in particular in the capital Luanda, where the people's committees ensured that South Africa could neither open a second front nor assume the internal political collapse of the regime. The people's committees were at least as significant in driving back South Africa as the Cuban troops were.

For the champions of Cuban internationalism, Angola is the keystone of their argument. They cite the initial decision to move troops, and the subsequent defeat of the attempted coup led by Nito Alves in 1977 (of which the Soviets had failed to warn the government despite their prior knowledge of it), as evidence of Cuban independence from Soviet strategic interests. The factional disputes, of which the attempted coup of 1977 was one, had a long history in the MPLA. The key issue is that the state that the Cubans stepped in to defend had suppressed the urban mass movements of the previous two years—the very organisations that had played such a significant role in 1975, though they had been written out of history subsequently. It was clearly committed to building a state capitalist regime along similar lines to Cuba's own post-1970 development. The anti-imperialist coalition of states that Cuba envisaged closely echoed the political objectives of the Soviet Union. And here, as in Latin America, the criterion for inclusion appeared to have little to do with levels of internal democracy or the pursuit of international working class solidarity—indeed the Soviets continually revised their descriptions of what constituted an acceptable regime, and the commitment to socialism was not one of their criteria. The Cubans had no difficulty, therefore, in defending the brutal and repressive regime of Equatorial Guinea. More crucially, Cuban troops also sustained Soviet foreign policy objectives in Ethiopia. When Russia announced new agreements with the brutal Derg government in Ethiopia, which was simultaneously conducting a war against the Eritrean liberation movement and a border war with Somalia, Cuban troops were made available to the Ethiopian government. They did not confront the Eritreans, but they did liberate Ethiopian troops to continue their savagery while Cuba guarded the Somali frontier.

The continuing Cuban presence in Angola represented the military support to 'progressive' regimes which lay at the heart of the Brezhnev doctrine and its attempt to exploit the post-Vietnam retrenchment of the United States to advance its own political and economic purposes in the region. The 1984 Nkomati Accord between Mozambique and South Africa was certainly a setback; but the Cuban presence was an important factor in determining that Angola did not follow suit. It was for that reason that South Africa, hitherto operating through its own UNITA surrogate, determined to launch another invasion late in 1987. South West Africa was again crucial to their decision; the hope was that a major thrust into Angola and the capture of the town of Cuito Canavale would enable UNITA to establish a rival centre of government to the MPLA. They were again defeated in the 1987-88 campaign; the crucial battle for Cuito Canavale was undoubtedly won by Cuban troops—though in the overall outcome Soviet and Eastern European air power was perhaps a decisive factor.

The result was a military defeat for South Africa. But the claims that this single battle transformed the situation in southern Africa and brought the end of apartheid, is absurd. The Angolan setbacks shifted South African government policy towards negotiation—or perhaps confirmed that direction. But subsequent events could in no way be described as representing a defeat for the government of South Africa. All parties agreed to enter peace negotiations late in 1988. The Soviets had no interest in seeing the defeat of Angola, but neither, in the era of Gorbachev, were they willing to engage in a protracted armed struggle which could fire the African powder keg. The negotiations of 1988 ended the war, but they represented a profound compromise, acknowledging South Africa's influence on events and giving the FNLA and UNITA some credibility as a result. As the American negotiator Chester Crocker put it:

There is no doubt that the Soviets have indeed used their role and influence, not on two, but on the three parties to the agreement (ie Cuba, Angola and South Africa).[50]

The negotiations were as much about US-Soviet detente as about the southern African scene. The withdrawal of Cuban troops from Angola was conducted in response to a new Soviet alignment towards the affairs of southern Africa, abandoning the Brezhnev doctrine of the search for zones of influence in exchange for economic and political cooperation with the West. Thus the closing of ANC offices in Angola and the compromises with UNITA were a price imposed upon the Angolans. In fact Angola too was anxiously seeking economic cooperation with Western banks and agencies.[51] And despite Castro's obvious dissatisfaction with some of the terms of the final agreement it was equally clear that the withdrawal of troops was imposed by a global situation over which Cuba had very little influence. The tone of Castro's speeches, full of dark hints at betrayal and compromise, suggest that he may once have seen Angola as an (illusory) opportunity to acquire an independent international stature.

Through its 13 year involvement, the Angolan intervention had also become a serious problem for the Cubans. Rising numbers of desertions and a deepening drug problem were one aspect; the swelling army of veterans whose expectations of work and housing on their return went unfulfilled were another. The 1,000 returning bodies bred disillusionment and despair in Cuba itself, all the more so when persistent stories (though the war was reported minimally in the press throughout its course) referred to the unpopularity of Cuban troops and the frequent and often violent friction between troops and the local population.[52]

At another level, Cuba's presence in Angola was not entirely disinterested. Angola is a major oil producer, and the cost of the Cuban presence in Angola was paid for in oil. A 1981 agreement gave Cuba a fishing base and important fishing rights in southern African waters.[53] Elsewhere, too, Cuban aid has been linked to Cuban exports. Construction (in Vietnam, for example) involved not only Cuban workers but also Cuban materials, particularly cement; and Cuban medical teams, invariably highly skilled, took Cuban medicines with them which were increasingly becoming important items in the list of exports.

Since 1970, Cuba has acted as a surrogate for Soviet foreign policy in Africa and Latin America. While Cuba has its own reasons, political as well as economic, for maintaining its presence in these areas, they coincide with Soviet interests at every turn. There is a line of consistency running from Castro's 1971 intervention in Algiers to the stout Cuban defence of the Russian invasion of Afghanistan in 1979. Cuba's arms are supplied free by the Soviet Union. The major cost to Cuba is in human resources, yet by the mid-1970s unemployment in Cuba was reaching 5 percent, and significant material incentives were offered to those prepared to go abroad. The pattern of Cuban international relations, therefore, has always corresponded to the needs and interests of the Cuban state seeking allies and supporters in the world.

In that sense, the Soviet interest was well served. When the United States began to pour military support into Central America in the wake of the Nicaraguan revolution of 1979, the Cuban role was again crucial in its influence on the leadership of both the FSLN in Nicaragua and the FMLN resistance movement in El Salvador. While Cuba sent technicians, teachers and trainers to both countries, it adopted a conciliatory role as the decade wore on. After the Grenada invasion in 1983, the Cuban message to the revolutionaries of El Salvador and the Sandinistas in Nicaragua coincided far more clearly with Soviet global interests. As the Central American peace negotiations wore on, Cuba actively encouraged them to participate and to accept whatever compromises were necessary. As the deputy foreign minister Ricardo Alarcon put it on 26 March 1984, 'If it came to an invasion of Nicaragua, it would be up to the Nicaraguans to defend themselves.'[54]

This position is quite consistent with a state seeking relations with other states in terms of its own survival, whatever the character of those regimes. It is certainly not consistent with proletarian internationalism. When in 1982, Castro played host to the Argentine foreign minister during the Malvinas war, the minister was the representative of a government that inherited the mantle of the 'dirty war'. Yet reasons of state overwhelmed all other considerations. And it is just those relationships which Cuba is now seeking to build across the 'non-aligned sector'. In the future, and with the evident cooling of relations with a new Russian regime ill disposed to maintain a distant economy, Cuba will seek friends wherever it can find them and without reference to their internal democracy or their class nature. When the Chinese government butchered its own students in Tiananmen Square, Cuba did not join the chorus of protest from around the world. A year later, Cuba reopened trade relations with China.

The history of the relations between Cuba and the Soviet Union reveal how disingenuous is Zimbalist's assertion that 'while not altogether benign, the effects (of the relationship with the Soviet Union) have been, on the whole, salutary'.[55] Stubbs describes Soviet 'assistance' as 'cooperation designed to bring the less developed countries closer to the levels of the more developed'.[56] If that was its purpose then it has signally failed. What is abundantly clear is that a consequence of Cuba's continuing economic dependence on the Soviet Union was its incorporation into Soviet strategic purposes across the world.

Rectification

In 1980 a wave of refugees took to the sea in an effort to reach Florida. These *Marielitos* were something of a propaganda coup for the United States. But in Cuba Castro denounced them as 'the scum of the earth', pushers, pimps, addicts and homosexuals. In fact, they included a large number of skilled workers who figured among the rising number of unemployed in Cuba. There were disillusioned Angola veterans, and dissidents of various kinds. Many were homosexual, tired of the systematic persecution of gays that has always been the case in Cuba.⁵⁷ Their numbers showed that something was seriously amiss in Cuba, whether or not the government dismissed that as so much imperialist propaganda.

What the refugees did reveal was how much was wrong. Though it was dismissed with scorn at the time, Castro himself confirmed many of the rumours and criticisms a few years later, at the beginning of the 'rectification' campaign. By the late 1970s, and despite the very good health and education provision, public sector spending was continually falling. While more consumer goods were available in general, the number who could afford them was diminishing, and the gap between the managers, bureaucrats, military officers and the rest of the population was growing.⁵⁸ The introduction of a limited private sector only served to underline the differences. Corruption, too, was spreading, as individual enterprise managers diverted both money and materials into the private sector where profits were higher. Discrimination against women, a backward step from the aspirations of the mid-1960s, was now embedded in a Family Code that assumed the place of women to be at home—an attitude brutally satirised in 20 year old films like *Lucia*, yet now officially sanctioned precisely in order to privatise the function of reproducing labour to relieve the state of its social obligations. Racial oppression was still widely acknowledged and experienced, despite its official abolition and the lack of any public acknowledgement of the problem. And the persecution of gays culminating in the effective quarantining of AIDS victims on the Isle of Pines had very little to do with socialism.⁵⁹ What criticism there was, was silenced and its perpetrators imprisoned or expelled—Ariel Hidalgo's exposure of the 'new class' in Cuba is only one case in point.⁶⁰

Furthermore, throughout this period, Cuba had been seeking both a rapprochement with the United States and avenues for collaboration with multinational capital—by 1982, in fact, not only was foreign capital allowed to own up to 49 percent of joint enterprise capital, it was also permitted to impose its own conditions of investment, including workers' conditions, wages and levels of organisation. Law number 32 of 1980 had finally removed any residual degree of trade union control in workplaces, giving administrators and/or managers full powers, including the right to dismiss workers. There were at least 4,900 political prisoners in Cuba by the end of the 1970s—and an unknown number of summary executions. More significantly in some ways the rate of 'ordinary' crime—theft etc—was growing rapidly, as was reflected in the extremely harsh Penal Code of 1979. This may well have covered too a dramatic rise in the number of cases of 'labour indiscipline' (from

10,000 to 25,000 cases between 1979 and 1985), culminating in the deliberate sabotage of the Vana telephone exchange by a dissident employee.[61]

The picture that emerges from behind the curtain of silence is of a society held down by rigid and absolutely inflexible structures of control, and without any forum or instrument for the expression of criticism or discontent. Where they were voiced, they were dealt with summarily and savagely. The source of the discontents did not lie in the behaviour or character of a leadership, but in the relationship between an identifiable ruling class, and a working class still asked to accept deepening exploitation, falling living standards and a steady decline in social provision in the name of a future transformation. Yet as the decade of the 1980s began, very little had changed. Cuba remained more dependent than ever on its sugar exports, more subject than ever to external controls from the world economy. The Russian connection had not produced an industrialised society nor a diversified economy—and the continuing scarcity was plainly unequally distributed between those who controlled and administered the economy and the active producers. By any token, this was not socialism—and the criticisms the refugees made, despite the use to which they were put, were real enough. Yet they were vehemently denied, and all expressions of dissent ruthlessly dealt with.

Six years later, in 1986, Castro announced the beginning of a process of 'rectification'. It was a pre-emptive response to *glasnost* and *perestroika*, and an alternative to any thoroughgoing revision of Cuban economic or political structures. Castro announced contemptuously that Cuba had no need of perestroika and embarked on a campaign conducted from above, without consultation or accountability, and seeking only ratification from the public. Its purpose was clearly to head off the impact of change in Eastern Europe to deal with what was public knowledge in Cuba—albeit never referred to above a whisper—namely the corruption and inequality that was the staple of Cuban daily life. Jean Stubbs' hagiographic account of Cuba, for example, rehearses the official arguments and reaches the extraordinary conclusion that, 'The role of the party and democratic centralism has always worked better from the top down than from the bottom up.'[62] That was almost certainly true, so long as there was no question of an advance towards socialism! Like many others she attributes Castro's unchallengeable power over nearly 30 years to an irresistible charisma—leading Cubans to voluntarily renounce their interest in democracy! The question that remains in my mind is why, in that case, such an elaborate apparatus of repression proved nonetheless to be necessary?

The problems of Cuban society which the 'rectification' was forced to finally acknowledge were not aberrations, but the constant features of the history of Cuba since the revolution. It remained a single product export economy; the only industrial development there had been had occurred in the area of mechanising sugar production. The bureaucracy now ruling Cuba had employed the state to impose internally the conditions of the world economy—deepening exploitation, the pursuit of accumulation at all costs. Faced with the periodic crises of the system, this state has mounted savage attacks upon its own working class while depriving it—in the name of revolution—of the means to defend and organise its own class interest.

Rectification was not in any sense a reversal of that direction but its continuation, as Castro was at such pains to underline. Preparing for the hardships to come, the state set out to put its own house in order.[63] Corruption was attacked at the highest level. In 1989, defence minister Arnaldo Ochoa, an Angolan veteran and a close friend of Castro, was tried and executed for drug trafficking along with two other senior officers. Another high official was found with half a million dollars in his Swiss bank account. Other examples of corruption and abuse of power were uncovered, prostitution and drug use denounced. Yet whatever the disclaimers from the Cuban leadership, all of this was public knowledge; there were shops where people could sell gold for dollars, supermarkets where all the scarce goods were available to those with dollars.[64] Castro had boasted for 30 years of his knowledge of every detail of Cuban political life—could he really have overlooked corruption and graft on a massive scale?

The official line here is that in Eastern Europe there were abuses, mistakes, errors. But what else could our party say other than it was errors. To say anything else would be to admit they lied to the people for 30 years about Eastern Europe.[65]

Yet the same article reports Castro as complaining:

No one else in the world buys Bulgarian forklifts. They are such garbage only we bought them. It's been difficult to talk about such things in the past.

And so, in an aside, the whole strategy for Cuban development is called into question.

As the events in Eastern Europe began to unfold, the Cuban government faced a series of problems. An economy founded on sugar production and dependent to such a degree on the USSR would have enormous difficulty in surviving the end of that relation. The economic and political crises were inextricably interwoven. In an immediate sense Cuba faced the problem of rising indebtedness (a foreign debt of $6.4 billion) coupled with a dependence on the USSR for exports, imports, machinery and above all, fuel. While a proportion of Russian oil was made available to Cuba for re-export in order to earn foreign currency, the arrangement worked in Cuba's favour only while the oil price was rising. The fall in world oil prices after 1986 only served to exacerbate Cuba's problems. As supplies began to diminish, the only available option was to cut domestic fuel consumption in order to re-export. Thirty percent of its food consumption was also imported—to convert land to production for domestic consumption would require conversion of land used presently for the production of sugar on which Cuba depended almost exclusively for its exports! The alternative was to depress consumption levels, to divert social spending, and at the same time raise levels of exploitation.

Yet the early 1980s had seen the encouragement of private enterprise, the use of material incentives, linking wages to productivity. The notion of shared benefit, or equal sacrifice, had now given way to a scornful dismissal of 'mistaken egalitarian notions'. Further, the same period had seen a growth in the number of state functionaries (from 90,000 to 248,000 in slightly more than ten years) and a doubling of the numbers of technical personnel. The early 1980s had seen improvements in living standards as sugar prices rose—but the beneficiaries were those managers and bureaucrats who gained individual profit from the new levels of economic activity. This decentralisation had produced corruptions, deepening differentials, but no transformation of the direction or structure of the economy. Now the engine of profit and private gain could not be sustained. How could austerity once again be justified?

Not for the first time, it was Che Guevara who came to the rescue of Castro's regime. Suddenly his name and image were re-evoked everywhere—the very embodiment of revolutionary selflessness and sacrifice. But this was not the 1960s, with the memory of Batista's overthrow still fresh and the promise of a better future still an inspiration. Whatever the external world said, Cubans themselves had few illusions left. And Castro's attempts to exploit his celebrated special relationship with the mass of Cubans and mobilise it against the state bureaucracy did not seem to work. The crowds for his speeches were smaller, the expressions of dissidence insistent. The only constant was the unyielding determination of successive US governments to bring Cuba to its knees—especially in the wake of Nicaragua and Panama.

For Cuban state capitalism, survival now depended on the ability to throw all resources into production and to effect cuts in the area of consumption. Rectification, like the early moral campaigns, had a directly economic purpose—to reduce the costs of production by persuading Cuban workers to voluntarily accept a catastrophic fall in living standards. And although this time it was particularly drastic, the dynamic of the situation was not different from the general demands of accumulation.

The Cuban economy now had to urgently seek new markets for its sugar, its biotechnology and its other export goods; to seek sources of currency and capital, in joint ventures with international agencies or multinational companies; to establish alliances with other developing states and mobilise some coordinated strength to mitigate the conditions of international debt repayment, a negotiation Cuba could not successfully conduct alone because of American pressure on the financial agencies. The urgent search for foreign currency will lead to a growth in tourism of various kinds; the need for fuel would be paramount. And although the USSR under Gorbachev did not immediately withdraw its support from Cuba, the shape of things to come was clear enough even though little was said. In 1987, Cuba's Eastern European trading partners required further dealings to be conducted in convertible currencies; in the same year *Moscow News*, clearly speaking with official sanction, launched a frontal attack on Cuban economic policy. Castro responded by banning the journal. Under the trade agreements of 1986-90 sugar prices were lower than in the previous five year plan, and while he signed a new friendship treaty, Gorbachev turned a deaf ear to requests to cancel the Cuban debt.

What strategies can Cuba now adopt? All of the options rest on an assumption of austerity for Cuban workers for a considerable time to come. Implementing the 'special period in time of peace' in August 1990, the dimensions of that austerity were set out. Provoked by a 20 percent drop in oil supplies, and the prospect of future shortfalls of at least those proportions, Castro announced measures to cut back drastically on industrial production. Electricity use would be cut by 10 percent, and fuel consumption by 50 percent in the state sector and 30 percent in private homes. Nickel production would be cut by half and over 300 factories would work half the week or only during hours of light.

Workers would be redeployed from industry to agriculture where presumably they would be set to raising the level of food production so that Cuba could cut back on the 30 percent of its food bill that was imported. Yet here a contradiction presented itself, or rather several at once.

More than 30 years after the revolution whose primary objective was to develop the economy, Cuba remained dependent almost entirely on sugar exports. Its levels of production had risen through the 1980s, despite worldwide overproduction, because it enjoyed a guaranteed market. Now, although Russia and Eastern Europe might still consume (drastically diminished) quantities of Cuban sugar it would no longer be on the basis of exchange. Cuba was now as locked into a network of

Eastern European technology as it had once been tooled entirely by North American manufacturers. Spare parts for its German computers or its Hungarian buses, neither of them particularly efficient and both expensive in comparative terms, rose in price by up to 50 percent in the course of 1990—and further, now had to be paid for in hard currencies. Somehow Cuba now has to find significantly greater amounts of currency. Its main export, sugar, must enter an overstocked market in which most supplies are sold through preferential agreements—and where the sudden arrival of several million tons of Cuban sugar will almost certainly bring the price plummeting down.

The alternative—new preferential agreements—is extremely limited. Cuba has signed a trade agreement with China for $417 million which entails an element of exchange of Chinese bicycles for Cuban sugar; beyond that China clearly sees Cuba as providing access to a wider market. Mexico and Venezuela will now supply oil on some kind of barter basis, but the price of their oil will be the market price. Biotechnology—the export of vaccines, for example—is a promising area of trade but one that is not likely to be significant for some years to come (its current value is about $150 million).

Joint ventures with French, Italian and Canadian multinationals under extremely favourable conditions for them have so far been limited to areas of oil exploration, nuclear power research and tourism. Indeed it is tourism that seems to offer some possibility of expansion. The 302,000 tourists who visited Cuba in 1988 spent $1,542 million; the hope is that the number will double in the current year and yield some $700 million in revenues. It will include the new area of 'health tourism', in which Cuban health facilities are made available to foreign patients.

The general pattern of the survival plan, whatever its detail, is grimly clear. All available resources will be directed into the export or currency earning sector. By 1990 living standards were down to prerevolutionary 1958 levels; they will almost certainly fall still further as funds are removed from consumption and social provision, although the government has insisted it will maintain minimum levels of nutrition, for example. As workers return to agriculture they will find themselves resuming the most primitive of methods—animals will replace tractors, hand tools will take the place of machines.

That is the paradox. For its very survival the Cuban bureaucracy, whoever is at its head, must turn outwards to the world market and accept the conditions that it imposes upon all its members for their survival. Like the rest of Latin America, it will compete for investment on the basis of its rate of exploitation and the guarantee of optimum conditions for external capital. And it will fall to a state that proclaims itself socialist to carry through that strategy and organise the deepening exploitation of its own working class.

How will it do so? In awakening the ghost of Che Guevara, Castro has tried to mobilise the population again around the ideas, of collective sacrifice for the general good, of hardship for the present as the prelude to a future growth, that functioned in the 1960s. But in the meantime the Cuban working class has seen its sacrifice benefit an increasingly visible minority of its own society and its labour produce surpluses spent in an unequal exchange of goods. The rewards that accrued to the majority were few.

While there had been no organised resistance to the priorities of the state, the signs of disaffection and protest were accumulating. Lisandro Otero, the veteran Cuban novelist, noted a persistent 'restlessness';[66] rock concerts and the unlikely medium of heavy metal music provided opportunities for protests by Cuban youth. In 1989 an art exhibition was closed down by Castro, and two years later the leaders of an Association for Artistic Freedom were jailed for dissidence. At the Panamerican Games late last year, 'rapid action detachments' roamed the streets in search of dissidents who might exploit the presence of foreign media to make their protests known.

This was the context of the party congress of October 1991. It left little doubt that Castro's defiant assertion that Cuba would never permit the hegemony of the party to be challenged, was a stance that did not enjoy that automatic agreement and support which have so often been claimed for Castro's arguments. The congress's 1,760 delegates appeared unmoved by the massively significant events inside and outside Cuba. They were unaffected by the turmoil outside, and devoid of doubts about the bleak austerity programme they were imposing. At least no such doubts were expressed at a meeting that greeted every pronouncement with unanimity. The 12 members of the Politburo who did not stand for re-election were replaced by younger members whose loyalty to Castro was unconditional—the majority of them were military men.

What was becoming clear was that the rhetoric of consensus and solidarity aside, the dominion of the Cuban Communist Party and its programme for national economic survival were to be enforced. No public debate would be tolerated, no public dissent expressed. The justification for such refusal to discuss the realities of the survival of an isolated state capitalism derived from the threat posed by imperialism.

No one would deny that imperialism's objectives are not to alleviate the conditions of exploitation but to obliterate resistance to them. And there are sections of the North American right who echo the Miami lobby in the demand for an immediate invasion to topple Castro. Some weeks ago, three men were arrested in just such an enterprise—one has already been executed. And while there is no suggestion that their mission was sanctioned, they would certainly not have been actively discouraged from their purposes by US officials. Yet even the neanderthals of the right must recognise that military action of that sort would be counterproductive. The threat of invasion combined with the systematic use of American economic power would do the job more efficiently and not run the risk of galvanising opposition across the continent. And the United States is indeed tightening the noose; remittances from Cubans living in the US have been cut by nearly half, while firms doing business with Cuba have been systematically excluded from North American ports. A private individual organising fishing trips to Cuba was recently prosecuted by the US government for breaking the embargo. But these are minor compared with the continuing embargo on trade and the use of American vetoes in all the international financial agencies.

In response the Cuban state has mobilised 15 percent of the population into the popular militias—ostensibly in anticipation of an invasion. Effectively, this means that a significant proportion of the population can be rapidly brought under military command—for whatever purposes the state may choose. With the prospect of increasing militarisation of economy and society, and the imposition of an internal state of siege for economic reasons, the militia can come to play a much more internal role.

It is true of course that hostility to the United States can still galvanise the bulk of Cuban workers. It seems unlikely that the vision of the US as a saviour holds much sway. It too is in deficit and those Cubans who have experienced the realities of life in the US are matched by those within Cuba who have seen the growing numbers who receive the benefits of advanced capitalism on the streets or in the shop doorways of New York. The idea that Castro's fall would bring massive amounts of immediate relief can hardly retain much credibility after the experience of Eastern Europe and, more particularly, of Nicaragua, where the anticipated large scale economic assistance after the defeat of the Sandinistas in 1990 simply never materialised.

In the search for markets, the Cuban bureaucracy has turned to Latin America, presumably in the belief that a new version of the non-aligned bloc can provide it with allies, some influence, and a status in the world. But their combined resistance to the punishing imposition of debt is all that they share; beyond that they are all, including Cuba, capitals competing for investment by seeking to provide the optimum conditions for exploitation. The notion that Cuba can somehow impose its own 'socialist' conditions upon the functioning of world capitalism, is absurd and dangerous. But Cuba is seeking allies and trade wherever it can.[67]

Will Castro fall? His position seems impregnable and dissident groups slow to organise—yet much the same could have been said of the Eastern European leaders weeks and days before their fall. Opposition exists, though it is dispersed. The Christian Democrats back *Criterio Alternativo* while a new group called AMOR (the word means love, and the acronym stands for the Marti Association in Opposition to the Regime) claims to have cells in the state apparatus and the army. Human rights liberals are meeting with their 'pro-dialogue' counterparts in Miami to urge elections. Within the party there seem very few dissenting voices; the most prestigious is Carlos Aldana, who has recently advanced a cautious suggestion that there might be room for other parties—but his public position is one of unequivocal support for Castro.

From the point of view of the working class, Castro's survival is not the key question. Immediately the issue will be how best to defend itself against the depredations that the world market has in store for Cuban workers, whoever administers them. For Castro and his detractors start from the same priorities—the survival of the national economy in the world system. The alternatives to Castro, therefore, are not this or that party or leader, all of whom share a willingness to represent the priorities of the market. Nor will an electoral system introduce a genuine democracy if the priorities of every ruling class are the same.

The hope for the future lies in the very reason why Cuba has come to occupy such an important place in the political symbolism of socialists. The Cuban working class has sustained the present state for over three decades. It is naive to imagine that this has been the product of sustained and spontaneous support for Castro's regime—if that were so, why the need for such an elaborate apparatus of repression, and why the absolute and rigid prohibition on all criticism or dissent. Yet at the same time, the Cuban working class rests on a history of anti-imperialist struggle, a tradition which Castro has exploited—but which is nonetheless real. That tradition provides a frame within which the ideas of revolutionary socialism can take root.

Cuba has symbolised and represented that tradition; it has also exemplified the consequences of a strategy for change that is limited to the national arena, and that ignores the force whose power on a world scale can transform the very world system that has brought it into being. Cuba at one level exposed the weaknesses of imperialism and offered a vision of a completely different world. At another level it exposed the inability of a strategy of national development to fulfil that vision. In the wake of the collapse of Stalinism, the question of how to transform the struggles for national liberation into the struggle for workers' power, for socialism, is once again on the agenda. An understanding of Cuba, an honest accounting of its reality, will be one of our most important weapons in the building of a new workers' movement.

Notes

1 See J Habel, *International Viewpoint* (29 April 1991) pp15-18.
2 See H Thomas, *Cuba or the Pursuit of Freedom* (London, 1971) (the standard right wing account but bursting with detail); L H Jenks, *Our Cuban Colony* (New York, 1928) and J Le Riverend, *Historia Economica de Cuba* (Barcelona, 1974).
3 See *The World Sugar Economy in Figures* (UN-FAO, 1961).
4 C Beals, *The Crime of Cuba* (Philadelphia & London, 1933) p84.
5 See F Mires, *Las Revoluciones Sociales en America Latina* (Mexico, 1988) p283. Also J O'Connor, *Origins of Socialism in Cuba* (Ithaca, 1970) ch2.
6 On this period generally see S Farber, *Revolution and Reaction in Cuba 1933-1960* (Middletown, 1976). See too L Aguilar, *Cuba 1933: Prologue to Revolution* (New York, 1974).
7 D L Raby, *The Cuban Pre-revolution of 1933* (University of Glasgow, Institute of Latin American Studies Occasional Paper 18, 1975), p18.
8 Ibid, p16.
9 On the history of the Communist Party of Cuba see J O'Connor op cit; K S Karol, *Guerrillas in Power* (London, 1971), and H M Enzensberger's essay on the Communist Party of Cuba in *Raids and Reconstructions* (London, 1976).
10 K S Karol, op cit, pp85-86.
11 For a sense of that world see G Cabrera Infante, *Three Trapped Tigers*.
12 F Mires, op cit, p296.
13 Ibid, p312.
14 F Castro, *History Will Absolve Me* (London, 1967).
15 T Cliff 'Permanent Revolution' in *International Socialism,* 61, p22.
16 Ibid.
17 See C Barker, Introduction to *Revolutionary Rehearsals* (London, 1987).
18 T Cliff, op cit, p27.
19 Ibid.
20 Ibid, p28.
21 On the agrarian reform programme see R Dumont, *Cuba: Socialism and Development* (New York, 1970). Also J O'Connor, op cit, ch5.
22 Ibid, pp27-57.
23 See P Brenner, *From Confrontation to Negotiation: US Relations with Cuba* (Boulder/London, 1988). In a broader sense see J Pearce, *Under the Eagle* (London, 1982).
24 See M Morley, *Imperial State and Revolution: the US and Cuba 1952-1986* (Cambridge, 1987). Also G Philip, *The Military in South American Politics* (London, 1985).
25 See L Huberman and P Sweezy, *Cuba: Anatomy of a Revolution* (New York, 1960), pp155-157. See also C Wright Mills, *Listen Yankee* (New York, 1960).
26 See Guevara's 'Our Industrial Tasks' in J Gerassi (ed), *Venceremos: Speeches and Writings of Che Guevara* (London, 1968), pp275-293.
27 In his introduction to J Habel's very important book, *Cuba: The Revolution in Peril* (London, 1991).
28 On the Missile Crisis see K S Karol, op cit, pp249-270. See also N Miller, *Soviet Relations with Latin America 1959-87* (Cambridge, 1989), pp58-90.
29 The trial and imprisonment of Anibal Escalante, once general secretary of the Cuban Communist Party, and his 'microfaction' created some tensions in the relationship,

and gave Castro an opportunity to assert his political independence. But it was essentially a sideshow to the main event—the reconciliation with the Communist Party.
30 In J Gerassi (ed) op cit, pp536-553. See also B Silverman (ed), *Man and Socialism in Cuba: The Great Debate* (New York, 1971) and B E Evans, *The Moral Versus Incentives Controversy* (University of Pittsburgh PhD thesis, 1973).
31 See, in this connection, N Harris, *The Mandate of Heaven* (London, 1978), pp48-59.
32 'Our industrial tasks' in J Gerassi (ed), op cit, p288.
33 T Szulc in his *Fidel a Critical Portrait* (London, 1987), attempts to address this problem, though he does not in the end provide a final answer. See also M Lowy, *The Marxism of Che Guevara* (London, 1973).
34 Cf Che's attack on Russian foreign policy in February 1965, where he suggested that 'socialist countries are to a certain extent accomplices in imperialist exploitation'. See T Szulc, op cit, p494.
35 For example the hagiographic account, J Stubbs, *Cuba the Test of Time* (London, 1989) suggests he is one of a series of Don Quixote type figures that emerge in Cuban history—a less than adequate account of the individual's role in history!
36 R Debray, a French writer, enjoyed access to Fidel and his *Revolution in the Revolution* (London, 1968) was an exposition of Che's ideas which received wide distribution. Later Debray was arrested and detained in Bolivia. On his release he interviewed Salvador Allende, and then produced *Critique of Arms* effectively renouncing his own past. In 1981 he became a political adviser to Mitterand.
37 On the growth of the working class in general see J Pearce, *Trade Unions in Latin America* (London, 1983). Beyond that there is a real dearth of systematic analysis of the working class movement in the period which testifies to the dominance on the left of ideas outside the socialist tradition. Particularly important, however, are the cases of Chile, where the growth of working class militancy underpins the rise of Allende's Popular Unity, and Argentina, where the extraordinary events of Cordoba and Rosario, where the working class briefly seized power in 1969, are often no more than a footnote in the political debates of the period.
38 See C Mesa-Lago 'Economic policies and growth' in C Mesa-Lago (ed), *Revolutionary Change in Cuba* (Pittsburgh, 1971).
39 J Stubbs, op cit.
40 On the whole course of Cuban agriculture up to the Great Offensive see R Dumont, *Cuba: Socialism and Development* (New York, 1970).
41 In this respect see P Binns 'Popular power in Cuba' in *International Socialism*, 21 (Autumn 1983), pp135-144. For the official view of that relationship see M Haernecker, *Cuba: Dictatorship or Democracy?* (Westport, 1980).
42 Figures quoted in P Binns and M Gonzalez, *Cuba, Castro and Socialism* (London, 1983), p26. In general see F Martinez Heredia, 'Cuban socialism' in *Latin American Perspectives*, 18/2, issue 69 (Spring 1991).
43 The term 'institutionalisation of the revolution' is commonly used by commentators —see J Stubbs, op cit, for example.
44 See C Mesa-Lago, *Cuba in the 70s*, (ed) op cit, pp26-28.
45 See M A Figueras 'Structural changes in the Cuban economy' in *Latin American Perspectives*, 18/2, issue 69, pp72-94.
46 Quoted in J Stubbs, op cit, p65.
47 Particularly D Bravo, the Venezuelan guerrilla leader, who denounced Castro's change of line in his 1970 *Letter to Fidel*. It was ironic that others like Hugo Blanco, the most important Trotskyist political leader in Latin America, who suffered directly as a result of Castro's new rapprochement with the government of Velasco, said little on the question—see H Blanco, *Peru: Land or Death* (New York, 1972).
48 See M Gonzalez 'The Chilean October' in C Barker (ed), op cit and R Debray, *Conversacion con Allende* (Mexico, 1972). In his introduction, Debray sets out very clearly the new lines of Cuban policy and defends them.

49 On Cuban involvement in Angola see S Eckstein, 'Why Cuban internationalism' in A Zimbalist (ed), *Cuban Political Economy* (Boulder/London, 1988). See too, J Habel, op cit, ch8. Also A Callinicos 'Can South Africa be reformed?' in *International Socialism*, 46 (Spring 1990), pp102-103.
50 Quoted in *International Herald Tribune* (15 December 1988).
51 See S Eckstein, op cit. Also *International Viewpoint* (March 1989), pp10-13.
52 See J Habel, op cit, ch5.
53 See S Eckstein, op cit, p172.
54 Quoted in N Miller, op cit, p115.
55 A Zimbalist 'Cuban political economy and Cubanology: an overview' in A Zimbalist (ed), op cit, p6.
56 J Stubbs, op cit, pp104-105.
57 Many of the Cubans in exile interviewed in L Geldof, *Cubans* (London, 1991) attest to this, see p172. But there is ample evidence—the systematic attacks on critical artists and writers are invariably attached to attacks on their sexual preferences—the case of Pablo Armando Fernandez, the outstanding novelist, is simply one among many.
58 See J Habel, op cit, ch2 and especially p65.
59 Faced with worldwide protests, the Cuban government has now said it will do something—nothing has materialised yet, nor has there been any public criticism of it. On the contrary, supporters of Cuba are quick to make claims for Cuba's success in controlling AIDS, without recognising that it has involved the virtual imprisonment of gay people for life.
60 See J Habel, op cit, ch7.
61 Quoted in J Habel, op cit, p205.
62 J Stubbs, op cit, p85. Fitzgerald in his 'Sovietisation of Cuba' in A Zimbalist (ed), op cit, makes the opposite assertion, 'The direction of change in post-1970 Cuba has been towards greater bottom-up expression...', p146.
63 See for example M Benjamin's sympathetic if critical piece in the first of two issues of *NACLA Report on the Americas* devoted to Cuba, 'Cuba facing change', XXIV/2 (August 1990), pp13-16. The following issue (XXIV/3) deals with the relations between the US and Cuba.
64 See M Benjamin, op cit.
65 In M Cooper's report 'Semper Fidel' in *Voice* (1 May 1990), p21.
66 Otero is quoted in the second of two articles by J Habel in *International Viewpoint*, 207 (27 May 1991), p13.
67 On the general economic picture in this period see J P Lopez's useful article 'Swimming against the tide', *Journal of Interamerican Studies*, 33/2 (Summer 1991), pp83-119.

The good old cause—an interview with Christopher Hill

LEE HUMBER AND JOHN REES

How do you see the development of the debate around the English Revolution over recent years? Would you agree that the revisionists have taken some ground?

They have made a lot of useful points, but their more extreme views are now being attacked by the younger generation of historians. Although the revisionists had all sorts of useful ideas they had a terribly narrow political approach in that they tried to find the causes of the English Revolution solely in the years 1639-41. This simply assumes what you are setting out to prove. If you look just at those years then of course it's a matter of political intrigue and not long term causes. I think people are reacting against that now. The better of the revisionists are themselves switching round a bit. John Morrill, for instance, who thought everything depended on the county community and localism, is now taking a much broader point of view. And Conrad Russell has become aware that long term factors have to be taken into account—he doesn't like it but he recognises that religion has some long term effects on what happened in 1640, a rather elementary point but he left religion out altogether in the early days. Now he's bought it in. He still leaves out the cultural breakdown in society of that period but he is moving a bit. I think a consensus will arise and then there will be another explosion in 20 years or so. These debates occur regularly—ever since 1640 people have been arguing about what it was all about.

Morrill has clearly reassessed his position on Cromwell, linking his political actions with his social circumstances in a way which one perhaps would not have expected.

People like Morrill and Russell are taking things aboard. Russell said of Cromwell, for instance, that he was the only member of parliament of whom we have records before 1640 who tried to help the lower orders in his work for the fenmen—but he doesn't draw any conclusions from that, yet this is one of the most important aspects of Cromwell. He had a much broader approach than most of the gentry.

English academics always hated revolutions so that there is an inbuilt pleasure in being able to get back, as some of them tried to do, to saying nothing important had happened. French, Russian and American historians have accepted revolutions as part of their tradition whereas we've always hushed ours up and transferred it to the Glorious Revolution of 1688.

Do you think the cycles of debate on the English Revolution are tied to political developments in Britain? Was the rise of revisionism tied to the rise of Thatcherism, for instance?

When I started as a historian the orthodoxy was that England was the centre of world history and that the whole of history was working towards the evolution of democracy of which England was the perfect example. That's the thing that my generation were gunning for—Anglo-centrism and concentration almost exclusively on political and constitutional history. So there has been a big change over time. Social and economic aspects became, in the Tawney years, almost the orthodoxy. It's that orthodoxy that the revisionists are trying to revise, to get away from too much sordid economics and back to the constitution.

Jack Hexter, for instance, who's not really a revisionist, has just founded an institute for the history of freedom and they've produced a volume of essays on parliament and freedom in the 17th century, showing parliament working for freedom. The book outlines the steps through which freedom emerges and it's all constitutional, nothing to do with social problems generally. So there are different aspects of this anti-revisionist process which are converging and producing strange allies. To find Trevor Roper, Jack Hexter and me on the same side was a unique experience—I don't think it pleased any of us very much!

What would you say about the emerging consensus amongst historians today? Would you agree that it has produced a sort of agnostic tone about the revolution, a recoil from the earlier more extreme positions, akin to Major's recoil from Thatcherism?

Or Kinnock's recoil from socialism! The emerging consensus amongst historians is based on a very cautious use of language. There are some phrases they want to avoid, like 'class struggle' or 'the bourgeoisie', often quite rightly since careless use of them can be misleading. Ann Hughes is probably on the right side with her latest book although cautious in her language. That's one of the things Conrad Russell has taught us. He caught a lot of us out, including me, with careless use of language. For instance, in the original edition of my *Century of Revolution* I used the phrase 'the opposition'. In the second edition I crossed out the word 'the' where it referred to parliamentary opposition in the 1620s, since Russell quite rightly pointed out that talk of 'the' opposition gives the impression of a much more organised parliamentary opposition than in fact existed. That's one of the useful things this latest debate has done, although Russell obviously hasn't taught Jack Hexter much since throughout his work he just assumes that 'freedom' always means freedom for property.

Consensus is probably exaggerating the position but it certainly is true that the better of the revisionists are toning their work down. The fierceness of the battle seems to be over. Most of the camp followers of the revisionists have just been discarded. The main debate still remains whether there were any long term causes or not. Russell still thinks it was all an unfortunate accident, although once you start to see that there had been problems with religion for 70 years that becomes more difficult. Then you have to define what you mean by religion of course. In my young days it was defined in terms of 19th century non-conformity, puritans were equated with 19th century non-conformists, which is not at all how I see it.

There is a marked trend to separate out various aspects of the revolution, so that cultural developments are seen in isolation to, say, economic ones, a trend which is part of a much wider debate taking in the arguments around postmodernism. Would you agree that this is also a great challenge to the economic and social interpretation of history?

Yes, all this linguistic stuff of the literary historians ignores the social context. I think that's a very unfortunate phase that literary criticism seems to be going through. I had thought that one of the good things of the last few decades was the way historians and literary critics seemed to be coming together on the 17th century and producing some sort of consensus. This is now in danger with all this linguistic guff. I suppose it's quite difficult for people trained in one discipline to take on board the lessons learnt in others, but any new consensus will have to be one based on looking at society as a whole including literature and religion.

I've recently finished a book that looks at the use of the bible in the 17th century, looking at some of the ways in which its myths were used for political purposes: Cain as the ruling class and Abel as the exploited class—god loves Abel and hates Cain, and Abel's day is coming—that sort of thing. I see literature and religion and economics and history as all part of a single picture.

Is that commitment to total history much more difficult for people who come to history solely with an academic background?

Yes, Ralph Samuel had a theory that all the historians who joined the Communist Party were interested in literature, E P Thompson and Victor Kiernan for example, and that this helped them a lot. I think he is quite right.

Would you agree that it is the political organisation that gives you that total outlook rather than any academic training?

Yes, the best academic historical training I ever got was from the historians' group of the CP where we discussed all of this—science and the revolution, literature and the revolution and so on. That gave me the sort of education that all historians ought to have, it showed me that all individual aspects of history are linked. It's very difficult when you study the personal letters of a gentleman from Bedfordshire in 1642 to spot the wider implications and references. They are there but you have to be on the look out for them.

Although we can't talk about the English Revolution being consciously planned would you agree that there was an emerging ideology on the parliamentarian side which helped shape events?

I think it's right to say that the revolution wasn't planned. One of the things that should be made more of is that no one in England in the 1640s knew they were taking part in a revolution. American and French revolutionaries could look back to England, the Russian revolutionaries had an ideology of revolution based on English and French experience, but no one in England could draw on such experiences. The very word revolution emerges in its modern sense in the 1640s. So that the English revolutionaries are fumbling all the time, they haven't got a

Rousseau or a Marx to guide them. The examples of the Netherlands and the French Huguenots were discussed in the 17th century as religious or nationalist revolts. The only text they could look to was the Bible, but of course the bible says such different things that you can get any theory out of it so that it proved totally unsatisfactory. One of my arguments in my new book is that it was the experience of its uselessness as an agreed guide to action in the 1640s and 1650s that led to its dethroning from its position of absolute authority. That was a major problem for the English revolutionaries, they had no theory to start from.

But the process of the revolution shows how quickly they developed one. The Putney debates for example testify to their progression.

Yes, the arguments there are wonderfully sophisticated, as are the ideas of Winstanley. They both suggest the widespread debate which must have been going on. Yet it's very difficult to establish that these debates were going on. In so far as those participating in the Putney debates have a text to work from, it is the bible. Millenarianism was the nearest they got to an ideology and of course that let them down since the millennium didn't come as expected—there are certain analogies with recent events in Eastern Europe perhaps.

They had a programme of bringing about the millennium which made all sorts of assumptions about what history was going to do which didn't come to fruition. We ought to try and find more evidence of the debate that was going on. We get occasional glimpses of it. Thomas Edwards, although very hostile to the radicals, is a wonderful source. He tells of William Erbery, one of the leading radicals, who was on his way to Wales in about 1645 and got involved in a discussion with other radicals in which he denied the divinity of Christ. The level of debate is astonishing, with copious references to scripture. Erbery defends himself by reference to the Greek original texts from which subsequent translations were taken, a very sophisticated level of discussion for a chance meeting en route and a hint of the level of debate taking place more generally around the country.

What strikes me, most forcefully through Cromwell, is the parallel between what we call theory and practice and what the 17th century knew as religious motivation at the level of principle and pragmatism at the level of politics.

Yes, but Cromwell wasn't conscious of it as, say, Lenin was. This is part of what I mean when I say they didn't realise they were taking part in a revolution, they hadn't any ideology to cope with this sort of thing.

Lenin had obviously thought about what happens in revolutions and what happens to revolutionary leaders; the English revolutionaries didn't have this luxury. It's amazing how well at least the better of them did. Of course we can't know how widely Cromwell's thinking, or that of participants in the Putney debates or Winstanley's ideas, were taken up. It must have been so different from conventional thinking. The consequences of Winstanley's theories were taken up by unemployed labourers but his ideas must have been a bit over their heads.

Would you say that contemporary events affect your interpretation of the English Revolution and, if so, is this a conscious decision on your part? *The World Turned Upside Down* **for example was written in the 1960s at a time of great social upheaval.**

It's difficult to know the true answer to that kind of question. I wrote *The World Turned Upside Down* at the time of massive student struggle and I was very consciously aware of parallels between say the Ranters and some of the way out student revolutionaries. To that extent it was conscious. But I didn't decide to write the book for that reason. I was invited to contribute to a series edited by Rodney Hilton. So there was no conscious decision to write the book because of the events at the time; but inevitably as I wrote I was seeing analogies between the 17th century and contemporary events all the time.

You said that you tend not to use the same sort of jargon which characterised your earlier writings but none of the essential method has gone. How important is the Marxist method in studying history?

I took a conscious decision in the 1950s to guard against political jargon after a lovely young woman from the Communist Party told me she thought my book on 1640 had done more harm than good because of the language I used. I've striven not to use sectarian language since. Some words can have an amazing effect on people. Using the word 'bourgeoisie' is a red rag to most academics. Even the most intelligent of them, Lawrence Stone for example, believe that the bourgeoisie must have something to do with the towns and that if you can prove that the gentry were the main capitalists in England in the 17th century you've disproved the idea of a bourgeois revolution. But to have to explain this every time you use the word bourgeois is a bore. It's much easier to just leave out the word bourgeois—but of course it's very easy to slide from dropping the word to dropping the idea. Initially I thought I had to drop the jargon in order to get people to take me seriously. I have changed some of my ideas, naturally, but not I hope my basic approach.

How did the Communist Party historians' group form and what influence did it have on you?

Anyone who was in it thinks it was the best academic and educational experience of their lives. There were beginnings of it just before the war. A few people got together and were thinking of a group and so after the war it naturally resumed. It was an entirely self appointed body. People brought others along to the discussions who they thought would be interested. It was primarily, but not exclusively, academics. There were technical relations with the Communist Party headquarters in King Street but it exercised no control over us. Dona Torr, who had King Street connections, was a member of the group. She was a marvellous historian and the least like a party dictator of anyone I have ever known. The most severe thing she ever said to me was, when she saw I had committed some terrible political deviation, 'I think, comrade, this has not yet reached its final formulation'. She was just one of us, taking part in discussion as an equal member of the group.

We were completely freelance, deciding amongst ourselves what we would talk about. We split up into sections: there was a 19th century section, a 17th century section, a medieval section and an ancient section. We all had our own discussions and worked out our own agenda and discussed what we wanted to discuss. We had a tremendous asset in the 17th century group in Victor Kiernan whom god created as a heretic who contradicted anything which he thought was verging on becoming an orthodoxy. He was terribly good at asking subversive questions about all our assumptions. We used to have fierce battles. There was no idea of imposing orthodoxy or a party line—which was one of the reasons why the discussions were so good. Victor Kiernan encouraged us to consider the possibility that Marxism might be wrong on this or that point. So we would have to argue it out and see whether he had a point. Quite often he did, although perhaps not what he intended. It was very stimulating.

We used to meet regularly in London from about 1946 onwards. Looking back it was clear it was losing a lot of its élan in the early 1950s before things started to go wrong in the party. With the benefit of hindsight of course it's easy to see there were signs, or an absence of signs, which told of things to come. I was very sad when I left it and I would have liked to have kept some sort of group like that going.

How did the group actually work?

The group didn't take any decisions on what particular people should write on. J C Davis thinks that Leslie Morton and I were told to play up the Ranters—utter nonsense. People may have discussed a book they were writing if it came up within the general group discussion and this could lead to modifications to the book if the author agreed. But there were no political decisions taken about subject matter, it was absolutely free for all in that sense. The stimuli were tremendous. I got interested in the history of science in a very amateurish way and things that I put into my *The Intellectual Origins of the English Revolution* arose out of our discussions on science. We were influencing each other but as individuals. After 1957 it was one of the things I most missed about leaving the party, in fact I may have been a little starry eyed about the party because of the group. We kept in touch with each other of course, including with people who stayed in the party. Eric Hobsbawm in some extraordinary way stayed on. I never quite understood why he did. I think he was daring them to expel him all the time. It didn't seem to make any difference to our relationship as friends.

Although your work has had a tremendous influence there isn't the same core of such committed people as you were then. How would you explain that?

It is perhaps because so much of Marxism has now been accepted by historians. It may be connected with the change in vocabulary. Both Eric Hobsbawm and myself discovered later that we changed how we expressed ourselves at about the same time because we both thought it was more important to be read than to use the 'right' jargon. But I really can't give an overall explanation.

Isn't it more to do with the fortunes of the organised left? Political organisation provides the framework within which people discuss and argue over problems, holding together Marxists and creating a forum for Marxist debate.

I think that is very important for developing ideas. One of the important things about the historians' group was that it formed about 1945, at a high point in left thinking in England. It was composed of pretty high level historians. The fact that we divided up into our four sections to discuss our specialisms, and each of the groups had high level professional discussions shows it as something a bit different from Marxist education. Students came along but the actual discussion was very professional and technical and I think that was its success and also perhaps why it didn't last. People started to drop away for all sorts of reasons during the 1950s. It had been a very fortunate conjuncture. A lot of left wing people had just left the army, they were fed up with everything, got together at that time full of excitement and optimism.

Were most of the people involved at the beginnings of an academic career?

Yes mostly. Some of us had been appointed in the 1930s. Maurice Dobb and Leslie Morton were of course well established. Leslie Morton was another good pricker of bubbles, good at telling academics when they were getting too academic. But mostly the others were just getting their first academic jobs or jobs as researchers. It was very fortunate that you could get enough young eager people who wanted to discuss at that sort of level. I'd love to have a group of people with whom to discuss any book I was writing. But, on the whole, English academics are not very good at that sort of thing. They like to do their own thing. The idea that you could write a better book if you sat down and argued about it is not very widely held. It is not part of the English academic tradition.

What does your new book cover?

It's got quite a lot about the importance of the English bible in connection with English nationalism. From very early days, the bible, Protestantism and nationalism went together. The bible was of tremendous use for Protestant propaganda, people learnt to read in order to read the bible. It was very important for the development of English literature in the 16th century. Translations of the psalms were important —everyone worth his salt tried his hand at translations of the psalms. Biblical drama was a popular propaganda aid in the reigns of Henry VIII and Edward VI.

Everyone in the 16th and 17th centuries tended to express themselves in biblical terms. The meaning of these terms becomes extended. Cain becomes not only a bad man, but a symbol of the ruling class. Nimrod becomes not only a bad usurping ruler, but again a symbol of any sort of tyranny or persecution. Everyone thought of politics in biblical terms and claimed biblical authority. Millenarianism, the main ideology of the radicals, was very important in bringing about regicide. When you have to go against the law of the land you can only do it with reference to a higher truth. John Cooke, the prosecutor of Charles I, says that the law is one thing but the law of god is something higher, and when necessary the law of god must overrule accepted legal judgement and precedents. At crucial stages the bible gave people the courage to do things they wouldn't have done otherwise. Cromwell genuinely believed that he and Christ's people knew what Christ wanted and they were going to do it.

An example is that Charles I was referred to as 'the Man of Blood', which just sounds like a term of abuse. In fact it's a very precise quotation from Numbers 33 which says that if a man sheds blood his blood must be shed or the blame will fall on the whole community. So after the second civil war which, it was clear, had been started by Charles, not by his evil advisers, it was argued that if the Man of Blood wasn't brought to justice the whole community was responsible, or at least parliament's army that fought in the second civil war was responsible. So the idea of the Man of Blood was decisive for regicides; it justified their determination to have Charles's head.

But there comes a point when so many people get so many things out of the bible that it becomes useless since it doesn't give any clear and agreed line. This is very important for the decline of the bible in the later 17th century as a political text as well as for the decline of radicalism. The radicals lost a very important focus. Again you might draw analogies with Eastern Europe. The lack of an agreed ideology makes you sceptical about the basis of your actions. They used to say it was god who called the Long Parliament, not Charles I, and it was god who executed Charles I. But then you had to say it was god who bought back Charles II in 1660. When you got to that the whole idea became a nonsense. Providential history is all right so long as your side is winning, but it's awful when it goes the other way. By the end of the 17th century the bible is no longer looked on as a guide for political action. In 1657 an MP was laughed at in the House of Commons for quoting the bible too often. That couldn't have happened ten years earlier. In 1697, in one of Vanbrugh's plays, Lady Brute is reminded that the good book says you should love your enemies; she answers immediately, 'That may be a fault in the translation'. In 1660 Samuel Fisher, an ex-baptist Quaker, published an enormous tome in which he proved that the bible couldn't be the word of god because it was so contradictory and inconsistent. This summed up two decades of biblical criticism. Spinoza read Fisher, and through him those ideas passed into the ideas of the Enlightenment.

The impasse of schematic dogmatism

ERNEST MANDEL

The attempted neo-Stalinist coup in the former USSR and its dramatic aftermath show we are entering a turning point in world history. The political tendency I belong to, the Fourth International, in common with the British SWP, condemned the coup from the start and applauded the mass workers' mobilisations which contributed decisively to its defeat. But now, as has been clear for a long time, the issue is posed whether capitalism will be restored in eastern Europe, the former Soviet Union, Cuba and China.

For us, contrary to the logic of Chris Harman and the SWP, such an outcome would signify a major victory for world imperialism. Capitalism can only be restored by inflicting major defeats on the working class. The bureaucracy in the deformed and degenerated workers' states is incapable of resisting capitalist restoration; indeed whole sections of the bureaucracy are preparing to find themselves a new niche as capitalists or in the state apparatus of a reconstituted capitalist system.

For us, the working class and the small minority of socialists in these states have to pursue a *double* struggle. First they have to fight against the bureaucracy to the end, ensuring its political defeat. While in some circumstances it may be possible to address, and to win over, sections of the base of the old Stalinist and neo-Stalinist parties, that is not the political heart of the matter. Politically, there must be a relentless struggle to defeat the old Stalinist and neo-Stalinist parties, and build mass independent unions and new workers' parties.

But at the same time, socialists must resist every attempt to destroy the collectivised property relations—concretely this means battling without reservation *against* attempts to privatise enterprises and destroy the social gains of the working class—the inefficient, unfair, chronically disorganised, but nonetheless real, gains of huge subsidies on rents and food, ultra-cheap housing and transport, free childcare and healthcare—and above all guaranteed employment. However disorganised and dilapidated these gains, imperialism demands their destruction to introduce full market relations; this has been a central demand as a precondition for economic aid to Hungary and Poland through the PHARE programme for example. The consequence of the integration of the GDR into West Germany has been a sharp attack on these gains—unemployment at about 40 percent, the abolition of free childcare, forcing women back into the home, rocketing rents and prices.

We have no nostalgia for Stalinism whatever. But every revolution engenders the danger of counter-revolution. Who could believe that the re-establishment of capitalism in the former USSR, China or Cuba could be anything other than a defeat? But for Chris Harman and the SWP, this is not the case. For them this would merely be a 'step sideways'—as Chris Harman (illogically) puts it from 'state capitalism' to 'multinational (!) state capitalism' (on this unique concept see Harman's article in *International Socialism* 46). The theory of state capitalism is incapable of responding to the needs of the dual struggle against Stalinism and capitalist restoration, because of the dogma of state capitalism and the fallacious theories of the development of modern capitalism devised by the SWP to justify it.

According to the SWP, developing the theories of Hilferding and Bukharin, all modern capitalism is one or other type of 'state capitalism', with capital increasingly fused with the state. This, in the epoch of the multinational corporation, we emphatically deny. The functionality of this theoretical operation is that the fundamental differences between non-capitalist and capitalist economies can be glossed over. In order to unravel this, we shall have to go back to a discussion about what Marx thought was specific about capitalism, and examine the reality of contemporary capitalism and its periodic crises.

Let us proceed then to an analysis of the SWP's mystifications about contemporary capitalism, after which we return in more detail to the political consequences of their theories.

The simplistic Marx and the logical Harman

Harman calls us 'simplistic in the extreme' because we see in contemporary capitalism the living proof of Marx's theories. This is a grave charge which just happens to be wrong.

Harman's overall case is that the crises in the former USSR can be considered a variety of *capitalist* crisis. This involves a series of far fetched propositions about the character of modern capitalism, and in particular the integration of capital with the state. As we shall see, this overestimation of the integration of capital with the state consistently led the Cliff-Harman school to overstate planning within contemporary capitalism, and thus to *underestimate* the possibilities of capitalist crisis.

Harman tries to deal with 'modern Western capitalism'. But that is an abstraction. There is an international capitalist economy, which is an organic (and contradictory) unity of imperialist and Third World countries. As Lenin explained to Bukharin[1], the ancestor, together with Hilderding, of Cliff's economic theories, you cannot detach the functioning of imperialism from the general laws of the capitalist mode of production, as laid bare by the three volumes of *Capital*.

Capitalism cannot exist without money, capital being the starting point and the end result of production for profit. Capitalism cannot exist without generalised commodity production, without the private and not immediately social character of labour, without the contradiction between use value and exchange value inherent in the commodity.

This is indeed Karl Marx's 'oversimplification' throughout the three volumes of *Capital*, the *Grundrisse* and the manuscripts of 1861-62. You cannot consider 'capitalist' any economic system in which these laws would not be valid anymore, in which 'the state' (why not 'the party', the general secretary, or any infallible Pope?) could somehow eliminate objective laws from functioning behind the backs of people.

Everybody has the right to consider themselves as revolutionary socialists while thinking that Marx's *Capital* is 'outdated' (a product of the 19th century). But nobody has the right to attribute to Marx ideas which not only he didn't share but against which he polemicised for more than a quarter of a century.

Marx's *Capital* makes it crystal clear that the reproduction of capital, and therefore capital accumulation, and therefore economic growth under capitalism, results from the *unity of a process of value (surplus value) production and of value (surplus value) realisation*. Produced but unsold commodities do not lead to capital accumulation. 'Say's Law' is nonsense. Under commodity production, output does not automatically create the demand for its own realisation. That is why crises of overproduction are inevitable for capitalism.

This is true in the 20th century as it was true in the 19th century. It will be true in the 21st century too, if capitalism survives till then. If an economy emerges in which this is not true anymore, then there would only be two possible conclusions: either that Marx's analysis of capitalism has been proven wrong, or that another economy than capitalism has emerged.

For the very same reason, as Marx precisely states in the *Grundrisse*:

> As value constitutes the basis of capital, and as it necessarily can exist only through exchange against all equivalent counter-value, [**Gegenwert** is the term used by Marx], it necessarily 'repulses itself from itself'. A universal capital, without alien capitals which it confronts and with which it exchanges [not with whom it conducts 'military competition' but with whom it exchanges—E M] is therefore an impossibility.[2]

Harman could object that he doesn't call Marx oversimplistic but only Mandel. After all, Mandel is not Marx. Of course he is not, he does not believe himself to be. But the objection would only make sense if Harman could prove that Mandel did not summarise correctly the central theses of Marx's *Capital*. He cannot. We did challenge Cliff and Harman before on this. We challenge them again. No explanation is going to be offered because it just cannot be offered.

In a complete reversal of Harman's position, Alex Callinicos accuses us of eclecticism and pragmatism instead of 'oversimplification'.[3] As he sees it, our rejection of monocausal explanations of economic booms and crises is incompatible with Marxism's aspiration to be a 'theory of the social totality'. Unfortunately, our rejection of monocausality is again a literal reference to Marx who wrote about the causes of economic crises:

> The world trade crises must be regarded as the real concentration and forcible adjustment of **all the contradictions of bourgeois economy**. The individual factors which are condensed in these crises must therefore emerge and must be described in each sphere of the bourgeois economy, and the further we advance in our examination of the latter, the more aspects of this conflict must be traced on the one hand, and on the other hand it must be shown that its more abstract forms are recurring and are contained in the more concrete forms.[4]

This is a far cry from any monocausal explanation of capitalist crises indeed.

Callinicos, harking back to Popper, contends that our way of explaining social developments through the dialectical interaction of the concrete and the abstract, the objective and the subjective, the general and the particular, the logical and the historical—which is but the reproduction of Marx's own dialectical method—'preserves its integrity at the price of the loss of any explanatory power'.[5] Really? He then cites as proof of that 'failure', what we consider as one of our main explanatory achievements: our prediction, in the midst of the post-war boom, in the mid-1960s, that a new 'long depressive wave' would start at the end of that decade, or at the beginning of the 1970s, with much more severe recessions, a much lower average rate of growth and constantly growing permanent unemployment. Isn't that what actually did occur? It should not have occurred, it could not have occurred, according to the Gospel of Saint Cliff. But it did occur.

So the shoe sits exactly on the other foot. It is the dogma of state capitalism which had no explanatory power. In order to prove the opposite, you have to go into sterile quote-culling, not looking for the real logic of ideas. It is unworthy of Alex Callinicos that he resorts to this kind of argument.

So we call upon all Marxists in and around the SWP to share our deadly sin: to prefer the sophisticated and painstaking Marx of the thousands of pages of the three volumes of *Capital*, the *Grundrisse*, and the manuscripts of 1861-62, to the 'logical' simplifiers and dogmatists of the Cliff-Harman-Callinicos school. Even if we shall burn at the stake, we shall still be shouting: *'eppur si muove'*. Experience shows us to be right.

Of course our (Marx's) thesis (hypothesis) is really scientific because it could (can) be perfectly falsified. If there had been no crises of overproduction for half a century or a century; if there had been no serious unemployment in any imperialist country; nor any rising misery in Third World capitalist countries again for half a century or a century; nor any serious 'new poverty' in the West, then the conclusion would be obvious: Marx and his minor disciples like Mandel would have been shown to be wrong. But is that the real trend of events of the last 20 years?

Fifty years behind reality

Harman insists on the fact that 'once capitalism enters its monopoly imperialist stage, it is dominated by gigantic concerns which certainly do not organise the processes of production inside them on the basis of exchange of commodities at market prices, but by a planned interaction of inputs and outputs'.

As a matter of fact, this is not only true for the 'gigantic' concerns of the imperialist stage. It was already true for any multi-divisional factory of the 19th century, for example steam engines or textile machines building plant.

But what happens when the products of these concerns leave the factory? Have they to be *sold*, or can they be distributed through a 'planned interaction of inputs and outputs'? Unfortunately for Messrs owners and managers of Ford, Philips and De Beers, unsold cars, and television sets and diamonds sold at steeply declining prices, mean less profit and less capital accumulation, in the stage of monopoly capitalism as in the stage of 'laissez-faire' capitalism.

Outside the factory, the law of value rules. And that rule reacts upon the international organisation of the factory too. Monopolies try to control markets (what they really succeed in achieving is avoiding permanent cut throat price competition). But they cannot eliminate the basic contradiction between growing objective socialisation of labour and private appropriation. You cannot overcome that contradiction within the boundaries of capitalism.

Let us grant (tongue in cheek) that, during a given stage, roughly 1890-1940, 'state monopolist trusts', to take Bukharin's formula, were actually the predominant forms of capitalist firms, and that during that period, the struggle between them on the world market 'is decided in the first place by the relation between their military forces'. But Harman does not seem to have noticed that these descriptions do correspond less and less to the capitalist reality since the end of the Second World War, ie for nearly half a century. The main new feature of 'late capitalism' is the growing internationalisation of the productive forces and, as a function of that, the growing internationalisation of capital itself.

But simultaneously, no 'international state' not to speak of a 'world state' have emerged. The main organisational form of capital today is not the 'state monopolist trust' but the multinational corporation, more and more independent of all states. Less than 700 of them dominate the world market. Competition between them is not decided in the first place by the 'relation between their military forces'. Otherwise, one would not understand why American based multinationals have steadily lost weight compared to Japanese and West German ones, why in other words US imperialism steadily lost its technological, industrial and financial advance compared to its competitors, while fully maintaining its military hegemony.

Of course, there is a complex concrete interaction between technological, industrial, commercial, financial, monetary, political and military competition. This has to be examined and re-examined during each specific sub-period (business cycle period, class struggle period) of the last 40 to 50 years. But it remains a fact that Harman's 'updating' contemporary capitalism is nearly half a century behind objective reality.

THE IMPASSE OF SCHEMATIC DOGMATISM

The dogma of 'state capitalism' just does not correspond to the reality of international capitalism today. Its four main features, the multinational corporation, the continuous over-exploitation of the 'Third World', the stepped-up tempo of technological innovation during the 'third technological revolution', and permanent inflation, were not taken into account by that theory. Divorce from reality in the name of defending the dogma is nearly complete.

The international capitalist economy floated towards prosperity on a sea of debt. The worldwide dollar debt alone is now estimated at $10 trillion. Germany's public debt is growing at thrice the pace of GNP. Every working day, currency speculation alone has a turnover equal to the annual volume of world trade. Yet Harman's article deals with modern capitalism without dealing with inflation, without dealing with debt, without even dealing with money.

We pointed out that the theory of state capitalism made its adepts unable to foresee the recurrent crises of overproduction which have occurred since the early 1970s, while we were able to predict them. Harman makes an embarrassed attempt to explain them away by saying that there were no real crises of overproduction but crises of stagnation (stop-go phenomena, as the British ideology has it). This just is not true.

There were real declines of industrial output and sales during the 1973-74 and the 1980-82 recessions. There is a real decline of output and sales during the present recession—incidentally in Britain more than in other industrial countries. Sticking at all costs to dogma becomes an impediment for seeing and understanding reality, even when facts stare you in the face.

Today in Britain you have a decline of industrial output of 6 percent, 3 million unemployed going towards 3.5 million, and thousands of small businesses going bankrupt. Yet Harman tells these millions of victims that this is no 'real' economic crisis of overproduction, but only 'stagnation'. The unemployed and bankrupt will greet this good news with great joy, you can bet on it!

The specific nature of the Soviet economy

We pointed out the best proof that the Soviet economy is not capitalist: for more than 70 years, it has not experienced a general crisis of overproduction. There is a specific systemic crisis in the former USSR, but it should be understood as a combined crisis of disproportionate allocation of resources and of underproduction of use values, especially of consumer goods. We summarised our argument by saying that you cannot explain empty shops to be just a variant of (over) full shops, underproduction of use values as a variant of overproduction of commodities.

Chris Harman answers: what we have in the former USSR is excess demand, which is just a phase of the capitalist business cycle. Of all Harman's arguments, this is certainly the most bizarre one. You might as well say that in the 19th century peasants in Tsarist Russia or in China were periodically hit by famine, or African peasants didn't have shoes, because of 'excess demand'. Harman does not seem to know that there is such a historical phenomenon as a chronic lack of supply (too low a level of output). He himself points out that this is precisely the case with agricultural consumer goods in the former USSR since Stalin's disastrous forced collectivisation policy, ie for a period of 60 years. So where is the 'logic'? What has 'excess demand' to do with this lack of food supply? And how does 'capitalism' (be it 'state capitalism') fit in here?

Can you imagine a situation in capitalist Britain in which for 60 years there is 'inadequate supply' compared with 'excess demand' for say meat, certain varieties of bread, oranges and bananas, children's shoes, well cut women's dresses and men's suits, colour television sets which do not break down, and private cars—without any capitalist doing anything about this, thereby foregoing huge immediate profits, either through manufacturing these commodities or through importing them?

Why would all the capitalists behave in such a stupid manner? Aren't they interested in maximising profits on a short or medium term basis, never mind the long term consequences? Are they perhaps motivated by a fanatical addiction to 'general economic equilibrium', the 'Generalkartell' or to the Hilferding-Bukharin-Cliff theories, rather than by the desire to maximise profits and thus increase their wealth, which is the concrete way in which capital is accumulated, again never mind the macro economic ultimate consequences of that behaviour?

Aren't they forced to try to maximise profits for fear of going bankrupt, while no such fear existed in the former USSR? Have you ever known real capitalists in the real world behaving in such an absurd way? Isn't the fact that the Soviet bureaucrats behave differently, are differently motivated, and operate in a different institutional framework, the reason why output in the former USSR was not adapted to demand in these fields for six decades? Isn't that proof that the bureaucracy is not a capitalist class? This is so obvious and so elementary that one really feels embarrassed to have to point it out to intelligent Marxists like Cliff and Harman.

Comrade Harman conducts a merciless war against common sense. He has got a point. In the extremely complex world in which we are living, common sense is certainly not enough to understand what is really going on. But it is one thing to say that it isn't enough. Quite another thing is to believe that it is useless. We give comrade Harman a piece of friendly advice: he should acquire a little bit of common sense. He will be more realistic and happier with it. According to common sense, consistent and lasting—60 years!—underproduction of use value, is structurally different from regularly recurrent crises of overproduction of exchange values, of commodities. It would not harm Harman to notice that difference.

Capitalism is generalised commodity production. This means that the law of value rules and periodically redistributes resources so as to adapt supply to demand. That is why under capitalism no 'excess demand' can exist for 60 years for whole groups of commodities (this does not imply that there cannot exist 60 years or even centuries of unsatisfied physical needs. But that again is characteristic of capitalism. Needs supported by 'demand', ie purchasing power, available money, are quite distinct from physical needs unsupported by money).

Under capitalism, as distinct from precapitalist commodity production, the law of value operates through the prism of the drive towards private profit maximisation (private in the sense of 'for each separate firm'). Capital flows out of branches and types of activity where profits are low(er), towards branches and types of activity where profits are high(er). In each branch, firms strive to have higher profits than their competitors, above all by cutting production costs, which is the basic motor both for increasing productivity of labour—'technical progress'—and for conducting the class struggle with the working class—for increasing the rate of exploitation.

In the Soviet economy, all these mechanisms did not function, or functioned only marginally. The law of value was not eliminated. But it does not rule, as little as it ruled the economy of classical China, which also had quite a lot of trade and where important amounts of money capital were being accumulated.

Contrary to what Harman alleges, the basic allocation of material and human resources in the former USSR indeed occurs in the form of *a priori* allocation by the state, ie by the top bureaucracy, on the basis of pre-established priorities.

These priorities are determined by the desire of the bureaucracy to maintain and extend its power and privileges, not by the profit motive. In that sense, yes, again contrary to what Harman alleges, the privileges of the bureaucracy in the field of consumer goods, intrinsically linked to its monopoly of power in the state and in the factory, motivate the bureaucracy's economic behaviour. If, in the light of all the evidence revealed by glasnost literature in the former USSR, you continue to deny this, you again fight elementary common sense.

A fatal flaw in Cliff's chronology of the origins of the bureaucracy's power and privileges appears in that respect.

For Cliff, the function of the bureaucracy as (state capitalist) masters of the Soviet economy and hence of their consumer privileges, is supposed to be the result of stepped up capital accumulation after 1928, under pressure of the world market, of competition with foreign capitalist powers. The real sequence of events is however different.

As Professor Potchekoldin, of the Institute of Marxism-Leninism revealed at the 1990 Wuppertal Bukharin Symposium, after having had access to the secret archives of the Central Committee, by 1923 a party functionary at *Gubernyia* level received nine times the income of an average worker. For a Central Committee functionary it was 30 times that income. These huge income differentials were anterior to any 'competition' with foreign powers. They were part of the basis of the Soviet Thermidor. And they were by and large circumscribed in the field of consumer privileges.

Indeed, 30 years ago we pointed out the long term disastrous consequences which would flow from the bureaucrats' basic indifference towards overall economic performance, at plant level as well as from a macro economic point of view. In the meantime, this has become a truism in the former USSR. Yet, caught in the impasse of his 'state capitalist' logic, Harman still refuses to understand this economic logic is basically different from that of capitalism.[6]

We never said that the Soviet economy is a 'waste economy' as some allege it is. We said that it *combines* economic growth with tremendous waste without a mechanism of correction of growing disproportions (a mechanism which, as Trotsky had already pointed out in 1932, could only result from a combination of socialist democracy and checks through the market).[7] Therefore, the rate of growth had to decline and the costs (losses, waste) of the system had to increase. Again, we pointed this out 30 years ago.

But the Soviet economy was not simply an economy generating 'waste'. It was also an economy characterised for a whole historical period by a higher average rate of growth than capitalism, an economy which, without being able to catch up with the USA, was indeed reducing the gap with the most advanced capitalist countries.[8] After much deliberation, Harman finally recognises this fact of life at least, and brings us a statistic on the average rates of growth in the period 1951-75 (he could as well have taken 1928 as a starting point) quite superior to that of the average of the advanced capitalist countries. And then, by an amazing flip flop, he tries to turn that very fact into an argument in favour of the theory of 'state capitalism'! He really has got a nerve after more than 40 years of debate on that very issue in which IS-SWP defended the opposite position, including his own argument in the initial article we polemicised against.

Not content with that first flip flop, he then adds a second one, actually underplaying the weight of the tremendous costs of bureaucratic misplanning, of the 'state (bureaucratic) command economy'. He accuses us of giving wrong information on agricultural fertilisers in the former USSR as compared to the USA and Western Europe. He hasn't got the point at all.

We never said that the former USSR consumes (uses) more fertilisers than the USA in the field. We said that it produces more, but that large parts of that production are not used, are not consumed, are wasted in uncovered shacks at farm level, overfilled warehouses, unloaded railways, cars etc.

All this is not the result of the functioning of the law of value. All that is not the result of socialist planning. All this is the result of arbitrary priorities in the allocation of resources by the *nomenklatura*, implying, among other things, that the part of resources devoted to the service sector and to transportation, is half or less than half of what it is in other industrialised capitalist countries. Again, this has become a truism today in the former USSR. Yet Harman sees fit to ignore it.

Harman, it is true, accepts another truism: that there are increasing bottlenecks in the Soviet economy. Generally, this truism is expressed through the formula that the Soviet bureaucracy has become unable to switch from extensive to intensive industrialisation (economic growth) when the former USSR's vast reserves of raw material, of relatively fertile soil, and of manpower, were drying up.

Thereby, the Soviet economy missed the boat of the third technological revolution. Its technology gap with the West was vastly growing instead of declining since the late 1970s,[9] with all the consequences thereof, including in the military field. This offers the materialist explanation of Gorbachev's closer co-operation with imperialism, as against the conspiracy theory type explanation.

But a simple question is then raised, to which Harman and Cliff cannot offer any answer. Why did this process unfold in that precise way? Why did the allegedly 'capitalist' Russian rulers not do what all the capitalists who had the means throughout the world did, and invest more in electronics, in a rather efficient way, rather than in steel, and concentrate on the most modern sectors of industry?

Why didn't they succeed in 'intensive industrialisation', as even Brazil and South Korea partially did, not to speak about Japan, West Germany, France, Italy? Why did Soviet oil production, the largest in the world, become more and more inefficient, while it became more and more efficient everywhere else?

Because of a lack of capital? But under capitalism, there is never an 'absolute' shortage of capital. There is always a combination of growing flows of capital to certain branches, and growing outflows from other ones (again, that's what the rule of the law of value is all about). So why didn't these flows occur in the former USSR in time and on a sufficiently large scale?

Because the Soviet workers didn't produce enough surplus value, ie were not exploited enough? Or because they were too much exploited? Or because there was too little food produced? Why would low agricultural output, or low real wages, prevent the production of 10 million computers, but not the production of 50 million useless tons of steel or 150,000 unused tractors?

Isn't the obvious answer that contrary to the capitalists, the Soviet bureaucrats have no vested interest in efficient output and successful competition? That it is not the profit motive which makes them tick? That conservative parasitism and not the relentless drive to increase production characterises them?[10]

The combination between huge initial successes of Soviet planning and increasingly dysfunctioning of the economic system reflects the combined, double nature of Soviet society in its totality. Its achievements are the products of what still survives of the October revolution. Its failures are the results of the stranglehold of the parasitic bureaucracy on society. If Harman finds that contradictory combination illogical, that only shows that there is something wrong with his 'logic'.

In *The Revolution Betrayed*, Leon Trotsky could summarise his view of that dual contradictory nature of the Soviet economy in a way, which, 50 years before the events, reads as a perfect anticipation of what is happening in the former USSR since the late 1970s and the early 1980s:

The progressive role of the Soviet bureaucracy coincides with the period devoted to introducing into the former Soviet Union the most important elements of capitalist technique. The rough work of borrowing, imitating, transplanting and grafting, was accomplished on the basis laid down by the revolution. There was, thus far, no question of any new word in the sphere of technique, science or art. It is possible to build gigantic factories according to a ready made Western pattern by bureaucratic command—although to be sure, at triple the normal cost. But the farther you go, the more the economy runs into the problems of quality, which slips out of the hands of a bureaucracy like a shadow. The Soviet products are as though branded with the grey label of indifference. Under a nationalist economy, quality demands a democracy of producers and consumers, freedom of criticism and initiative—conditions incompatible with a totalitarian regime of fear, lies and flattery... Behind the question of quality stands a more complicated and grandiose problem which may be comprised in the concept of independent, technical and cultural creation... The socialist culture will flourish only in proportion to the dying away of the state. In that simple and unshakeable historic law is contained the death sentence of the present political regime in the former Soviet Union. Soviet democracy is not the demand of an abstract policy, still less an abstract moral. It has become a life-and-death need of the country.[11]

Yet these prophetic words were developed on the basis of the theory that the former Soviet Union is a bureaucratised workers state. Maybe that theory isn't so wrong after all.

Harman is making a lot of capital out of the fact that today, the growth of the Soviet economy is grinding down to stagnation and even going into negative growth. But this is a *result* of the gradual decomposition of the way that economy functioned for 60 years, not a reflection of that functioning. If a bridge is, through lack of maintenance and repair, in danger of collapsing, and traffic is therefore gradually reduced on it, that is no proof of the fact that traffic was never dense there in yesteryear, or that the bridge served no useful purpose from the start.

In the same vein is his allegation that today's shops in Poland which are full of commodities (exchange values) which find no customers, are the products of yesterday's empty shops. They are not. They are the results of the decomposition of a system which, for decades, was characterised by a shortage of consumer use values, caused by insufficient and inadequate output, and to which is now substituted a system of increasing output of exchange values.

Bureaucrats and capitalists

The particular character of behaviour of the Soviet bureaucrats, especially at plant level, quite different from that of capitalists, can be explained by their material interests and by the basic features of the Soviet economy after the victory of the bureaucratic political counter-revolution, the Soviet Thermidor.

The power of the bureaucracy is based upon the usurpation of power from the working class, its de facto disenfranchisement and elimination from all exercise of power, in the state as well as in the economy. It also implies a severe limitation (in the first stage even a severe restriction) of workers' consumption. Under these circumstances, only the immediate material interest of the bureaucrats could become the direct motor for the implementation of the bureaucratic plan.

To believe otherwise, to believe that people act as direct embodiments of objective social laws, including the need of capital accumulation, without the mediation of their private interests, is a naive rationalistic (in reality idealistic) illusion. Under capitalism also, the laws of capital accumulation are realised through the mediation of individual capitalists trying to further their private interests, not independently from these.

In the former USSR, the realisation of the plan is dependent upon the private interests of the bureaucrats in a twofold way. Precisely because they are not private owners of the means of production, the individual bureaucrats in the first place crave for stability of tenure. The threat of losing their jobs (under Stalin: losing liberty if not life) or the possibility of career advancement is a very real one. The income of the bureaucrats is directly tied to this stability of tenure, which gives them access to many non-monetary advantages.

In addition, the money income they receive depends upon fulfilment and 'overfulfilment' of the plan. A small difference say between fulfilling the plan, realising only 98 percent of the foreseen target, or overfulfilling at 102 percent, can make a difference in the bureaucrats' income of as much as 50 percent if not more through various premiums etc.

But bureaucratic planning was characterised from the start by huge disproportions, as indicated above. These led to permanent irregularities in supply, chronic scarcities, constant interruptions in production. All these features of bureaucratic—as opposed to socialist—planning make it difficult to fulfil and overfulfil the plan.

In order to defend their material interests, the bureaucrats have recourse to a typical reaction, quite distinct from the normal behaviour of capitalists. They will systematically try to hoard reserves (of raw material, manpower, equipment) regardless of cost.[12] It is simply not true that Soviet industry is characterised by a constant overstretching of resource use, by an extreme lack of reserves (of stocks of 'productive factors') as so many commentators allege. There are huge reserves. But they are generally scattered over a great number of production and distribution units. They are not at the disposal of the central planning authorities (of the state).

Furthermore, to be able to have these 'cushions' available, the individual bureaucrats chronically give false information to the centre. They not only hide these reserves in their reports. They will also systematically undervalue the existing productive capacity and overestimate the need for receiving additional resources. Their logic is simple. The lower the recognised production capacity of the plant, the lower the predictable plan targets, the easier these will be realised, and the higher will be their incomes and their chances of keeping their jobs and continuing their upward careers. The same applies, roughly speaking, for the requested additional resources. The higher these will be, the easier will it be to fulfil and overfulfil the plan.

But the central authorities know all that. They therefore start from the assumption that the information they get from the production and distribution units is partially false. Their reaction is again twofold.

First, they send an army of controllers to the units, in order to check the data. Second, they change systematically and in a quite arbitrary way, the mass of data received from below when they formulate the plan targets. *Systematic misinformation becomes generalised.* Here you have the secret of the bureaucratised planned economy, of the hypertrophy of department III (unproductive expenditures, a huge army of controllers-checkers-policemen of all types) and of the growing dysfunctioning of the economy.

Yet Harman's representation of the Soviet economy even formally denies the existence of department III. It mixes the output of machines and raw material used for expanded reproduction, ie capital accumulation, ie economic growth, together with the output of weapons, rusting steel hoards, cotton never delivered to textile factories, luxury 'Culture Palaces' for the bureaucracy, potatoes rotting on the fields, in a single department I. How such goods contribute from the point of view of use values to expanded reproduction and economic growth remains a mystery. Here the 'state capitalist' theoreticians' disregard for the basic contradictions of the commodity, the contradiction between use value and exchange value, between private labour and social labour, and of capitalism as being generalised commodity production, really comes into its own.

Contrary to the logic of socialist planning, bureaucratic planning has a built in element of opacity, of lack of transparency, not corrected by the market and by the law of value. Paradoxically, the Soviet economy was characterised as much if not more by a lack of real planning, by semi-planning or pseudo-planning, as it was characterised by a lack of socialist democracy (workers' control) and of necessary checks through the market.

One should add that the basic logic of any bureaucracy—including a capitalist one, in bourgeois society—and the basic logic of capitalism are quite different. Bureaucrats operate on the basis of an economy of *a priori* allocation of resources (*Zuteilungswirtschaft*). They therefore have a vested interest in spending these resources entirely, regardless of results, lest the allocation be automatically reduced for the following year. They also have a vested interest in demanding more resources, regardless of results.

Capitalists on the contrary get their income only *a posteriori*, when the goods they own are sold. For that reason, as well as in function of the general pressure of competition they are submitted to, they have a vested interest in cost cutting and exact cost accounting. They are unable to operate 'regardless of cost'.

This does not mean that their economic behaviour is more 'rational' than that of the bureaucrats. What is 'rational' on a micro-economic scale, at the level of the individual firm or trust, can have extremely irrational effects from a macro-economic and macro-social point of view.[13] What is 'rational' in the short run can be extremely irrational in the long run.

We only state that the behaviour of bureaucrats and that of capitalists is basically different, because they are embedded in different socio-economic frameworks and submitted to different constraints, not that the one is 'better' than the other.

The Soviet economy and the world market

Derek Howl makes a half hearted attempt to save the relation of the 'state capitalist' theory with Marxism—ie the question of the function of the law of value in the Soviet economy—by stating that the Soviet bureaucracy 'compares' the production costs in Russia with those of its foreign 'competitors'[14] and in that way submits to the law of value. Unwittingly, he thereby puts his finger on a key weakness of the 'state capitalist' dogma.

A capitalist firm certainly 'compares' its production costs with those of its national and international competitors. But precisely under capitalism, 'comparison' is only the starting point of the process, and in no way its decisive aspect.

Whatever the mistakes these comparisons may contain—they always involve predictions, projections, extrapolations, ie strong margins of error—the real test is that of realisation of profit. Under capitalism, only those firms are successful in competition which have a higher than average rate of profit. And one of the key contradictions of the system is precisely the tendency of the average rate of profit to fall, not in the first place because of 'oversupply of capital', as Howl alleges, but as a result of the increase in the organic composition of capital.

Surplus value production (valorisation of capital) is only introduced in Marx's analysis of the tendency of the rate of profit to decline as a countervailing force unable to stop the rot, because basically, the increase in surplus value production cannot be proportional to the increase in the organic composition of capital in value terms.

But this whole central part of volume III of *Capital* isn't even mentioned by Howl. After presenting us with the mystification of a capitalism without money, we now get from the SWP leadership the additional mystification of a capitalism without the tendency of the average rate of profit to decline.

But the attempt to explain 'capitalism' (be it 'state capitalism') through relations with the world market ('comparisons with foreign competitors') has another unreal and reality distorting aspect, which we already pointed out in our debate with Michael Kidron in the late 1960s.[15] The pre-revolutionary Russian economy, like the economy of the East European states (with the exception of the Bohemian part of Czechoslovakia), was an underdeveloped economy, unable to fully modernise and industrialise in the framework of the world market.[16]

'Competition' with foreign 'powers' meant in practice that these countries had semi-colonial economic structures. They were condemned to specialise in the output and export of raw materials and agricultural products. Their modernisation was largely blocked through that dependence.

If they could break out of that dependence in Russia first, in Eastern Europe later, it was precisely because they largely could free themselves from dependence upon the world market, because they despotically suspended 'competition' with 'foreign powers'. This is exactly the way in which the rule of the law of value was eliminated in these countries. For the law of value rules in the first place through the world market.[17]

The decisive test of the restoration of capitalism today would be precisely such a restoration of the rule of the law of value through the world market, ie large scale reversal of these countries to a semi-colonial pattern of output, to their specialisation in those sectors of production where they are relatively more competitive than in more modern industry. The future of a capitalist Poland, Hungary, Lithuania, Georgia, Ukraine and Russia would be closer to Portugal, Greece and Turkey than to that of Italy or Finland. The social implications would be similarly disastrous.

The acid test of practice

The SWP leaders have argued for decades that not accepting the 'state capitalist' nature of the former USSR would lead socialists to wrong, if not counter-revolutionary, positions in front of workers' uprisings in that and similar countries. We have already shown that this prognosis has not been borne out by history. Harman comes back to this issue in his second article. But he introduces two red herrings.

First he alleges, against all the facts, that we somehow had illusions about the possible self reform of the bureaucracy, and that we even preferred, at least in the case of Poland and Hungary, such self reform ('revolution from above') to revolution from below, ie the overthrow of the bureaucratic dictatorship by mass action. As we said before, this is slander pure and simple. Not for one day since we started to deal with the question of the nature of the former USSR in the mid-1940s, did we abandon the perspective and the fight for political revolution following Trotsky's and our movement's tradition since 1932.[18]

The quotes which Harman uses to try to insinuate that this is untrue, do not prove that at all. They just state that there is an inevitable interaction between rising mass discontent and rising mass action in these countries on the one hand, and internal divisions inside the bureaucracy on the other hand. Experience has borne that out. Nobody can deny that Rakosi, Gero, Kadar and Pal Maleter did not take an identical position towards the Hungarian revolution of 1956.

In fact, not only were they fighting on *different* sides of the barricades, but Gero and Kadar had Nagy and Maleter shot. To note these facts, independently from the correctness of precise predictions in that respect, is not in any way to 'capitulate' before Stalinism, any more than noting the post-war long boom meant capitulating to Stalinism. Everything depends upon the political and practical conclusions you draw from recognising these facts of life. The conclusions we drew from these observations about the divisions inside the bureaucracy were to continue the struggle for defending the workers' interests and the fight to political revolution.

Then Harman introduces a second red herring. Some people associated with the general approach of 'workers' statism' are alleged to have actually developed quite wrong positions. He then goes on insinuating that this is somehow the 'logical' outcome of 'workers' statism'. This is presented without any causal proof or empirical evidence. It is just demagogic mud slinging. It is based on one of the classical sophisms of deduction: the abusive and unsubstantiated generalisation of single cases. It goes as follows: 'When I disembarked in Calais, I saw a red headed woman. As this woman was French it follows that all French women are red headed.' No, it does not follow at all.

'Jacek Kuron, as cabinet minister of a reactionary pro-capitalist government, has been responsible for mass unemployment and the reduction of the Polish workers' real wages by 35 to 50 percent. As Jacek Kuron has been and continues to be a resolute defender of the theory that the former USSR is state capitalist, it follows that this theory leads to radical anti-working class policies.' No, it does not follow at all.

Or better still: 'Stalin committed terrible crimes. As he referred to himself as a Marxist, it follows that Marx and Marxism throughout the world leads to terrible crimes.' No, it does not follow at all.

The use of such polemical gimmicks serves no positive purpose whatsoever for socialists and the struggle for socialism. It should be radically banned from any serious theoretical and political discussion by all responsible socialists. It is totally counter-productive. It can only discredit those who use it.

In fact, if one wants to 'infer' anything from how different revolutionary currents reacted to changes in Eastern Europe and the former USSR, the inference goes in exactly the opposite direction of what Chris Harman alleges. All sections of the Fourth International, without a single exception, rejected the perspective of self reform of the bureaucracy. All sections maintained and maintain their course towards political revolution. But all sections also maintained their analysis of the former USSR and similar societies as bureaucratised workers' states, societies frozen in transition between capitalism and socialism by the bureaucratised dictatorship. So, 'workers' statism' does not 'logically' lead to any concession to the idea of possible self reform of the bureaucracy.

We are ready to take responsibility for everything we wrote and did, and everything which the movement to which we belong wrote and did, including its mistakes, and try to correct these and discover their roots. But we don't take any responsibility for what Isaac Deutscher, who left the Trotskyist movement in 1938 and therefore never was a member of the Fourth International, did or wrote after that date, while we respect his writings and the service he has obviously rendered in rehabilitating Trotsky in the eyes of a large international audience.

And even less can we take responsibility for what Fred Halliday or Val Moghadan write or do, who have never been members of the Fourth International or even Trotskyists.

But the real issue is very important indeed: what are the practical political implications of the two different positions regarding the social nature of the former USSR and similar societies on the way revolutionary socialists have to intervene in the unfolding social conflicts in these countries?

Harman cites two insignificant episodes of the alleged usefulness of the 'state capitalist' position for correct intervention in Eastern Europe. His examples are not convincing. In the concrete case of the ex-GDR, our comrades of the Revolutionary Socialist Group (in Eastern Germany) who support the position that the former USSR is a bureaucratised workers' state, were also in favour of supporting the mass demonstrations to which Harman refers.

The issue of privatisation, which is a central issue of social and political struggles in the former USSR and in several eastern European countries, is a thousand times more decisive for judging political orientation than the question of whether to participate or not in this or that particular demonstration. The SWP comrades consider that vital question as a 'side issue'. That is utterly preposterous and irresponsible.

If large scale privatisation of big industry occurs in the former USSR, there will be between 30 and 40 million unemployed. Initial privatisation has already led the ex-GDR to the highest level of unemployment any European country has known, higher than in the 1929-33 crisis: nearly 50 percent. Can a responsible socialist or even trade unionist be indifferent or neutral on that issue?

Dragging their feet, the SWP leaders finally say that they are also against privatisation, like they are against privatisation of nationalised industries in Britain. But this does not get them off the hook.

For as Cliff himself correctly pointed out since the Attlee government, nationalisation of certain branches of British industry was in the interests of the private sector of British capitalism, was indeed necessary to prop them up. State property in the former USSR cannot be interpreted as propping up any private sector in that country. Nationalised industries in Britain did not prevent large scale unemployment from arising precisely for that reason. Nationalised property *did* prevent large scale unemployment in the former USSR for over half a century.

Harman and Cliff are caught in the trap of their qualifying state property in the former USSR as 'capitalist'. If it really is, then its suppression certainly does not make any important difference. But unfortunately for comrade Harman, it makes a tremendous difference for tens of millions of workers in the former USSR and millions in eastern Europe. It has already given rise and will give rise to massive struggles. In this fight, we are unconditionally on the side of the workers who oppose privatisation in practice, regardless with what ideology and regardless whether a section of the bureaucracy also supports them.

We do not accept the choice of the neo-liberal pro-capitalist: either privatisation or state despotism. We reject both state despotism and despotism of the market (of private wealth). We stand for a third economic model: planned democratic self management—Trotsky called it 'producer/consumers democracy'—in which the masses decide themselves, in a democratic way, the priorities of what to produce, how to produce it and how to distribute it.

We stand for collective, social property as against private property of the great means of production and exchange. How that collective property will be organised, what could be the articulation of control of workers of each factory, of each industrial branch, of each town, of each region, of each republic, of the union in its totality, on the means of production and on current output, this is a question to which nobody has any definite answer, and on which the Soviet workers and revolutionary socialists will have to learn from new practice and many current debates.

Harman then raises a rhetorical question:

For a workers' state, however deformed or degenerate, to become a capitalist state must be a step back historically, a stage in a counter-revolutionary process which Marxists should oppose. But if this is so, should Marxists not be supporting those sections of the **nomenklatura** *most resistant to such a change—supporting Ligachev when he argues against privatisation, supporting the Stalin-lover Nina Andreveva when she denounces Gorbachev's 'restorationist' tendencies, supporting Iliescu when he crushes the Bucharest students? Should Marxists perhaps have supported Honecker's efforts to use force against a movement which fell so easily under West German hegemony?*

But this 'logic' again corresponds to a formalistic, mechanistic schema, distorting the real historical process and the real historical alternatives.

The collapse of the bureaucratic dictatorships in Eastern Europe, and the deep systemic crisis in the former USSR, occurred under the direct impact of huge mass mobilisations in Eastern Europe and of rising mass mobilisations in the former USSR. Thereby a dynamic of political change, a pre-revolutionary dynamic, has started. This dynamic can have three different outcomes: a reconsolidation of the bureaucratic dictatorship, which would be a defeat for the working class, a political counter-revolution; a restoration of capitalism, ie social counter-revolution, which would be an even graver defeat for the working class; a victory of the political revolution which would mean the victory of the working class.

We are convinced that only a militant, self active, self organised and increasingly politically conscious working class can prevent a restoration of capitalism. We are convinced that the Ligachevs, Honeckers, Ceausescus, Deng Hsiao-Pings et al are totally unable to prevent this. On the contrary: any repression of the mass movement, irrespective of its immediate effects and of its motivations, will assist the restoration of capitalism by driving the great majority of the masses politically into the pro-bourgeois camp.

Given all the disastrous political, ideological, moral consequences of the bureaucratic dictatorship on the present level of class consciousness of the Soviet working class, that class needs more time and the de facto enjoyment of democratic freedoms in order to accumulate the necessary experience in the struggle for reconquering its capacity to fight for power.

For that reason, the defence and extension of already existing democratic freedoms—never mind whether you call them glasnost or not—is an absolute precondition for a successful struggle against the restoration of capitalism. Whenever these freedoms are threatened by whatever force, socialists have to oppose these threats as resolutely as they

oppose privatisation, again irrespective of whether any section of the
bureaucracy joins in that fight, and under what ideological banners the
workers defend democratic freedoms.

In other words: socialists in the former USSR and eastern Europe
have to fight on two fronts: against privatisation and for democratic
rights (freedoms, space of operation), regardless of whether different
sections of the bureaucracy join in these different struggles.

This might appear 'illogical' for formalists. But it corresponds to the
immediate and historical needs of the working class, in the former
USSR and on a world scale.

Any radical privatisation of large factories in the former USSR but
also any radical suppression of de facto existing freedoms, return to a
Brezhnev not to say a Stalin type dictatorship, would be a disaster for
the Soviet and the international working class.

This position is completely coherent with the Fourth International's
view of the historical place of the political revolution in the process of
world revolution. But this we do not need to develop here.

But where is the civil war without which a victorious restoration of
capitalism, a victorious social counter-revolution, would be impossible,
according to Trotsky and the Fourth International, thunder Harman and
Derek Howl?[19]

Trotsky and the Fourth International supporters of the theory of bureaucratised workers' states in fact never said that a civil war was *unavoidable* in order to restore capitalism in the former USSR. They only
said that on the road of restoration of capitalism, the resistance of the
working class would have to be broken. What form that would take
would obviously depend on the dimension and the political awareness
of that resistance. Here is what Trotsky wrote on the subject in 1936:

*If—to adopt a second hypothesis—a bourgeois party were to overthrow the
ruling Soviet caste, it would find no small number of ready servants among
the present bureaucrats and privileged circles in general. A purgation of the
state apparatus would, of course, be necessary in this case too. But a bourgeois restoration would probably have to clean out fewer people than a revolutionary party. The chief task of the new power would be to restore
private property of the means of production. First of all it would be necessary to create conditions for the development of strong farmers from the
weak collective farms, and for converting the strong collectives into producers' co-operatives of the bourgeois type—into agricultural stock companies.
In the sphere of industry, denationalisation would begin with the light industries and those producing food. The planning principle would be converted for the transitional period into a series of compromises between state
power and individual 'corporations'—potential proprietors, that is, among
the emigre former proprietors and the Soviet captains of industry.*[20]

This reads as a near total description of what is going on today in eastern Europe and what has started in the former USSR. There is no mention here of civil war.

A good illustration of the differences in method

The underlying differences in method, schematic formalism and dogmatism as opposed to scientific dialectical thinking, are clearly revealed in Callinicos's critique of our analysis of the Second World War as 'five wars in one'.

Again trying to turn our strong points against us, Callinicos accuses us of 'syncretism' and 'scholasticism':

> *the subtle skills of a medieval school man to distinguish relevant factors— for example to distinguish no less than five distinct wars within the Second World War... The effect is to deprive social theory of the interaction with potentially disconfirming observations.*[21]

The last sentence is a perfect non-sequitur, and a near perfect refutation of the dialectic. If you note contradictory elements of reality, you are supposed to 'deprive social theory of the interaction with potentially disconfirming(?) observations'. You are forbidden to start from the assumption that reality is contradictory and condemned to assume that really existing contradictions automatically 'disconfirm' social theory. All references made to formalistic monocausal schemas, ie preconceived dogmas, not to the real living world and to attempts to develop 'social theories' which take in advance into account the existence of these contradictions and try to explain them. The rejection of dialectical thought is finally based upon the rejection of the dialectical nature of objective reality itself.

In the night, all cats are grey. You can then develop monocausality into a systematic attempt to reduce 'totality' to a single colour scheme, ie the rejection of the colour spectrum. But like the great dialectician Goethe wrote: 'Eternally green is life's golden tree'. In the real world's rich totality to which Marx refers—which is never monocausal or monocoloured—people are said to be colour blind, if because of an obsession with a 'single basic principle', they only distinguish one colour, grey, or in the best of cases, two colours: black and white.

So let us move on from schematic formalism to the 'eclectic' question of what happened in the real historical process.

Yes, the Second World War was predominantly an inter-imperialist war, which didn't fulfil any progressive function, which had to be condemned and opposed by all socialists. But it was not only that.

The war of the Chinese people against their attempted enslavement by Japanese imperialism was not an inter-imperialist war. It served an eminently progressive purpose. It was a just war, which had to be supported by all socialists.

Likewise, the war of the Soviet peoples against enslavement and mass slaughter by Nazi imperialism—we repeat: *the Generalplan Ost* implied the planned slaughter of 100 million Slav, Jewish, Asian *Untermenschen*—was not an inter-imperialist war. It served a highly useful purpose. It was a just war which socialists the world over, and in the first place the Soviet workers, had to support 100 percent (as Trotsky consistently called upon them to do, and as they happily did).

Likewise the Indian, Algerian, Indonesian, Indo-Chinese, Filipino peoples' uprisings against their imperialist overlords and butchers was not an inter-imperialist war. Again, it served a highly progressive purpose. Only lackeys of imperialism could oppose these uprisings and wars.

And finally, the uprising of the Warsaw ghetto, of the Yugoslav, Greek, Italian, Polish masses against the Nazi butchers, was not an episode of an inter-imperialist war. It was a just and legitimate revolt against a mass murder and overexploitation. It was perfectly legitimate, highly useful and had to be enthusiastically supported by all socialist internationalists.

So there you have your five wars in one. Before you crack cheap jokes about these distinctions involving the fate of a billion and a half people, please try to refute the concrete analysis. You'll have a hard time doing that. The fact that these five wars were up to a certain point enmeshed does not suppress in any way the specificity of each of them—except if you substitute schematic formalism to the concrete analysis of a concrete situation. Lenin *dixit*.

Opportunists make a pretext of the undeniably particular nature of Nazi and Japanese imperialism to arrive at the conclusion that the Indian, Indonesian, Algerian oppressed people had no right to rise against their imperialist overlords, as long as the world war was going on, lest they 'objectively' strengthen the Nazi and Japanese imperialists (which wasn't even true 'objectively'). They likewise argued that the American, British, Australian, Canadian workers had no right to defend their class interests and class independence, lest they 'objectively' help Hitler and Togo (which was slanderous nonsense).

Sectarian dogmatists on the other hand make a pretext of the predominantly inter-imperialist character of the Second World War— which is undeniable—in order to negate any relative autonomy of the peoples and mass struggles of the four other wars going on simultaneously. 'Objectively' these wars and uprisings they said, could only help one of the two imperialists camps (which again was 'objectively' totally untrue).

So parallel to the opportunists they preached abstentionism, ie submission to overexploitation and mass slaughter, as long as the 'imperialist war' had not ended everywhere, presumably by instantaneous, simultaneous revolution in all countries.

The uneven, combined and contradictory character of real mass struggles is explained away in the name of a 'unifying principle'. In practice, and in spite of all good intentions, this amounts to preaching passivity and resignation to fatality.

We believe that the duty of revolutionary socialists is exactly the opposite one: encouraging and supporting resistance, rebellion, popular uprisings and revolutions, while trying to unfold class independence and self activity, but without transforming the acceptance of these political contents into an ultimatistic precondition for giving critical support to progressive, just, legitimate mass struggles.

Incidentally, while the First World War was undoubtedly more 'homogeneous' and 'unilaterally' inter-imperialist than the Second World War, Lenin, who was light years away from schematic dogmatism, perfectly recognised the seeds of 'several wars in one' even then. He wrote in July 1916, in a polemic against his fellow revolutionary internationalists Rosa Luxemburg and Herman Gorter, in a long article entitled 'Balance sheet of a discussion on the right of nations to self-determination':

> *If in 1917 Belgium was annexed by Germany and it rose up in 1918 to free itself...while refusing to support the insurrection of the annexed regions, objectively we become annexers..*[22]

He continues by declaring that the uprising of the Irish people against British imperialism is just, like all uprisings in the colonies, in spite of them taking place within an imperialist war (there you have already 'embryonically' three wars in one). And then he makes a more general point:

> *To believe that the social revolution is conceivable without insurrection in the small colonial and European nations, without revolutionary explosions by a part of the petit-bourgeoisie with all its prejudices, without movement of the proletarian and semi-proletarian masses who don't possess an anti-capitalist, an anti-clerical, anti-monarchical or anti-nationalist consciousness—is to repudiate the social revolution. It is like imagining that an army would take up a position and say, 'We are in favour of imperialism', and that that would be a social revolution! It is only by starting from this pedantic and ridiculous point of view that you could abusively call the*

Irish insurrection a 'putsch'. Whoever waits for a 'pure' social revolution won't live long enough to see it. They would be a revolutionary only in words, who understands nothing of what a real revolution is.[23]

Ridiculous pedantism! Revolutionary in words, who does not understand a real revolution! It is not we who are saying it but Lenin—and the attitude of the SWP comrades towards what happened during and after the Second World War in Yugoslavia, China, Algeria, India, Indonesia, Indo-China etc, comes dangerously close to justifying Lenin's harsh judgement. There you have the two different methods of approach nicely illustrated.

Following numerous bourgeois, neo-Stalinist, Eurocommunist, social democratic and sectarian critics, Alex Callinicos takes on Trotsky for his allegedly mistaken predictions about world developments in 1939. He again accuses Mandel of transforming Marxism into a theory which has lost any explanatory power[24] by trying to 'save' Trotsky's prediction through changing the life span.

But what is the truth here? In what way was Trotsky's alleged 'urgency' tied to the inner logic of his analysis about capitalist decline?

The famous sentence from 'The USSR in War' is most often only quoted partially—including now by Callinicos. It does not say that there would be a worldwide slave totalitarian society in case the war did not end in victorious revolutions. It does say: 'If, however, it is conceded that the present war will provoke not revolution [Trotsky does not say victorious revolutions—E.M.] but a decline of the proletariat, then there remains another alternative' (our stress).[25]

That prediction (its 'explanatory power') has already been shown to be much less wrong than Callinicos and other critics lightmindedly alleged. After all, the war did provoke revolutions, if not in the 'pure' form the pedants think social revolutions can only occur. And the war did not provoke a decline but a new rise of the proletariat, again not in the same form as after 1916, but still a new rise, not a decline. So the succinct formula did give us after all some 'explanatory power' to explain what actually happened from 1945 till 1949.

But what about the narrow time limit, Trotsky's alleged 'urgency'?

In the autumn of 1939 Trotsky formulated his initial thought in few words, in the midst of a faction fight and in order to deal with the central historical alternative raised by that faction fight. A few months later, he returned to the same subject in a more elaborate and thorough way, correcting any impression that the alternative had to be resolved at short notice. In his political testament, the May 1940 *Manifesto of the Emergency Conference of the Fourth International*, he wrote:

> *There remains the question of leadership. Will not the revolution be betrayed, this time too, inasmuch as there are two Internationals in the service of imperialism while the genuine revolutionary elements constitute a tiny minority? In other words: shall we succeed in preparing in time a party capable of leading the proletarian revolution? In order to answer this question correctly, it is necessary to pose it correctly.* [It is as if Trotsky had foreseen critics of the Callinicos type]. *Naturally, this or that uprising may end and surely will end in defeat owing to the immaturity of the revolutionary leadership. But it is not a question of a single uprising. It is a question of an entire revolutionary epoch. The capitalist world has no way out, unless a prolonged agony is so considered. It is necessary to prepare for long years, if not decades, of wars, uprisings, brief interludes of truce, new wars and new uprisings... The question of tempos and time intervals is of enormous importance; but it alters neither the general historical perspective not the direction of our policy.*[26]

Has that analysis, without any short term urgency embodied in it, but based on the 'general historical perspective', no explanatory power for what really did happen after the Second World War?

Again the shoe fits the other foot. In his obsession with 'unified theory' and 'monocausalism', Alex Callinicos does not seem to notice that at the end of the Second World War, we did after all have revolutions—or the beginning of revolutions—in Yugoslavia, Greece, Italy, Indo-China, Indonesia, China, as well as pre-revolutionary crises in India and France.

In the 1950s, we did have the Bolivian revolution, the Algerian revolution, the Hungarian revolution, the revolution in South Vietnam, the Cuban revolution. In the 1960s we did have May '68 in France and its aftermath in Italy. Then we had the Portuguese revolution and the Nicaraguan revolution. And this list is by no means exhaustive.

In the meantime we have also had 'local' wars which have already cost more deaths than the whole First World War. So has Trotsky's analysis prognosis proven to have been wrong?

It is true that Trotsky and the Fourth International seriously underestimated the duration of the 'brief interlude of truce' inside the imperialist countries, ie the long post-war boom and the impressive development of the productive forces (including the main productive force: the proletariat) which corresponded to it. We corrected that mistake a bit late, but not so late, in 1953. But Trotsky's overall analysis was certainly more correct than that of all those tendencies who said: revolution is out, full stop; or: revolution is out for a whole historical epoch, full stop; or capitalism is prosperous on a world scale...or the proletariat is historically on the decline, full stop.

Incidentally, it would be easy to prove that Trotsky and the

Trotskyist movement developed the theory of at least 'four wars in one' (ie the progressive nature of the war of self defence of Russia and China against imperialist aggressors and or uprisings of colonial people, as distinct from the reactionary nature of the inter-imperialist war) years before 1939-40. And before dying, Trotsky started to express himself clearly in favour of judging progressive the resistance struggles of the European peoples against Nazi occupation too. So far from being a theory developed after the facts to try to be 'right in any case', the theory of five wars in one was actually developed before the events, predicted them correctly, and created the basis of adequate socialist intervention in them.

Permanent revolution in 'Third World' countries

Again: this is not a moot academic question. It raises key problems of judgement, policy, intervention, action, by revolutionary socialists. If you have an essentially ideological approach to class struggles, mass struggles and genuine popular revolutions, ie revolutions with massive participation of toiling masses, then you can of course dismiss the Indo-Chinese, the second Vietnamese, the Yugoslav, and especially the Chinese revolutions as being no social revolutions at all, because they were manipulated, channelled, led by Stalinists and finally resulted in bureaucratic dictatorships. If it can be proven that these uprisings are guided by 'petit-bourgeois' or 'bourgeois' ideas and (or) organisations, then they are not workers' uprisings at all but bourgeois uprisings. *Ergo* the working class equals the bourgeoisie (for the state caps, the working class equals the bureaucracy in said revolutions).

For Marx social classes are objective categories, independent from the level of their self consciousness. Roman slaves were certainly a social class, even if they had no 'slave consciousness' and were not conscious of being a class.

In bourgeois society, given the specific nature of socialist revolution, the level of class consciousness is a decisive element for determining the outcome of the class struggle. But it is not a decisive criterion for determining whether a given struggle represents a form (stage) of class struggle. And the same applies *mutatis mutandis* to the societies in transition between capitalism and socialism.

Callinicos sees a 'drift to Stalinism' in the fact that we recognised social revolutions taking place in countries like Yugoslavia, China etc, not to speak about Cuba and Nicaragua. For him, these were only 'movements for national liberation'. He thereby joins all those—Mensheviks and Stalinists—opponents of the theory (better: the strategy) of permanent revolutions, all those advocates of a revolution by stages, who argue that it is possible to realise the central tasks of the national-democratic revolution (national independence and radical land reform) without destroying the class rule of the bourgeoisie-cum-landlords-cum-foreign capital, and without destroying the bourgeois state.

Confusing the class content of the state with the nature of its political leadership, Callinicos tries to defend the idea that the states in Yugoslavia, China, Cuba etc remained bourgeois, ie that there was no qualitative difference between the state of Chang Kai-shek and the state of Mao Tse-Tung, between the state of Batista and the state of Fidel Castro. Again a case of colour-blindness.

You do not need to love Mao Tse-Tung or to transform him into a proponent of direct workers' power or of socialist democracy, in order to grasp that genuine fundamental questions are involved here. Should revolutionists have been neutral in the civil war between Mikhailovitch and the Ustachi on the one hand and Tito on the other hand? That would have been an openly counter-revolutionary position. Should the 'bourgeois' state of Mao Tse-Tung be considered a 'lesser evil' compared to the bourgeois state of Chang Kai-shek for political reasons? But Mao did not create any form of 'democratic' state. His state was a viciously dictatorial one. So whence the lesser evil?

Wouldn't critical support to the People's Liberation Army be justified precisely because we were confronted not with a political but with a social revolution, in which tens of millions of peasants (and quite a few workers too) fought against their class enemies, be it under a bureaucratic leadership? Wasn't the abolition of the comprador-landlord-imperialist rule a gigantic historical step forward for China? Or should one perhaps say that it was a 'side issue'?

The identification of genuine social revolutions with 'pure' leaderships, 'pure' ideologies and 'pure' forms, ends in the preposterously sectarian conclusion that no 'genuine' social revolution is possible without a conscious Marxist leadership—thereby even denying the Paris Commune the nature of the dictatorship of the proletariat. Life has proven to be much more complex and much richer than the dogmatic schemas of such pedants.

The case of Cuba and Nicaragua is still clearer. By no stretch of imagination can one consider the Castro and Sandinista leaderships 'Stalinist' when they were conducting the civil war, with enthusiastic support of the great majority of the toilers (including in Cuba an important urban proletariat which followed the call for a general strike by the Castro leadership).

In fact, they conducted their struggle against the strenuous and at times openly treacherous, counter-revolutionary opposition of the local Stalinists and the Kremlin. Would potential supporters of the 'state capitalist' dogma in Cuba and Nicaragua have fought on the side of the

Fidelista and the Sandinistas? Or should they have joined the Stalinist absentionists, paraphrasing their argument that social revolutions were not on the agenda (with a different rationale: there is no genuine Marxist leadership)?

Or should they have striven as we advocated, to have the struggle for breaking the bourgeois army and the bourgeois state and suppressing at least large parts of private property? What was wrong with such an approach? Isn't that what actually did occur?[27]

Of course we had to add to those demands that of the organisation of a democratic workers' state, based upon freely elected workers' councils and multi-party democracy. But such a state did not exist any more in Russia in 1922 either. Was Soviet Russia therefore a bourgeois state already in 1922?

The implications of these two different approaches in today's mass struggles in 'Third World' countries are numerous. The defence of the specific immediate interests of the working class is a central element of our general strategy in 'Third World' countries. But, after all, it was also a central piece of the Menshevik strategy in Russia too. That was not the main dividing line between Menshevism and Bolshevism.

The main dividing line was the understanding, by the Bolsheviks, that the genuine and radical fight for the implementation of the national-democratic demands cannot be realised without a political break with the 'liberal' bourgeoisie and the fight for power.

The decisive addition to that position which is expressed in Trotsky's strategy of permanent revolution, and which has been thoroughly confirmed by nearly 80 years of historical experience (either positively, where it was applied, or negatively, where it wasn't), is that it is impossible to achieve the full realisation of the national-democratic tasks of emancipation (of the revolution) and a full break with the 'liberal' bourgeoisie, without pushing the emancipatory (revolutionary) process through to the point where you destroy the bourgeois army and the bourgeois state.

Whether you like it or note, that is what Tito, Mao, Castro and the Sandinistas did in practice, independently of their ideologies, initial intentions and later political developments. Anybody who wants to explain what really happened, and not stick to 'theories' completely unable to interpret reality, will have had a hard time denying that obvious fact. This is even more true for the formula that these leaderships led these revolutions to victory 'under the pressure of the masses'. While that pressure was undeniable, it is not sufficient to explain what happened. It underestimates the key role of the subjective factor, and the undeniable merits of initiative and orientation of said bureaucratic leaderships.

Was there less pressure of the masses in Greece than in Yugoslavia?

Yet in Greece the Stalinists saved the bourgeois state and gave up their weapons. In Yugoslavia, the CP led a popular revolution to the destruction of the bourgeois state and the bourgeois army. Again: was there less mass pressure in Indonesia than in Vietnam and in China in 1945-49? Yet in Indonesia, the CP allowed the bourgeois army and the bourgeois state to retain power, which led to one million people killed by the counter-revolution. In China and Vietnam, the CP overthrew the bourgeois state through defeating the bourgeois army. Is that only a 'minor' difference?

Lack of genuine proletarian-democratic programme and principle has disastrous results, sooner or later. But in order to build strong efficient genuinely proletarian-democratic revolutionary organisations in a revolutionary situation, you have to know in what camp you stand, with what arguments you operate and what is the hierarchy of your tasks.

Building the Fourth International or retreating into 'national communism'

Harman tries to justify the constitution of little groups in several countries, cloned on the British SWP, by referring to the need of having theory serve as a guide to action; without a correct theory, no correct action. So far, so good. He even points out to some good interventions which the followers of the SWP are supposed to have made in the general strikes in Greece and in the anti-fascist struggle in France.[28]

But the argument boomerangs: how can one seriously argue that you need the theory of state capitalism in order to understand the tasks with which revolutionary socialists are confronted in a general strike in Greece or in the anti-fascist struggle in France? Weren't these tasks also fulfilled by comrades who have different positions on the social nature of the former USSR? Does not the same conclusion apply to Great Britain too?

What is the relevance of the theory of state capitalism existing in Russia to the anti poll tax struggle, to the struggle against Bush's and Major's Gulf War, to a correct assessment of what a Labour government would do to the working class, of what the attitude of British workers should be towards capitalist Europe, and to practically all problems of the immediate and future class struggle in Britain?

Harman accuses us of preferring to 'fudge' the question of the nature of Stalinism. We don't fudge that question. We make a more general point. We say that the programmatic questions on which advanced workers have to organise—and on which you have to build separate organisations—are the central problems of our epoch, the problems relating to world revolution of overthrowing capitalism. On these questions you have to build separate organisations, lest the working class suffers terrible defeats, nay lest humankind become annihilated. These questions turn around the key issue of how to prepare and organise the workers to take and exercise power in the economy and the state. Only inasmuch as the question of the nature of the former USSR and of Stalinism is relevant to that central problem, is it of vital importance.

So it is Harman who is really fudging the issue. Is it justified, is it responsible to use the issue of state capitalism for the purpose of splitting revolutionary organisations intervening in current struggles, supporting and developing struggles for immediate and transitional demands, with the conscious purpose of preparing the ground for workers' power? Is it responsible to subordinate the general movement towards the overthrow of capitalism to the special fight over the state capitalist dogma? Isn't that exactly what Marx meant when he defined a sect as people addicted to their special *point d'honneur* instead of putting the general interests of the class first?

Precisely because of the predominant trend towards internationalisation of capital and towards 'globalisation' of the key life and death questions, which confront humankind, the struggle for world revolution for a Socialist World Federation, is the central issue for our epoch. Whatever the ups and downs of the class struggle, in the long run it too will become more and more international. It is totally utopian to believe the European working class, including the British working class, could meet the challenge of the EEC by retreating into self defence measures on a national scale, in whatever form. Only the growing unity of action with the workers of the other European countries, with the workers of the rest of the world, can enable them efficiently to oppose the actions of the multinational corporations, inside Europe and outside Europe.

But in order to operate efficiently on an international scale, you need an international organisation. We are no fetishists of the Fourth International as it is today. We know quite well that it is much too weak. We are in favour of a revolutionary mass International, composed of revolutionary mass parties in the key countries of the world. Of that future mass international, the present Fourth International will probably be only one of several components.

But that revolutionary mass international unfortunately does not yet exist. No important organisation anywhere in the world, literally not a single one, is ready to put its creation immediately on the agenda. Under these circumstances no useful purpose can be served by giving up building the Fourth International. We shall continue to build it while at the same time facilitating all moves towards national and international regroupments of revolutionaries on a principled basis. As experience has shown, building the Fourth International favours such regroupments far from representing an obstacle to them.

You will not increase the consciousness of the need to proletarian internationalism basing itself upon an international organisation, without showing in practice how such an organisation can operate, should operate and can develop. This is not in the first place an organisational question. It is certainly not a question of tactical choice. It is at the very heart of the Marxist programme and of the Marxist tradition.

It is sufficient to recall what Marx, Engels, Lenin, Rosa Luxemburg, Trotsky, Gramsci, Bukharin and innumerable others wrote on that issue: 'The International is our real fatherland'.

You cannot be an advocate of international socialism and of world revolution and simultaneously put the building of the International off into the distant future as a secondary or even irrelevant question today. You cannot be an advocate of the strategy of permanent revolution and simultaneously relegate the building of the International to 'better times'. And you can especially not centre the building of an international organisation on the issue of 'state capitalism', forgetting that such an International can only be built on the relevant class struggle problems of every country or at least most of the countries of the world.

Karl Marx historically summarised the reasons why you have to build simultaneously national parties and an International 120 years ago, in his Amsterdam speech of 1872:

> *Let us think of the basic principle of International Solidarity. Only when we have established this life-giving principle on a sound basis among the numerous workers of all countries will we attain the great final goal which we have set ourselves. The revolution must be carried out with great solidarity, this is the great lesson of the French Commune, which fell because none of the other centres—Berlin, Madrid etc—developed great revolutionary movements comparable to the mighty uprising of the Paris proletariat.*
>
> *So far as I am concerned, I will continue my work and constantly strive to strengthen among all workers the solidarity that is so fruitful for the future. No, I do not withdraw from the International and all the rest of my life will be, as have been all my efforts of the past, dedicated to the triumph of the social ideas which—you be assured—will lead to the world domination of the proletariat.*[29]

The great merit of the Fourth International as it exists, in spite of its weakness, is precisely that it does just that. It is the only existing organisation which expresses the common and particular interests of the toilers in all countries—as we say in our jargon, 'in the three sectors of the world revolution' or of 'world reality'—and tries to unite them in practice.

There are a lot of people on the left in the West, the East and the

South who enthusiastically support either the liberation struggles in the Third World, or the mass struggles against the bureaucratic dictatorships in the East, or workers (and feminist and ecological) struggles in the West. But outside revolutionary Marxists, essentially the Fourth International, no political organisation or current is ready to support all of them simultaneously, alike, without reservation, and without subordinating any of them to others. This is a very great source of strength. This creates a homogeneity in basic programme and intervention much higher than anything the workers' movement has known in the past.

The Fourth International has not been split in its basic attitude towards any war during the last three decades. Isn't that remarkable? Isn't that something new? Shouldn't that be recognised with genuine pride?

When we say that the Fourth International is still much too weak, we must add that it is stronger than many people assume. Harman has got his membership figures wrong, because he chalks up losses but forgets to add gains. The fact that the Fourth International is growing in a whole series of countries, on four continents—not in all countries, it is true—is quite significant in a world in which the left generally is in total disarray and steep decline. It proves that in our own modest and limited way, we already fill a need. Militants and organisations in various countries join us on the basis of their own class struggle experience, and the political and programmatic conclusions they draw therefrom. That is quite relevant to our debate, comrade Harman.

What the SWP is doing by refusing to join in that common effort is really retreating into 'national communism'. It has developed into a serious and relevant organisation in Britain, but in Britain only. It is now saying in practice, never mind the verbal cover up: our main purpose is to consolidate and expand the SWP erected upon the basis of the theory of state capitalism. To that purpose, we subordinate any effort of building the International. That is why we limit ourselves to cloning in some countries our own organisation, refusing to link up with thousands of revolutionary socialists who have come to common programmatic and practical conclusions on the basis of their experience with the problems of class struggle with which they are confronted in their respective countries and internationally.

During the last months, the objective dialectic of 'national communism' has started to reveal itself dramatically in the case of two of the largest organisations claiming to be Trotskyist outside the Fourth International: the British Militant group and the Argentine MAS (followers of Moreno).

In both of these organisations, sectors of its leadership suggested gravely erroneous national tactics as a result of a wrong assessment of the world situation and its impact on a national scale. They thought there was a rise of political mass radicalisation of the working class on a national scale, whereas in reality there is a predominantly rightward political evolution of the class, under the impact of the worldwide capitalist offensive and the worldwide crisis of credibility of socialism, strong defensive mass struggles notwithstanding.

These wrong tactics brought parts of the Militant and MAS leadership in head on collision with parts of the working class and of their own organisations' workers' basis.[30]

Any national grouping not sufficiently implanted in the international working class through membership and mass movements in an international organisation really functioning as such, is condemned to make similar mistakes sooner or later. For it is condemned to elaborate analyses of world developments from behind office desks, by reading newspapers and books, without having these analyses checked and rechecked by political and organisational practice.

If you stick to your retreat into 'national communism' this will sooner or later lead to disaster in Britain too, comrades of the SWP. You cannot reach an adequate level of internationalist consciousness among your membership without an adequate level of international practice, which presupposes an adequate level of international organisation.[31]

Let us illustrate our thesis by an 'extreme' example. Imagine a situation in which the workers of any country—yes, why not, including the former Soviet Union—are unfolding mass struggles of such a scope that workers' and popular councils are arising and that the question of their centralisation is immediately on the agenda. Admittedly, this is not likely to happen in the immediate future. But the comrades of the SWP firmly believe, as we do, as all revolutionary Marxists do, that it will happen sooner or later, never mind the time scale.

Now add to that first hypothesis a second one: imagine that the great majority of the revolutionary socialists in that given country, actively struggling for that centralisation of workers councils and preparing the working class for power, are opposed to the theory of state capitalism? Wouldn't it be irresponsible to the extreme, nay criminal, to split their forces on the issue of state capitalism and to weaken them in relation to all the opponents of workers' power even at the even of the struggle for power? Or would you seriously argue that it is impossible for the workers of that given country to take power without having first accepted the dogma of state capitalism?

One could answer: this is after all a moot question, for the direct struggle for workers' power is not on the agenda in any country just now (perhaps with a couple of exceptions). But this does not weaken our case. The struggle for workers' power does not suddenly fall from the sky. It can only be the final link of a whole chain of intermediate links, experience and conclusions drawn by advanced workers first, broader masses later, from their current struggles, growing self assurance and class consciousness assisted by adequate socialist propaganda and education.

In all these fields, the revolutionary organisation's activity plays an important role. It is most probable that we shall not see workers' councils emerge without previous experiences of elected strike committees and of their tendential centralisation, that we shall not see revolutionary mass parties emerge without the revolutionary socialists' increasing implantation and authority gained inside these initial forms of self organisation of the class as such.

Today's propaganda and incipient implementation of the central idea that socialism in the final analysis is self activity and self organisation of the working class, is the struggle for democratically, ie pluralistically elected workers' councils, is the struggle for democratically articulated self management and planning in the economy, represents the only way to overcome the terrible crisis of credibility of socialism which all of us are confronted with worldwide. Do we stand in the same camp on that vital issue? If so, what is the purpose of not building together one International based upon it?

Notes
1 See Lenin's comments on Bukharin's draft party programme in Lenin: *Collected Works*, vol 29.
2 *Grundrisse*, p234 of the German edition of 1939—our own translation.
3 A Callinicos, *Trotskyism,* (Open University Press, 1990), p41.
4 Marx *Theories of Surplus Value*, vol 2, p510. Our stress. See likewise ibid, p534: 'In world market crises, all the contradictions of bourgeois production erupt collectively'.
5 A Callinicos, op cit, p44.
6 It would be interesting to analyse the large similarity between the 'state capitalist' interpretation of contemporary capitalism and the Stalinist 'state monopolist capitalism' theory. Even more striking are parallel political conclusions concerning the absence of revolutionary perspectives in the imperialist countries for a long historical period.
7 L Trotsky: *The Soviet Economy in Danger*, pp273-279, in *Writings of Leon Trotsky 1932*, (Pathfinder Press).
8 The basic economic fallacy of 'socialism in one country' (later in one 'camp') was the illusion that the former USSR could 'catch up with and overtake' total output, per capita output, and average productivity of labour of the USA and the leading capitalist industrial nations, ie maintain a higher rate of growth for an indefinite period.
9 From a certain point on, late 1970s or early 1980s; estimates differ in that respect, the US economy grew more rapidly than that of the former USSR.
10 Of course relative paratisism, not absolute parasitism. We take up that question further in this article.
11 L Trotsky, *The Revolution Betrayed*, (New Park Publications, 1967) pp275-276.
12 The top of the *nomenklatura* tried to prevent or at least to limit this indifference with regard to real costs by imposing on the managers' different planning objectives: physical quantities of output; physical quantities of raw material inputs; wage costs; even net financial results—*khozrashot*—from the mid-1930s on. But various objectives were contradictory and even mutually exclusive. In practice, the priority was given to

attaining output goals in physical terms. And the pressure from the top went essentially in the same direction, as the system of bureaucratic planning had as its key feature the concentration of efforts on prioritised sectors (goals), at the expense of a proportionate development of the economy and society as a whole.
13 Under capitalism, this is expressed most clearly in the elimination from cost calculations at firm level of all 'externalities' for which the firm does not have to pay. But even when these get a 'price', the socially irrational character of economic decisions measured in purely money terms is not suppressed. Its real character is only expressed more clearly. Investment decisions implying human deaths are considered worthwhile as long as the 'rewards' are higher than the costs, the 'cost' of human lives being discounted in the form of lost incomes. And what about the 'cost' of dead babies, whose potential profession and income are unknown? The inhuman character of this macro-social irrationality is undeniable.
14 D Howl, 'The law of value and the former USSR', *International Socialism* 49, Winter 1990.
15 In *Readings on 'State Capitalism'*, (International Marxist Group pamphlet, 1970, 1973).
16 Russia was a special case combining the character of the (most backward) imperialist country with that of the (most developed) underdeveloped country.
17 This does not represent in any way an option in favour of autarchy, which Trotsky systematically opposed. It represents an option in favour of a monopoly of foreign trade. Whether that monopoly should be in the hands of the state or of a central organ of workers' self management bodies is another question.
18 The Theses 'Decline and Fall of Stalinism' as well as the Manifesto adopted by the 5th World Congress of the Fourth International in 1957 are entirely centred around the concept of the political revolution from below, by mass action, in the bureaucratised workers' states. An editorial note appearing in the June-July 1957 issue of *Quatrième Internationale* and entitled 'From the 8th to the 9th Plenum of the Polish Workers Party' states: 'In our preceding issues, we indicated the character of the Gomulka leadership: in October (1956), it used the workers, the intellectuals and the students which rose in revolt against the police regime. But the Gomulka leadership was and remains a bureaucratic leadership, which does not try to stimulate revolution by the masses, but to channel these precisely in order to avoid revolutionary upheavals'.
19 D Howl, op cit, p109; C Harman, in *International Socialism* 49, pp80-81.
20 L Trotsky, *The Revolution Betrayed*, op cit, p253.
21 A Callinicos, op cit, p43.
22 V I Lenin, *Collected Works* vol 2, p237. A Belgian revolutionary socialist would of course have to combine such support to a national insurrection in Belgium with unconditional support to all movements for democratic demands, including national independence, directed against Belgian imperialism in the Belgian Congo.
23 V I Lenin, op cit, p383.
24 A Callinicos, op cit, pp41-42.
25 L Trotsky, *In Defence of Marxism*, (original Pioneer Publishers edition) p99.
26 L Trotsky, *Writings 1939-44*, (Pathfinder Press), pp217-218. Our stress.
27 Contrary to the USSR under Stalin, Cuba has the most progressive working class labour legislation of the world, more radical even than that of the Scandinavian countries or Austria.
28 It is simply not true that our French section had to wait for actions by the tiny 'state capitalist' sect in France before taking anti-fascist anti Le Pen initiatives.
29 K Marx in *Marx-Engels Werke*, Band 18, p161.
30 It is obvious that socialists have to oppose the Labour leadership's witch hunt without reservations, in spite of any tactical difference they may have with this or that victim

of the witch hunt. The criticism of the Militant's tactics in the Liverpool by-election is precisely that it helps the leadership to get away with the witch hunt.
31 The SWP's tendency towards sectarianism also expresses itself in activity in Britain. It counterposes itself systematically to the Labour Party, in spite of the fact that that organisation still enjoys the loyalty of the overwhelmingly majority of the organised British working class—a loyalty which could only be upset by a political mass radicalisation which has not yet occurred. This leads the SWP to make recruitment to its own organisation the main objectives of its intervention in mass struggles like the anti poll tax movement.

The Socialist Workers Party is one of an international grouping of socialist organisations:

AUSTRALIA: International Socialists, GPO Box 1473N, Melbourne 3001
BELGIUM: Socialisme International, Rue Lovinfosse 60, 4030 Grivengée, Belgium
BRITAIN: Socialist Workers Party, PO Box 82, London E3
CANADA: International Socialists, PO Box 339, Station E, Toronto, Ontario M6H 4E3
CYPRUS: Ergatiki Dimokratria, PO Box 7280, Nicosia
DENMARK: Internationale Socialister, Ryesgade 8,3, 8000 Arhus C, Denmark
FRANCE: Socialisme International, BP 189, 75926 Paris Cedex 19
GERMANY: Sozialistische Arbeitergruppe, Wolfsgangstrasse 81, W-6000 Frankfurt 1
GREECE: Organosi Sosialistiki Epanastasi, c/o Workers Solidarity, PO Box 8161, Athens 100 10, Greece
HOLLAND: International Socialists, PO Box 9720, 3506 GR Utrecht
IRELAND: Socialist Workers Movement, PO Box 1648, Dublin 8
NORWAY: Internasjonale Socialisterr, Postboks 9226 Grønland, 0134 Oslo, Norway
POLAND: Solidarność Socjalistyczna, PO Box 12, 01-900 Warszawa 118
SOUTH AFRICA:
International Socialists of South Africa, PO Box 18530, Hillbrow 2038, Johannesburg
UNITED STATES:
International Socialist Organization, PO Box 16085, Chicago, Illinois 60616

The following issues of *International Socialism* (second series) are available price £2.50 (including postage) from IS Journal, PO Box 82, London E3 3LH.

International Socialism 2:55 Summer 1992
Alex Callinicos: Race and class ★ Lee Sustar: Racism and class struggle in the American Civil War era ★ Lindsey German and Peter Morgan: Prospects for socialists—an interview with Tony Cliff ★ Robert Service: Did Lenin lead to Stalin? ★ Samuel Farber: In defence of democratic revolutionary socialism ★ David Finkel: Defending 'October' or sectarian dogmatism? ★ Robin Blackburn: Reply to John Rees ★ John Rees: Dedicated followers of fashion ★ Colin Barker: In praise of custom ★ Sheila McGregor: Revolutionary witness ★

International Socialism 2:54 Spring 1992
Sharon Smith: Twilight of the American dream ★ Mike Haynes: Class and crisis—the transition in eastern Europe ★ Costas Kossis; A miracle without end? Japanese capitalism and the world economy ★ Alex Callinicos: Capitalism and the state system: A reply to Nigel Harris ★ Steven Rose: Do animals have rights? ★ John Charlton: Crime and class in the 18th century ★ John Rees: Revolution, reform and working class culture ★ Chris Harman: Blood simple ★

International Socialism 2:52 Autumn 1991
John Rees: In defence of October ★ Ian Taylor and Julie Waterson: The political crisis in Greece, an interview with Maria Styllou and Panos Garganas ★ Paul McGarr: Mozart, overture to revolution ★ Lee Humber: Class, class consciousness and the English Revolution ★ Derek Howl: The legacy of Hal Draper ★

International Socialism 2:51 Summer 1991
Chris Harman: The state and capitalism today ★ Alex Callinicos: The end of nationalism? ★ Sharon Smith: Feminists for a strong state? ★ Colin Sparks and Sue Cockerill: Goodbye to the Swedish miracle ★ Simon Phillips: The South African Communist Party and the South African working class ★ John Brown: Class conflict and the crisis of feudalism ★

International Socialism 2:49 Winter 1990
Chris Bambery: The decline of the Western Communist Parties ★ Ernest Mandel: A theory which has not withstood the test of time ★ Chris Harman: Criticism which does not withstand the test of logic ★ Derek Howl: The law of value In the USSR ★ Terry Eagleton: Shakespeare and the class struggle ★ Lionel Sims: Rape and pre-state societies ★ Sheila McGregor: A reply to Lionel Sims ★

International Socialism 2:48 Autumn 1990
Lindsey German: The last days of Thatcher ★ John Rees: The new imperialism ★ Neil Davidson and Donny Gluckstein: Nationalism and the class struggle In Scotland ★ Paul McGarr: Order out of chaos ★

International Socialism 2:47 Summer 1990
Ahmed Shawki: Black liberation and socialism in the United States ★ Fifty years since Trotsky's death ★ John Rees: Trotsky and the dialectic ★ Chris Harman: From Trotsky to state capitalism ★ Steve Wright: Hal Draper's' Marxism ★

International Socialism 2:46 Winter 1989
Chris Harman: The storm breaks ★ Alex Callinicos: Can South Africa be reformed? ★ John Saville: Britain, the Marshall Plan and the Cold War ★ Sue Clegg: Against the stream ★ John Rees: The rising bourgeoisie ★

International Socialism 2:45 Autumn 1989
Sheila McGregor: Rape, pornography and capitalism ★ Boris Kagarlitsky: The market instead of democracy? ★ Chris Harman: From feudalism to capitalism ★ plus Mike Gonzalez and Sabby Sagall discuss Central America ★

International Socialism 2:44 Autumn 1989
Charlie Hore: China: Tiananmen Square and after ★ Sue Clegg: Thatcher and the welfare state ★ John Molyneux: *Animal Farm* revisited ★ David Finkel: After Arias, is the revolution over? ★ John Rose: Jews in Poland ★

International Socialism 2:42 Spring 1989
Chris Harman: The myth of market socialism ★ Norah Carlin: Roots of gay oppression ★ Duncan Blackie: Revolution in science ★ International Socialism Index ★

International Socialism 2:41 Winter 1988
Polish socialists speak out: Solidarity at the Crossroads ★ Mike Haynes: Nightmares of the market ★ Jack Robertson: Socialists and the unions ★ Andy Strouthous: Are the unions in decline? ★ Richard Bradbury What is Post-Structuralism? ★ Colin Sparks: George Bernard Shaw ★

International Socialism 2:40 Autumn 1988
Phil Marshall: Islamic fundamentalism—oppression and revolution ★ Duncan Hallas: Trotsky's heritage—on the 50th anniversary of the founding of the Fourth International ★ Ann Rogers: Is there a new underclass? ★ Colin Sparks: The origins of Shakespeare's drama ★ Mike Gonzalez: Introduction to John Berger on Picasso ★ John Berger: Defending Picasso's late work ★ Alex Callinicos: The foundations of Athenian democracy ★ Norah Carlin: Reply to Callinicos ★

International Socialism 2:39 Summer 1988
Chris Harman and Andy Zebrowski: Glasnost, before the storm ★ Chanie Rosenberg: Labour and the fight against fascism ★ Mike Gonzalez: Central America after the Peace Plan ★ Ian Birchall: Raymond Williams ★ Alex Callinicos: Reply to John Rees ★

International Socialism 2:36 Autumn 1987
Dave Beecham and Ann Eidenham: Beyond the mass strike—class, state and party in Brazil ★ Chris Bambery :The politics of James P Cannon ★ Norah Carlin: Was there racism in ancient society? ★ Paul Kellogg: Goodbye to the working class ★ Lutte Ouvrière: A critique of the SWP Analysis of the French railway workers' strike ★ Gareth Jenkins: A reply to Lutte Ouvrière ★ Ian Birchall: A comment on Colin Sparks on film theory ★

International Socialism 2:35 Summer 1987
Pete Green: Capitalism and the Thatcher years ★ Alex Callinicos: Imperialism, capitalism and the state today ★ Ian Birchall: Five years of *New Socialist* ★ Callinicos and Wood debate 'Looking for alternatives to reformism' ★ David Widgery replies on 'Beating Time' ★

International Socialism 2:31 Winter 1985
Alex Callinicos: Marxism and revolution In South Africa ★ Tony Cliff: The tragedy of A J Cook ★ Nigel Harris: What to do with London? The strategies of the GLC ★

International Socialism 2:30 Autumn 1985
Gareth Jenkins: Where is the Labour Party heading? ★ David McNally: Debt, inflation and the rate of profit ★ Ian Birchall: The terminal crisis in the British Communist Party ★ replies on Women's oppression and *Marxism Today* ★

International Socialism 2:29 Summer 1985
Special issue on the class struggle and the left in the aftermath of the miners' defeat ★ Tony Cliff: Patterns of mass strike ★ Chris Harman: 1984 and the shape of things to come ★ Alex Callinicos: The politics of *Marxism Today* ★

International Socialism 2:27 & 28
Special double issue published in conjunction with Socialist Worker ★ Alex Callinicos and Mike Simons on ★ The Great Strike: the Miners' Strike of 1984-5 and its lessons ★

International Socialism 2:26 Spring 1985
Pete Green: Contradictions of the American boom ★ Colin Sparks: Labour and imperialism ★ Chris Bambery: Marx and Engels and the unions ★ Sue Cockerill: The municipal road to socialism ★ Norah Carlin: Is the family part of the superstructure? ★ Kieran Allen: James Connolly and the 1916 rebellion ★

International Socialism 2:25 Autumn 1984
John Newsinger: Jim Larkin, Syndicalism and the 1913 Dublin Lockout ★ Pete Binns: Revolution and state capitalism in the Third World ★ Colin Sparks: Towards a police state? ★ Dave Lyddon: Demystifying the downturn ★ John Molyneux: Do working class men benefit from women's oppression? ★

International Socialism 2:18 Winter 1983
Donny Gluckstein: Workers' councils in Western Europe ★ Jane Ure Smith: The early Communist press in Britain ★ John Newsinger: The Bolivian Revolution ★ Andy Durgan: Largo Caballero and Spanish socialism ★ M Barker and A Beezer: Scarman and the language of racism ★